DATE DUE

FRANCISCO DE IBARRA
AND NUEVA VIZCAYA

Francisco de Ibarra
and Nueva Vizcaya

BY

J. LLOYD MECHAM

Associate Professor of Government in the University of Texas

GREENWOOD PRESS, PUBLISHERS

NEW YORK   1968

To

MY WIFE

PREFACE

The history of the Spanish conquest and colonization of New Spain in the sixteenth century comprised three periods. The first was marked by the spectacular exploits of Hernán Cortés in the capture of Tenochtitlan, and it may be said to extend from 1519 to 1521. The second was characterized by expansion in all directions from Mexico City and fell between 1522 and 1542. The third period extended from this last date to the end of the century and was especially distinguished by the development of Nueva Galicia and the conquest and organization of the frontier provinces of Nueva Vizcaya and Nuevo León.

The narration of the fall of the Aztec Empire may be regarded as definitive, for we have not only Prescott's classic, but also the exemplary works of Sir Arthur Helps and F. A. MacNutt. The second period does not fare so well in its historians. Here we encounter no classics or monumental works, but exceptional contributions have been written on various phases by Bancroft, Bandelier, Lowery, Winship, and others. For the third period, with the exception of Bancroft's very meritorious but frequently inaccurate accounts, and Bolton and Marshall's excellent, but necessarily too brief treatment, there is practically a void.

This book aims to remove a portion of this deficiency in the third period by bridging the gap on the northwestern frontier which separated Francisco de Coronado from Juan de Oñate. (The story of the founding of Nuevo León, the province on the northeastern frontier, must be reserved for future relation.) The discovery by the writer of original manuscript materials in the Archivo General de Indias at Seville has made it possible to tell now for the first time the

complete story of the founding of Nueva Vizcaya, as northwestern New Spain was then called. An account of the
exploration, settlement, and organization of that region becomes in large measure a biography of Francisco de Ibarra,
the first governor of the province. For convenience of treatment as the central figure, the facts relating to the history
of Nueva Vizcaya have been assembled about Ibarra, but
a rigid adherence to a formal biographical sketch has not
been attempted, for it is the aim of this book to present a
comprehensive view of the vast region under consideration.
Such a result could not be obtained without a broad background, as is presented in Chapter II; an exposition of
frontier economic organization, as in Chapter VIII; and
other digressions from an account restricted solely to Ibarra's
career.

The numerous expeditions which crossed and recrossed
the frontiers went in search of gold and silver. Mining was
the magnet which drew thousands of adventurers into the
northern provinces. Some of the greatest cities of Mexico
owe their origin to the mining "rushes" of the middle sixteenth century. Guadalajara, the old metropolis of Nueva
Galicia and now the capital of Jalisco, prospered because of
the mines of Guanchinango, Jacotlán, and Ixtlán. Zacatecas
owed its origin to the discovery of the rich veins of San
Bernabé, La Albarrada, and Pánuco. Durango, once the
capital of Nueva Vizcaya and now the capital of the state

of Durango, was supported at first by the returns from a
particular mine in Aviño. San Luís Potosí, the beautiful capital of the state of that name, was founded following the
discovery of one of the richest mineral deposits in New
Spain. The mines of Zacatecas, Guanajuato, and the Durango district were one of the chief sources of the flood of
silver which had such a profound effect upon economic,
social, and political conditions in the Old World. The sub-

ject here treated—the discovery of those mines—is one of prime importance in the history of Spanish America.

Although the sedentary Indians of the American Southwest and the advanced types of the Valley of Mexico have been the subjects of intensive ethnological research, the Indians of the Mexican northwest have been almost totally neglected. Accordingly, an effort has been made to identify and locate all Indian tribes mentioned in the documents, and it is the hope of the writer that his findings may be of assistance to future ethnological investigators.

The author takes the opportunity here to acknowledge his indebtedness to the Order of the Native Sons of the Golden West, which made it possible for him to spend a profitable year of foreign residence and research in the archives of Spain. The purpose of the Native Sons' Traveling Fellowships is to assist the development of Southwestern American History, and since the present monograph furnishes a portion of the background for that study, the writer hopes that he may have been instrumental in contributing in a substantial measure to the definitive history of the Great Southwest. He also wishes to thank the officials and attendants of the Archivo de Indias at Seville for their kind offices. Finally, he acknowledges his debt of gratitude to Professor Herbert E. Bolton, who suggested the present work and who offered helpful criticism, unfailing sympathy, and inspiration throughout its preparation.

J. LLOYD MECHAM.

UNIVERSITY OF TEXAS,
Austin, Texas.
March, 1926.

TABLE OF CONTENTS

MAPS

FRANCISCO DE IBARRA
AND NUEVA VIZCAYA

CHAPTER I

The founding of the Spanish colonial empire was in large measure the work of individuals who undertook the conquest of certain regions in the New World by virtue of special arrangements with the Spanish crown. These impresarios, who bore variously the titles of adelantados, governors, and captains-general, were men of means who obligated themselves to bear most of the expense of conquering and peopling the wilderness in return for wide powers, extravagant titles, and extensive economic privileges. This was true in the early sixteenth century of Diego Velásquez, Hernando de Soto, Pedro de Mendoza, and Ponce de León. The later sixteenth century was still within the age of the proprietary conquerors and could boast such names as Menéndez de Avilés, Miguel López de Legazpi, Juan de Oñate, and Francisco de Ibarra. The career of the last-named conquistador is without doubt the least known and his achievements the least appreciated. But it was due to his initiative, enterprise, qualities of leadership, and financial support that the whole of northwestern Mexico, or New Spain, as it was known under the Spanish régime, was explored and secured for the Spanish crown.

The ancestry of Francisco de Ibarra may be traced to the Provincias Vascongadas, a division of northeastern Spain composed of the provinces of Álava, Vizcaya, and Guipúzcoa. This fact is significant because certain noteworthy qualities are said to be inherent in the "Señores de Vizcaya." Splendid physical specimens, easily recognized from among the other inhabitants of the Iberian Peninsula, the Basques possess rugged characteristics reminiscent of their land and its history. The isolation of the provinces, the mountainous and easily defended nature of the country, the rocky seacoast looking out upon the stormy Bay of Biscay, the meager tillable soil, all tended to develop a hardy, abstemious, proud, and self-reliant race. It was the proud boast of the Basque that he had never been conquered. It is indeed true that the Moslem invasion of the eighth century did not extend to the Basque provinces; it was there in their mountain fastnesses that the stalwart bands of Christians held out against the Moors; and later it was they who initiated the counter-attack which was not to end until the fall of Granada in 1492. Though no conqueror ever stamped out the indomitable spirit and customs of the Basques, they were rarely independent. They were connected variously with the kingdoms of Asturias, Navarre, and Castile. Eventually the provinces were consolidated with the Castilian crown in the following order: Guipúzcoa in 1200, Álava in 1332, and Vizcaya in 1370.

Another boast of the Basques was that they were all nobles! This status was legally recognized by laws before and after the union with the Castilian crown. Some Basque settlements which pretended to the nobility of their inhabitants even went to the extreme of refusing to permit foreigners to dwell among them unless they too were of noble rank. Nevertheless, in actual practice there was a denial of equal rank, for the familiar social differences existed. Since the near-universality of noble titles was typical, not of Vizcaya alone, but of all of Spain, the absence of base blood among the conquistadores is understandable. The common boast that they belonged to the nobility, or were scions of ancient and noble houses, meant nothing unless the claims were substantiated by evidence to show that the titles were of high degree. This last was true with respect to the House of Ibarra.

Francisco de Ibarra was born in the province of Guipúz-coa, probably in 1539. The exact date and place of his birth are unknown. The House of Ibarra was said to be one of the oldest and most noble in Guipúzcoa. The truth of this is substantially attested by the high governmental and ecclesiastical positions that were held by numerous members of the family. There were three main limbs on the Ibarra family tree: the oldest was located in Hergueta; the second was in Villa de Ybar; and the youngest was settled in the city of Durango. Francisco was a member of the Ybar, or Hibar, branch, for the family estate which he mentioned in has last will and testament was situated in the village of that name. It is to be presumed, therefore, that he was born in the same place.[1]

Francisco's father, Pedro Sánchez de Ibarra, was a man of considerable prominence who held many official positions, among them that of Inquisitor of Toledo. The father of Pedro Sánchez, Francisco's paternal grandfather, had also been engaged in the public service; at one time he went to Peru on a royal mission. Another member of the family, an uncle of Pedro Sánchez, had served as constable and governor of Castile during the revolt of the communes in the beginning of the reign of Charles V. Diego de Ibarra, who played an important rôle in the early histories of Nueva Galicia and Nueva Vizcaya, was a younger brother of Pedro Sánchez. Another brother was Inquisitor of Navarre and Calahorra. Regarding Francisco's mother, Doña María de Arandía, and her family, nothing is known beyond her name. In addition to a sister, whose name we do not know, Francisco had two brothers, Martín Ybañes de Ibarra and Juan de Ibarra. The former did not come to America until several years after Francisco. With respect to lineage,

[1] Other famous Guipúzcoans in the history of Spanish colonial exploration were Sebastián del Cano, first man to circumnavigate the globe, and Miguel López de Legazpi, adelantado of the Philippines.

therefore, Francisco de Ibarra was a member of the higher
nobility, but in this he differed in no essential respect from
most of the great conquistadores of the New World. In only
a few notable exceptions were royal commissions conferred
upon applicants of common origin. The fortunate circumstance of noble birth was the open sesame to opportunity in
his Catholic Majesty's new dominions—particularly when
blue blood was accompanied by wealth.[2]

The career of Francisco de Ibarra can be conveniently
and logically divided into three periods: first, 1539 to 1554,
the early years of his life preliminary to his activities on
the frontiers of New Spain; second, 1554 to 1562, the
years of his first explorations, conducted as private enterprises, of the region between Zacatecas and Durango; and,
third, 1563 to 1575, the years of his greatest work as governor and captain-general of Nueva Vizcaya. Reserving for
future discussion the two last-named periods, let us first
turn our attention to a consideration of his boyhood and
early training. Concerning the early life of Francisco de
Ibarra, nothing has been known, up to the present time.
The brief information noted below, therefore, serves to
fill an absolute void in prior accounts of the conqueror of
Nueva Vizcaya.

[2] For the genealogy of Francisco de Ibarra, cf. A. G. I., 60-1-3, Información de oficio sobre q dió el Bachiller Ant. de Ybarra, México, 8
de agosto de 1591; A. G. I., 1-1-3/22, Crónica, comentario y narativo por
Baltasar de Obregón; A. G. I., 87-5-1, Un libro que tiene 1341 Informes
de conquistadores de México y otras partes de N. España; A. G. I., 67-
1-2, Testimonio de Francisco de Ibarra, Pánuco, 18 de agosto, 1575.
(Note: The manuscripts in the Archivo General de Indias (A. G. I.)
are wrapped and tied in bundles (legajos) which, in turn, are to be found
in large cases (estantes), and the shelves (cajones) of the cases are
numbered. The meaning of A. G. I., 60-1-3, is, therefore, Archivo General de Indias, estante 60, cajon 1, legajo 3; indicative that legajo 3 is
to be found on shelf 1 of case 60 of the Archive. Since the manuscripts
in a legajo are generally numbered and unbound, the only semblance of
order being a loose chronological arrangement, it has been found necessary to cite solely by document title within the legajo. For a brief
explanation of the classification of documents in the Archivo General
de Indias, cf. A. S. Aiton and J. L. Mecham, "The Archivo General de
Indias," in *The Hispanic American Historical Review*, IV. 533-568.)

At a very early age Francisco left his native Vizcaya and sailed for New Spain. The date of his departure and the circumstances of his voyage are unknown. In Mexico City he was entrusted to the care of his uncle, Diego de Ibarra, who in fact became a foster-parent to the boy. Why a mere child, certainly not beyond ten years of age, should have been sent to the New World is a matter of interest. Were his parents dead? We have reason to doubt it. Who accompanied the boy to America? This we do not know, excepting that he was not accompanied by his uncle, Diego, who was already in New Spain at the time of the Mixton War (1542). Francisco was reared and educated in the household of his uncle in Mexico City. Later he was made a page in the viceregal court of Luís de Velasco, second viceroy of New Spain. This preferment is explicable if we recall that Diego de Ibarra was a son-in-law of the viceroy.[3] Francisco's term of service in the court was not long, certainly not longer than four years, for Velasco became viceroy in 1550, and in 1554 the young conquistador began his career as an explorer in Nueva Galicia. It is to be presumed that, in view of his powerful patronage, the training of the youth was the best that the capital of New Spain afforded; Francisco de Ibarra developed into a refined, intelligent, and extremely well-trained young man—"a wise and good Christian deemed capable of winning both laurels and riches for his sovereign and for himself in enterprises demanding wisdom, prudence, and daring."[4]

The territorial limits of Nueva Vizcaya, the province explored and settled by Francisco de Ibarra and of which he was commissioned first governor and captain-general, were during his lifetime but ill-defined. It comprised approximately the modern Mexican states of Durango, Chihuahua,

[3] A. G. I., 66-6-17, Información de Diego de Ibarra, 9 de agosto de 1582.
[4] A. G. I., 1-1-3/22, Obregón, Crónica.

Sinaloa, and Sonora. The vast expanse of this frontier province can be appreciated to best advantage if we pause to note that the 236,382 square miles of the four Mexican states are slightly in excess of the combined areas of New England, New York, Pennsylvania, and Ohio.

The dominant physiographic feature of the region is the great central Cordillera, the Sierra Madre Occidental, which runs nearly parallel with the Pacific seaboard and divides the states of Sonora and Sinaloa from Chihuahua and Durango. To the eastward another range, the Sierra Madre Oriental, passes through Coahuila, Nuevo León, San Luís Potosí, and continues in a southerly direction until it is united with the western range at the Isthmus of Tehuantepec. These mountains form a great central plateau, beginning at Mexico City at an altitude of about eight thousand feet and sloping off to the north into the desert lands of Chihuahua. Fully half of the old Spanish province of Nueva Vizcaya was a part of this table-land. It does not constitute a continuous level stretch, however, but is intersected by two ridges: first, a range which rises in Jalisco and crosses in a northeasterly direction into San Luís Potosí where it merges into the eastern Sierra Madre; and, second, the mountain divide which crosses from Durango to Coahuila. At the intersection of the Durango, Chihuahua, and Coahuila boundary lines, there occurs a great depression of barren desert and marsh lands known as Bolsón de Mapimí. The elevations of the following cities named in order of their location from south to north illustrate the decline in altitude as one proceeds from Zacatecas to El Paso: Zacatecas, 8050 feet; Durango, 6850 feet; Chihuahua, 4635 feet; and Ciudad Juárez (adjoining El Paso), 3600 feet.

The Sierra Madre Occidental consists of several parallel ranges; the most eastern of these is known as the Sierra Tarahumare and Sierra del Durango and the most western as the Sierra del Nazareno, Sierra Yaqui, and Sierra Fuerte. They converge in southern Sinaloa and Durango to form the Sierra Nayarit. The average height of the sierras is six to eight thousand feet. In the Sierra Nayarit occurs the highest peak, the Nevado de Colima (14,363 feet). The Sierra Madre Oriental consists of a broken chain of ranges which are rather low until they converge south of Tampico in a single lofty range. Both of the slopes of the western sierras are very abrupt, thus making it extremely difficult to cross them. The passes are not numerous, and their elevations are great. A fortunate physiographic feature, however, which facilitates the crossing of the sierras, is the system of waterways on the Pacific slope. Though none of the rivers, the Sonora, the Yaqui, the Mayo, the Fuerte, the Tamazula, or the Mazatlán, are navigable, nevertheless they penetrate far into the mountains, burrowing out great transverse canyons. The Spanish explorers invariably followed the rivers to their sources, whence they worked their way over the mountain ridges to the central plateau. No rivers of importance are to be found east of the sierras. The Río Conchos, which rises in southern Chihuahua and flows north to its junction with the Río Grande del Norte, is dry most of the year. A large part of Durango is drained by the Río Nazas, which empties into the salt lake of Mayrán in the Bolsón de Mapimí. Southern Durango and northern Zacatecas are drained by the Aguanaval and the Nieves, which also find an outlet in the Coahuila marsh lands. Even at the time of the first appearance of the Spaniards, the central plateau of Durango was quite arid; for they frequently alluded to the dry bed of the Nazas and other rivers of the region.

Although the area under consideration lies between the twenty-fourth and the thirtieth parallels of north latitude, the climate is not uniformly semitropical. There, as in other portions of Latin America, it is conditioned not by latitude, but by altitude. The climate of Durango can hardly be surpassed in its tonic properties; the temperature is remarkably even, and the atmosphere is ever clear and dry. Farther to the north, in Chihuahua, however, the variations in summer heat and winter cold are more marked. The climate of the coastal plain of Sinaloa and Sonora, although very pleasant in winter, is notably warm in the summer months. Hermosillo, for example, is decidedly warmer than Yuma, the warmest meteorological station in the United States. The ordinary midday summer temperature is about one hundred and ten degrees in the shade; the night temperature at the same season is usually fifty to seventy-five degrees. Because of the great altitude of the Sierra Madre Occidental, it is almost impassable at times, due to the snows and the bitter cold. In several of the diaries of the conquistadores there is mention of men and horses being frozen to death while crossing the sierras.

A climatic characteristic of the Mexican northwest is the two relatively humid seasons coinciding with the two principal inflections of the annual temperature curve, i.e., in January-February and July-August respectively. Precipitation is chiefly in the form of rain; in the winter snow falls frequently in the sierras, but rarely on the outlying ranges or on the plains. The mean annual precipitation is about thirty inches toward the crest of the sierras, and diminishes with decreasing altitude. On the coastal plain the average rainfall is five to ten inches. In northern Sonora it is less than two inches. On the north central plateau it varies from two to ten inches. The distribution of precipitation is erratic both in time and in space; some spots may receive half a dozen rains within a year, while other spots may remain rainless for several years; and the wet spot of one series of years may be the dry spot of the next.

"No part of the world can be truly understood without a knowledge of its garment of vegetation, for this determines not only the nature of the animal inhabitants but also the occupations of the majority of human beings."[5]   The flora of Nueva Vizcaya illustrates in a striking manner the adjustment of vegetal life to an unfavorable environment. The prevailing vegetation is perennial, of slow and stunted growth and unequal distribution.   Nearly all of the plants have roots of exceptional length and are protected from heat and animals by glazed epidermis and by thorns.   Broadly speaking, the vegetation of Nueva Vizcaya falls into two classes, the cordillera coniferous forest and the desert plants. Since the moisture in the southern sierras lasts only three or four months, the forests are quite different from the forests of the American Northwest.   The trees are not so vigorous, so green or moss-covered, so dense in growth or in foliage, or so large.   As the mountains merge into the plains and the desert, the stately pines are replaced by scrub.   The desert predominates.   Its arborescent vegetation represents two distinct types: (1) trees and shrubs related to those of moister lands but modified to fit arid conditions; and (2) distinctive forms peculiar to the desert, such as cacti and related plants.   In the first class we encounter mesquite, paloverdes, and the straight-trunked paloblanco.   Interspersed among the larger trees and also in drier and more alkaline areas are a number of woody shrubs, some with thorns and some without thorns; in the latter class fall the sage and greasewood.   Cacti in a score of forms grow throughout the region.   The plateau of Durango, which is semidesert (i.e., partially grassland), is particularly adaptable to pastoral purposes; thus, soon after the country was opened up to the miners, cattle-raising became the occupation

[5] Ellsworth Huntington, *The Red Man's Continent*, New Haven, 1919, p. 88.

second in importance. Indigenous edible vegetation will be discussed later.

The fauna of the region is scarcely richer than the vegetation. Spanish explorers marched over vast areas of plains and mountains without encountering traces of bird or animal life. This condition was especially true of the eastern slope of the Cordillera and the Sonora and Chihuahua deserts. In other localities game was found in varying quantities. The larger land animals are the mountain goat, lion, puma, and jaguar in the higher sierras; the mule-deer and white-tail deer in the mid-height plains; and the coyote, antelope, and peccary ranging over the lower expanses. Of the smaller animals, the hare, rabbit, and squirrel are most common. The buffalo never penetrated, in historic times at least, south of the Río Grande del Norte.[6] Quail and doves are fairly common and wild turkeys to a somewhat lesser degree. The aquatic fauna of the waters washing the shores of Sonora and Sinaloa is, in contrast with the meagerness of the land fauna, most abundant and varied. In addition to innumerable varieties of fish, especially abundant and large are the green turtles on which the Seri Indians chiefly subsist.

The most valuable natural resources of northwestern Mexico are the minerals, which are widespread in their distribution. The precious metal found in greatest abundance is silver, and, indeed, the total production of silver in Mexico has far exceeded that of gold. "The historic mines are grouped about the central plateau; the axis of the metalliferous region lies on a line which might be drawn from

[6] "Originally the bison ranged from the Alleghanies to the Rockies and even farther west into Oregon and Nevada, and from Great Slave Lake southward nearly to central Mexico" (L. Farrand, *Basis of American History,* New York, 1904, p. 62). The author is not in agreement with Dr. Farrand, for the first Spaniards to enter Texas speak with surprise of the "cows" or buffalo which they found on the plains; this was their first view of the bison.

Guadalupe y Calvo in southern Chihuahua through Mexico south to Oaxaca. The chief deposits of metal lie in the Pacific range. Until the period of the Revolution the output of silver represented one-third of the world's production, coming, as it did in the colonial epoch, mainly from the mineral districts of Guanajuato, Zacatecas, and San Luís Potosí, regions which even during the recent period of unrest continued great production."[7] Other mineral resources are: gold in the sierras, but especially in northern Sonora; copper in Durango and Sonora; tin and cinnabar in Durango; and coal widely distributed. Excepting silver, and gold to a certain extent, the great mineral wealth of Nueva Vizcaya was untouched by the Spaniards.[8]

The indigenous population of the area which was once the province of Nueva Vizcaya, though not numerous or greatly advanced in culture, presents an ethnological problem which up to the present time has not been satisfactorily solved. The great diversity of idioms and range of cultural development render classification an extremely difficult matter. One of the earliest classifications was that made by H. H. Bancroft in 1883.[9] He grouped under the general term "New Mexicans" the Indian nations of New Mexico, Arizona, Lower California, Sonora, Sinaloa, Chihuahua, Durango, Coahuila, Nuevo León, northern Zacatecas, and western Texas. He admitted that as a groupal designation this name was neither more nor less appropriate than some others. Although he does not state explicitly, it is presumed

---

[7] H. I. Priestley, *The Mexican Nation,* New York, 1923, p. 12.

[8] For references on the physiography of northwestern Mexico, cf. H. H. Bancroft, *Resources and Development of Mexico,* San Francisco, 1883; Bureau of American Republics, *Mexico, a General Sketch,* Washington, 1911; Farrand, *Basis of American History,* chaps. i-iii; A. de Humboldt, *Political Essay on the Kingdom of New Spain,* London, 1811, I, Book I; Huntington, *The Red Man's Continent,* chaps. ii-iv; M. Orozco y Berra, *Apuntes para la historia de la geografía en México,* Mexico, 1864.

[9] H. H. Bancroft, *The Native Races,* San Francisco, 1833, I, chap. v.

that Bancroft's classification was based on both cultural similarity and racial and linguistic affinity. These "New Mexicans" were in turn subdivided into: (1) *Apaches,* all the savage tribes roaming through New Mexico, northwest Texas, and a small part of northern Mexico and Arizona; (2) the *Pueblos,* the partially cultivated townspeople of New Mexico and Arizona, and the non-nomadic Pimas, Maricopas, and Papagos; (3) the *Lower Californians,* those occupying the peninsula of Lower California; and (4) the *Northern Mexicans,* the natives scattered over Sonora, Sinaloa, Chihuahua, Durango, Coahuila, Nuevo León, and northern Zacatecas. The Northern Mexicans were the original inhabitants of Nueva Vizcaya; it is with them that we shall be concerned.

Since linguistic and cultural limits do not always coincide except in the case of small families, we find that Clark Wissler, noted ethnologist of the American Indian, has two classifications for the natives of the Southwest.[10] The natives of New Mexico, Arizona, and northern Mexico are grouped into "The Southwestern Cultural Area." In this area there are what appear to be two types of culture, the *pueblos* and the *nomadic tribes;* but Wissler contends that in reality there is no serious distinction, since the differences are chiefly those of architecture and social grouping. Certain dominant traits for the whole area far counterbalance minor differences; these are: main dependence upon maize and other cultivated foods, use of the grinding-stone or *metate* instead of the mortar, the art of masonry, the loom or upward weaving, cultivation of cotton as textile material, and domestication of the turkey. It is significant that this cultural classification is almost identical with Bancroft's "New Mexican" group.

[10] Clark Wissler, *The American Indian,* New York, 1922, chap. xlv.

Linguistically, nearly all of the natives of the Mexican northwest and central interior are classified by Wissler, after Thomas and Swanton,[11] as Nahuatlans. Here we note a radical departure from the cultural classification in that the Indians of New Mexico and Arizona are omitted, whereas many more tribes even as far south as the valley of Anáhuac are included. Under the generic term Nahuatlan, the following tribes are listed: (1) Piman (Pima Alto, Pima Bajo, Pima Bamoa, Potlapigua, Tepehuane Villages); (2) Ópata (Eudeve, Jova or Ova); (3) Tarahumare; (4) Seri; (5) Yaqui; (6) Zoe (Baimena, Tepehue, Tepehuana); (7) Acaxée (Xixime, Sabaibo, Teloca); (8) Cora; (9) Huichol; (10) Tepecano; (11) Concho; (12) Zacateco; (13 Guachichile; (14) Nio; (15) Aztec; (16) Pipil; (17) Niquiran; (18) Sigua.

Basing our conclusions on the foregoing, we find that there existed a cultural and linguistic bond among the natives of Nueva Vizcaya. Disagreement of ethnologists applies only to the Indians who lived north and south of Nueva Vizcaya —areas which do not at present concern us. Although it is very dangerous to indulge in generalization, certain recognized characteristics and traits can be detected in the North Mexicans (adopting Bancroft's groupal name). Physically, the North Mexicans were splendid types. With few exceptions, notably the Ópatas and Chicoratas, they were robust and well-formed, with fine chests, slender but sinewy limbs, though the hands and especially the feet were large; their heads were round, and average in size; their features quite regular; their hair luxuriant, straight, and coarse, ranging from jet-black to tawny in color, and worn long. In complexion they were dark brown; a few, notably the Yaqui, being light brown. The Seri are especially fine

[11] C. Thomas and J. R. Swanton, *Indian Languages of Mexico and Central America*, Bureau of American Ethnology, *Bulletin*, No. 44.

physical specimens and have for centuries been reputed a
race of giants. The mean stature of the adult Seri may be
estimated at about six feet for the males and five feet nine
inches for the females.[12]

The character of the raiment of the North Mexicans at
the time of the Spanish conquest certainly did not approxi-
mate uniformity. It ranged from a piece of tanned deer-
skin worn in front of their persons by the Tarahumares to
the rather complex cotton garments worn by the Ópatas.
From the New Mexican pueblo area down to Peru, cotton
was the great textile fiber. It is significant that the distribution of cotton coincided with regions of higher culture; at least it was not found among the non-agricultural
people. Bast fiber, especially that of the agave, was also
used for weaving. Among different tribes, therefore,
clothing was made variously from skins, both tanned and
untanned, cotton, vegetal fibers, and feathers. Their habitations ranged from the rocky caverns of the nomadic Tarahumares to the rather substantial timber and adobe dwellings
of the Conchos, Yaqui, and Ópatas.

As was noted above, Wissler cites as a dominant trait of
the natives of the "Southwestern Area" "the main dependence upon maize and other cultivated foods." This characteristic was quite true of the North Mexicans, although
exception must be noted on the coast of Sonora, where there
was no maize and the natives lived on pulverized rush,
straw, fish, and game; and on the eastern plains, where
the nomadic tribes lived almost solely on game. Agriculture
was practised by the majority of natives, and, because of
the almost universal scarcity of rainfall, irrigated agriculture
was the prevailing type. This was by no means exceptional,

---

[12] W J McGee, *The Seri Indians*, Bureau of American Ethnology,
Seventeenth Annual Report, Washington, 1898, Part I, p. 136.

for the art of irrigation was known from Arizona to Peru.[13]
In addition to maize, the natives cultivated varieties of beans,
squash, pumpkins, melons, the agave, and the prickly-pear or
the Indian fig. Widespread cultivation was impossible, both
because the natives lacked iron tools and also because they
lacked draft animals. Throughout the length and breadth
of the two Americas, the llama of the high Andes was the
only animal that could take the place of the horse. As a
matter of fact, the llama and the dog were the only native
American domesticated animals.

The weapons used by the Indians in their wars and on
their hunts were the bow and arrow, clubs, and a short lance.
The arrows were sometimes provided with chipped stone or
bone points; some tribes possessed flint knives. The natives
of northern Sonora smeared the points of their arrows with
a deadly poison. The poisoned arrows of the Sonora tribes
filled the Spaniards with terror and seriously retarded exploration and settlement in that area.

Regarding political organization among the North Mexicans, Bancroft says: "I find nowhere in this region any
system of laws or government. There are the usual tribal
chieftains, selected on account of their superior skill or bravery, but with little or no power except in war matters."[14]
Since personal prowess and ability were the requisites of a
chieftainship, the office usually died with the holder. Unlike
the case of the well-organized Pueblo Indians, the duties
and authority of the chiefs of the North Mexicans were
very indefinite. Certain it is, however, that with the passing
of the emergency the chief tended to lapse back to the level
of the other members of the tribe. The most significant
organization within the tribe was the kinship group or the
clan. In most of the tribes descent was traced through the

[13] Wissler, *The American Indian*, p. 28.
[14] Bancroft, *Native Races*, I. 584.

mother, and new-born children were assigned to the clan of the mother. In Mexico, as among the Indians within the present limits of the United States, the ownership of property depended upon the clan organization; land was the common property of the group. There was private ownership of personal property, but the right of inheritance lay in the clan.

In conclusion, the cultural level of the North Mexicans was rather low. They lacked much in comparison with the Pueblos in social organization and in the arts. On the other hand, they were as developed as the Indians of the northern plains, and perhaps more so. Although certain tribes, such as the Seri and the Salineros of Sonora, were degraded and vile and deserved Arlégui's sweeping condemnation as being "totally barbarous and of gross intelligence,"[15] nevertheless, many nations deserved exemption; noteworthy among these were the Ópatas, Yaqui, Mayos, and Acaxées. Detailed accounts of distinctive tribal characteristics will be reserved for succeeding chapters.[16]

[15] José Arlégui, *Chrónica de la Provincia de S. Francisco de Zacatecas,* Mexico, 1737, p. 149.

[16] In addition to manuscript titles cited in the succeeding pages, too numerous to be enumerated here, the following references were consulted for the ethnology of the Indians of northwestern Mexico; A. F. Bandelier, *Historical Introduction to Studies Among the Sedentary Indians of New Mexico,* Boston, 1881; also, *Final Report of Investigations Among the Indians of the Southwestern United States Carried on Mainly in the Years from 1880 to 1885,* Cambridge, 1890-1892; also, *Contributions to the History of the Southwestern Portion of the United States,* Cambridge, 1890; Bancroft, *Native Races,* I; D. G. Brinton, *The American Race,* New York, 1891; McGee, *The Seri Indians;* J. W. Powell, *Indian Linguistic Families,* Bureau of American Ethnology, *Seventh Annual Report,* Washington, 1891; Wissler, *The American Indian.*

CHAPTER II

An account of the exploration, settlement, and organization of Nueva Vizcaya becomes in large measure the biography of Francisco de Ibarra; but not solely through a biographical sketch can the founding of Nueva Vizcaya be chronicled. Although Ibarra was the central figure, he by no means monopolized the field, for he was assisted by several able lieutenants whom he often dispatched on individual enterprises. In the later years of Ibarra's governorship, when he was physically incapacitated, he put a greater dependence on these men than would have ordinarily been the case. Certain pioneers in Nueva Galicia must also be accorded their legitimate credit, for they paved the way for the exploration and settlement of the northern hinterland.

Since the founding of Nueva Vizcaya constitutes a natural phase of the expansion movement in New Spain which was inaugurated after the Cortesian conquest, it seems necessary to review somewhat fully the steps in the occupation of the frontiers north and west of Mexico City. These preliminary events centered for the most part in the kingdom of Nueva Galicia, that region from which were dispatched most of the organized expeditions into the northern interior in search of the Seven Cities of Cíbola, Gran Quivira, the Amazons, and other fantasies which constituted the "Northern Mystery." Thus, since the exploration and settlement of Nueva Galicia was a necessary preliminary to the development of Nueva Vizcaya, an account of these beginnings cannot be summarily dismissed.

With the conquest of the capital city of the Montezumas by the intrepid Cortés and his handful of equally courageous followers, the first phase of the conquest of the mainland of North America was finished. Then was inaugurated a second stage of the Spanish advance, one which in many respects vastly overshadowed the first. For two decades Spanish activities were directed east, south, and west from the valley of Mexico and then northward into California, New Mexico, and Florida. In expansion the second stage was markedly superior to the earlier period because of the great range of "the northern will o' the wisp," and the inexhaustible zeal and fortitude with which numerous conquistadores pursued it. Although no marvelous land of fabulous riches was discovered, the latent wealth of the northern borderlands was infinitely greater than that of the Montezumas stored up in the palaces of Tenochtitlán. Nor is there lack of romance in the conquest, though it has had no Prescott to tell its story.

The northward expansion began, not from Mexico City, but from Michoacán, which had been founded in 1522 by Cristóbal de Olid, a lieutenant of Hernando Cortés. In that year Olid dispatched Álvarez Chico and a small company of men to Zacatula, but they turned aside to conquer Colima, where great riches had been reported. Before Álvarez reached the coveted province, a dispute arose in the ranks, and some of his men deserted him and set out independently for Colima under the leadership of Ávalos. They marched to the north and east of Lake Chapala through an area since called, in honor of its discoverer, Ávalos Province. Álvarez, in the meantime, approached Colima by a more direct route, but after being defeated by the Indians of that region, he hurriedly retreated and proceeded to Zacatula, his original destination. A settlement was planted at Zacatula in May, 1522. When Cortés was informed of the defeat of Álvarez, he ordered Olid to chastise and subjugate the Indians of

Colima. After a hard-fought battle Olid defeated the native cacique and his allies, and, to assure possession of their country, he founded the town of Colima. Ávalos was left in charge of the new settlement.

Colima became the base of the next advance into the region which became known as Nueva Galicia. In 1524 Francisco Cortés, a kinsman of the great conquistador and alcalde mayor of Colima, was sent in search of the rich islands of the Amazons, which were said to be a ten days' journey up the coast from Colima. With about eighty men Francisco Cortés marched through Chimalhuacán, or western Jalisco, as far north as the Río Tololotlán (Río Grande). There he secured the allegiance of the "queen" of Jalisco, but discovered no Amazon Islands and but little gold. Disappointed by the absence of riches, Francisco Cortés returned to Colima. In the meantime, Ávalos had also ventured as far north as Guadalajara. Preparations were made to resume exploration in the north, but they had to be postponed for various reasons.[1]

As early as 1522 Hernando Cortés began building ships in Zacatula. He planned to sail north, then west, and finally south until he should reach India; he hoped to discover in the course of the voyage the "secret of the strait." He encountered numerous obstacles in building and launching the ships, and it was not until 1526 that he was ready to start. Then came a royal order to Cortés on June 20, 1526, to dispatch immediately an expedition to the Moluccas to the relief of Loaisa. As haste was necessary, the plan of following the coast to India was abandoned. Three vessels under the command of Álvaro de Saavedra were sent from Zacatula on October 31, 1527, direct to the East Indies.

[1] H. E. Bolton and T. M. Marshall, *The Colonization of North America,* New York, 1920, pp. 36-37; H. H. Bancroft, *The North Mexican States and Texas,* San Francisco, 1844, I. 12-15; V. Riva Palacio, ed., *México á través de los siglos,* Barcelona, 1888-1889, II. 49-81.

Before undertaking the hazardous transpacific voyage, Saavedra tested his ships by making a trial voyage in July, 1527, up the coast as far as Santiago, which is situated near Manzanillo in Colima. Barring this one voyage, which skirted the coastline, the northwest region was not visited by white men from the time when Francisco Cortés discovered Jalisco until Nuño de Guzmán became active in Nueva Galicia.[2]

An important though bloody chapter in the history of northwestern New Spain was written by Nuño de Guzmán in the years 1530 to 1535. Guzmán was an able and even brilliant lawyer, a man of great energy and firmness, but insatiably ambitious, aggressive, wily, and cruel. He had served successively as governor of Pánuco and president of the first audiencia of Mexico. His tenure of office as president of the audiencia was short-lived, due to the bitter opposition aroused by his misrule. Moreover, the expected return from Spain of Hernando Cortés, the sworn enemy of Guzmán, helped to convince him that he should leave Mexico City for safer climes. He refused to flee ignominiously, but proposed to recoup his waning fortunes by conquering for himself and his sovereign a new kingdom in the northwest land of mystery.

At the head of a force of five hundred Spaniards and numerous Indian allies, Guzmán left Mexico City in December, 1529. He had with him as one of his captains Cristóbal de Oñate, a man who was to become one of the most important figures in the history of the northern frontier of New Spain. Cristóbal de Oñate was an hijodalgo of illustrious parentage. He was a native of Vitoria, in the Basque province of Álava, and a descendant of López Díaz de Haro, "Señor de Vizcaya," chief and captain-general of the Andalucian frontier, and conqueror of the city of Baeza from the

[2] Riva Palacio, II. 253-265; Bancroft, *North Mexican States and Texas,* I. 15-25; F. A. MacNutt, *Cortés and the Conquest of Mexico,* New York, 1909, pp. 43-67.

Moors in 1227. For this achievement the descendants of López Díaz adopted the surname of Baeza. Cristóbal de Oñate came to New Spain in 1524. He married Doña Cathalina de Salazar, daughter of Gonzalo de Salazar, first factor of real hacienda in New Spain. An issue of this marriage was Juan de Oñate, conquistador of New Mexico.[3]

Guzmán's line of march lay by way of Michoacán and Jalisco to the vicinity of modern Guadalajara. In marching through that territory he ignored the prior rights of discovery of Ávalos and Francisco Cortés and pursued a policy intended to make it appear that the country had never been conquered. Therefore the natives were provoked to revolt in order that they might be subdued; this end was accomplished by plunder, carnage, and enslavement. At Tepic Guzmán left a garrison; then he crossed the Río Tololotlán on May 29, 1530. He was now on virgin soil, insofar as it had never before been visited by white men. He took formal possession of this territory and named it Greater Spain. This proud title was later changed by royal order to Nueva Galicia.

Guzmán and his followers then pushed up the coast beyond the Río San Pedro to Azatlán on the Río Acaponeta, where they went into winter quarters. From that place a reconnoitering party under Lope de Samaniego, in November, 1530, effected an entry into the province of Chiametla. In the words of H. H. Bancroft, "This was the first entry of Europeans into the territory since called Sinaloa, the first crossing of the line which marks the territorial limits of this volume"; i.e., *The North Mexican States and Texas.*[4] In like manner, Samaniego's expedition constituted the first

[3] B. Q. Cornish, "The Ancestry and Family of Juan de Oñate," in H. M. Stephens and H. E. Bolton, eds., *The Pacific Ocean in History,* New York, 1917, pp. 452-467.

[4] Bancroft, *North Mexican States and Texas,* I. 30.

entry of white men into the region which later became Nueva
Vizcaya, the territorial limits of the present volume.

A few weeks after the return of Samaniego, Guzmán,
with his force somewhat augmented, marched to Chiametla.
He remained there for about a month, and in January, 1531,
resumed his journey in a northwesterly direction. By April
the explorers reached the Culiacán country at the junction of
the Humaya and Tamazula rivers. Several scouting parties
were sent out; one followed the Río Culiacán almost to the
sea; another penetrated into the mountains some distance
beyond the Río Humaya; and still another, under Samaniego, went as far north as Río de Petatlán, now known as
Río de Sinaloa. There is mention, but unfortunately not
satisfactorily substantiated, of expeditions sent by Guzmán
under Cristóbal de Oñate and José de Angulos which supposedly crossed the mountains to the east and reached the
Guadiana Valley.[5] Disappointed in his search for the rich
Amazon Islands, Guzmán now turned to the other of his
two original destinations; that is, the Seven Cities of Cíbola.

In May the explorers started to cross the Sierra Madre
Occidental and were almost over the mountains when they
were met by a reconnoitering party which had been sent
ahead. Their report was most discouraging, for they said
that they had marched nearly two hundred miles through
most unpromising country and were of the opinion that a
continued advance would be futile. It is to be presumed
that these scouts had ascended the Tamazula, crossed the
sierras, found a branch of the Río Nazas, and traversed a
portion of central Durango. They were the first Europeans
to enter the state of Durango. On being advised of the

[5] M. de la Mota Padilla, *Historia de la Conquista de la Provincia de
la Nueva Galicia*, Mexico, 1870, pp. 76, 82; F. Frejes, *Historia breve
de la conquista de los estados independientes del Imperio Méjicano*,
Mexico, 1839, pp. 11-114; P. Beaumont, *Crónica de la Provincia de S.
Pedro y S. Pablo de Michoacán*, Mexico, 1873-1874, III. 488.

futility of further search for the Seven Cities in that direction, Guzmán abandoned with reluctance this, his second goal, and returned to Culiacán.

After the founding of San Miguel de Culiacán and the appointment of Captain Diego de Proaño as alcalde mayor of the new settlement, Nuño de Guzmán returned to Jalisco. On his return march he planted in Chiamatla a small settlement which maintained a precarious existence for several years. Henceforth that portion of Nueva Galicia north of Río Grande de Tololotlán received scant attention from Guzmán, who established himself in 1531 in his capital city, Santiago de Compostela. The gradual settlement of Nueva Galicia continued. La Purificación on the Colima frontier was founded, and, under the orders of Guzmán, Cristóbal de Oñate founded a Spanish villa at Nochistlán. This town, named Guadalajara after Guzmán's birthplace, was moved in 1533 to a site near the present Cuquio, and finally, in 1541, it was transplanted to its present site.[6] Guzmán's harsh rule brought a train of well-deserved reverses upon him; in 1536 he was deprived of his governorship and forced to retire from Nueva Galicia; subsequently he died in poverty and disgrace. Cristóbal de Oñate was left in charge of the province until 1537, when Diego Pérez de la Torre assumed the reins of government. Torre governed but a short time, for he was killed in an Indian uprising in 1539. The next governor of Nueva Galicia was the famous Francisco Vázquez de Coronado.

The Spaniards left by Guzmán in San Miguel de Culiacán had not remained inactive. Shortly after Guzmán's departure, Proaño sent Sebastián de Evora on an expedition to the north on which he discovered the Río Mocorito, which was known during the colonial period as Río Sebastián de

---

[6] Mota Padilla, *Nueva Galicia*, pp. 23-107; Bancroft, *North Mexican States and Texas*, I. 26-70.

Evora. In July, 1533, Diego de Guzmán led another expedition from Culiacán. He marched up the coast past the Sinaloa and Fuerte rivers, and in August arrived in the land of the Sinaloas who lived between the Fuerte and the Mayo. From Sinaloa he continued past the Río Mayo to the Río Yaqui, which was explored from its mouth up to Nevame. Guzmán and his followers then returned to San Miguel.[7] Little more is known concerning northern Nueva Galicia during these years other than that the Indians, because of Spanish oppression, revolted in San Miguel and in Chiametla. The revolts were put down, but the Spanish oppression did not end. As a result, the natives ceased to cultivate their fields, deserted the settlements, and fled to the mountains. Because of these outrages, Captain Proaño was removed from office, and Cristóbal de Tápia was appointed alcalde mayor of San Miguel. Tápia in turn was succeeded by Melchior Díaz, who held the office in 1536 and 1537.

Between 1532 and 1536 ships belonging to Cortés touched at several points along the coast of Nueva Galicia. Diego Hurtado de Mendoza was the first to navigate the waters of the Gulf of California. In 1532 he was put in command of two ships and was ordered by Cortés to sail up the coast for one hundred and fifty leagues. He succeeded in sailing as far north as the Río Fuerte, where he was killed by the natives. Cortés, undeterred by the death of Mendoza and the loss of one of his ships, dispatched two more vessels up the coast in 1533. This expedition had no better luck than the first one; one of the ships was lost, and the other sailed into the port of Chiametla with only four survivors.

In 1534-1535 the indefatigable Cortés sent three more ships from Tehuantepec to Chiametla, at which place he joined them a little later with a large force. He had

[7] Bancroft, *North Mexican States and Texas*, I. 26-70.

entered Nueva Galicia in spite of the protests of Nuño de Guzmán. From Chiametla Cortés set sail to the northwest. The subsequent history of this expedition bears no relation to Nueva Galicia and Nueva Vizcaya.

The next event of moment on the northern frontier was the advent in Culiacán of the famous overland travelers, Cabeza de Vaca and his three companions. These, the only survivors of the ill-fated Narváez expedition to Florida (1528), after enduring nearly six years of slavery among the Indians of the Gulf region, escaped and crossed Texas, Chihuahua, and Sonora, and finally, in 1536, reached Culiacán. Cabeza de Vaca and his companions, after wandering over Texas, reached the Río Grande at about Presidio del Norte (the junction of the Conchos and the Río Grande). They continued up the Río Grande for some distance, then struck westward across Chihuahua to the headwaters of the Río Yaqui, where they found an Indian pueblo, named by them Corazones. There they heard of other men like themselves, which gave them renewed hope that they were nearing Spanish settlements or *tierra de paz*. As they descended the Río Yaqui they not only heard more reports about the white men, but discovered traces of Spanish invasion. At last Vaca and his companions met a party of slave-raiders from San Miguel on the Río Petatlán. They arrived in San Miguel on April 1, 1536, and were hospitably received by Melchior Díaz, the alcalde mayor. From Culiacán they went to Compostela and then to Mexico City.[8]

The arrival of Cabeza de Vaca in Mexico reawakened intense interest in the northern interior. This interest culminated in keen rivalry between Viceroy Mendoza and Hernando Cortés for the exclusive right of exploring the new lands. Mendoza forestalled Cortés by acquiring the Negro

[8] Cf. A. F. Bandelier, *The Gilded Man*, New York, 1893, pp. 125-162; and A. F. and Fanny Bandelier, *The Journey of Cabeza de Vaca*, Trail Maker Series, New York, 1905.

slave Stephen, one of Vaca's companions, and sent him with a Franciscan friar, Marcos de Niza, on a reconnoitering journey. In March, 1539, Friar Marcos and the Negro left San Miguel and traveled in a northerly direction. After being sent ahead, Stephen reported to Friar Marcos that he had found the Seven Cities of Cíbola. The credulous monk hastened after the slave and crossed over the mountains of northern Sonora into the Gila Valley. It is conjectured that he went by way of Magdalena, or Vacupa, in the valley of the upper Río Magdalena. From the Gila he continued in a northwesterly direction until he reached the vicinity of the Zuñi pueblos in western New Mexico.[9] Friar Marcos, believing the pueblos to be Cíbola, did not attempt to enter them, because the natives had risen and killed the Negro. On returning to the Spanish settlements, he grossly exaggerated the wealth and importance of Cíbola.[10]

When Cortés heard Friar Marcos' marvelous tales, he became alarmed lest Mendoza should be the first to acquire those fabulously rich lands. He therefore hastened to dispatch three vessels under Francisco de Ulloa with orders to explore to the northward. Baltasar de Obregón, principal chronicler of the exploits of Francisco de Ibarra, who has also given us a detailed account of the Coronado expedition, cites an additional motive to explain the interest of Cortés in the northern lands. According to Obregón, Cortés acquired certain Aztec chronicles and maps which referred to the early home of that people. It was in the hope of making important scientific discoveries, and perhaps acquiring accu-

---

[9] According to Obregón (A. G. I., 1-1-3/22, Obregón, Crónica), Friar Marcos "traveled through Michoacán, Chiametla, Culiacán, Sonora, and Corazones until he reached the province of Líboro, called by the Spaniards, Cíbola."

[10] For the work of Friar Marcos cf. G. P. Winship, "The Coronado Expedition," 1540-1542, in Bureau of American Ethnology, *Fourteenth Annual Report*, Washington, 1896, Part I, pp. 353-367.

mulated treasure, that Cortés organized the expedition.[11] The voyage of Ulloa is important in that for the first time Spanish navigators skirted the entire coastline of Sinaloa and Sonora as far as the Colorado River. It is probable that the port of Guaymas was entered; several islands north of it were discovered.

The Ulloa expedition was the last one organized by Cortés, for soon afterward the conquistador went to Spain to press his claims of exclusive right in the matter of northern exploration. He never returned to the New World. Over the petitions, claims, and protests of several contestants, the Council of the Indies decided that the next entrada should be made under direct supervision of the crown. Accordingly, Viceroy Mendoza organized a great expedition under the command of Francisco Vázquez de Coronado, governor of Nueva Galicia. The viceroy went to Compostela and there supervised personally the preparations for the expedition.

Before setting out with the main body of his army, Governor Coronado sent ahead Melchior Díaz and Juan de Zaldívar to blaze a trail. They followed practically the same route that had been taken by Friar Marcos and reached Chichilticale, which was probably located on the Gila River.[12] A little later, in February, 1540, Coronado left Compostela at the head of one of the finest exploring forces yet assembled in the New World. He had six hundred well-armed soldiers, mostly mounted, and a great following of natives. When he arrived in Chiametla, Coronado was rejoined by Díaz and Zaldívar. Some of the cattle, which had been left in Chiametla because of their exhausted condition, multiplied so extensively that, when Francisco de Ibarra visited Chiametla years later, he found vast droves of wild

[note]

[11] A. G. I., 1-1-3/22, Obregón, Crónica.
[12] Winship, "The Coronado Expedition," p. 387.

cattle. Here, as in other parts of Nueva Galicia, the rich
and important grazing industry was founded on accidental
beginnings.

At San Miguel Coronado put Captain Tristán de Luna
y Arellano in command of the main force, while he with fifty
picked horsemen went ahead. When he came to the Yaqui
River, he ascended the valley of that stream to Corazones.
From the headwaters of the Yaqui he crossed the mountains
to Chichilticale and from there went to the Zuñi pueblos.
Arellano, with the main body, left San Miguel in April,
1540, and also marched to Corazones Valley, where he
founded the town of San Gerónimo, which was put in charge
of Melchior Díaz. "The site [of San Gerónimo] was soon
changed to the Valley of Señor, or Señora, perhaps the original form of the name Sonora, still applied to the valley as to
the state. The site was probably in the region between the
modern Hermosillo and Arizpe, but all details of exact location in the different authorities are hopelessly confused."[13]
After Arellano set out to join Coronado at Cíbola, Díaz left
San Gerónimo, hoping to find Hernando de Alarcón, who
had sailed up the coast with two vessels to coöperate with
Coronado by water. Díaz descended the Yaqui to its mouth
and then marched up the coast to the Colorado River. He
arrived too late to find Alarcón. The navigator had sailed
up the coast from Acapulco, putting in on the way at Santiago in Colima. From there he directed his course to Guay-
abál, the port of San Miguel de Culiacán, where he procured
a third ship and then continued north, noting several harbors
on the way. Finally, he arrived at the head of the Gulf of
California (1540) and ascended the Colorado River beyond
the mouth of the Gila River. Finding no trace of Coronado,
Alarcón gave up his search and returned to Acapulco.

[13] Bancroft, *North Mexican States and Texas,* I. 87; according to
Obregón (A. G. I., 1-1-3/22, Obregón, Crónica), Diego de Alcaras was
left in charge of the new villa with one hundred men.

Coronado, in the meantime, was experiencing a series of disappointments in New Mexico. The rich cities which had constituted his lure failed to materialize; but in searching for them he explored a vast expanse of territory. To the north of Zuñi the Moqui pueblos were discovered by Tovar, and farther to the northwest Cárdenas found the Grand Canyon of the Colorado. From Zuñi the explorers went to Tiguex, the pueblos of the Río Grande, where, in the course of the winter, an Indian revolt was put down with great severity. In the following spring, 1541, Coronado marched east to the Pecos River, descended that stream for some distance, and then ventured into the buffalo plains of western Texas. He continued in a northerly direction as far as Gran Quivira, which was probably located near Wichita, Kansas. He then returned to Tiguex, from whence he went back to Mexico in April, 1542. Obregón says of the return of the conquistador:

Coronado then returned from Quivira to his camp on the River Tibuex. There he fell from his horse which disarranged him mentally as well as physically, and so he determined to return from the land that he might easily have settled. Others give as the reason for his return his desire to rejoin his beautiful wife and his children in Mexico City. Some of Coronado's officers opposed his return, but he was obstinate, and so he returned with all his expedition to the City of Mexico by the route he had taken in going out. When he reached Mexico he had with him one hundred soldiers, some Indian servants, and fewer friends than when he left the city.

After making his report to the viceroy, Coronado returned to Nueva Galicia to resume his duties as governor.[14]

When men were being recruited for Coronado's expedition, it was not without reason that settlers in Nueva Galicia protested against the departure of their most able protectors.

[14] Winship, "The Coronado Expedition," is the standard authority on Coronado. Obregón's Crónica, however, gives a detailed account of the expedition and adds considerable to Winship. Cf. also, Bolton and Marshall, Colonization of North America, and F. W. Hodge and T. H. Lewis, editors, The Spanish Explorers in the Southern United States, 1528-1543 (Original Narratives of Early American History), New York, 1907.

There was great fear throughout the province of a general native insurrection, and, indeed, scattered revolts were already in progress. Guzmán had left Nueva Galicia in a terribly distraught condition; the natives had been so maltreated that they were marking time, waiting for an opportunity to throw off the hated yoke. This spirit was accentuated by the forced levies in men and supplies for Coronado's expedition. Native sorcerers and secret plotting added fuel to the fires of discontent.

Cristóbal de Oñate, the lieutenant-governor in charge of Nueva Galicia during Coronado's absence, sensed the coming trouble and took steps to protect the province. His measures, however, were futile, for suddenly, in April, 1541, the most serious native revolt in the history of New Spain had broken out, and temporarily the Spaniards were overwhelmed. The Indians killed their encomenderos, destroyed the settlements and the crops, and then sought refuge in the *peñoles,* or fortified cliffs, of Mixton, Nochistlán, Acatic, and other places near Guadalajara. Oñate sent Captain Miguel de Ibarra with a few Spaniards and an army of Indians to treat with the rebellious natives, but they refused to negotiate and treacherously attacked Ibarra and put him and his men to flight. The uprising spread like wildfire, and soon the natives about Culiacán, Compostela, and La Purificación were in open revolt. The uprising having become general and beyond his control, Oñate appealed to Mexico for aid.

Pedro de Alvarado was at that time in Navidad with a fleet making preparations to sail to the Spice Islands. The great adelantado could not resist Oñate's appeal for aid, as this was not only an opportunity to further the royal interests, but, equally important, it afforded the fiery conquistador the sort of adventure he loved. He accordingly hastened to Guadalajara in June, 1541, with a relief force of two hun-

dred men. Then, despite the prudent advice of Oñate, the
headstrong Alvarado refused to await reinforcements from
Mexico, but marched immediately against the Juchipila Indians. He was accompanied by Cristóbal de Oñate, Miguel
de Ibarra, Luís de Castilla, Pedro de Tovar, Juan de Zaldívar, and others. At the *peñol* of Nochistlán several
thousand Indians attacked the Spaniards with such ferocity
that they were forced to retreat with heavy losses. In the
confusion of the retreat Alvarado lost his life.

The natives, elated by their victory, were now able to
enlist in their cause many other tribes that had hitherto held
aloof. With overwhelming numbers they advanced upon
Guadalajara and invested the city; but, after a series of
sorties, the defenders were able to drive off the enemy. "In
one of the sorties," says Obregón, "forty horsemen opposed
fifteen thousand natives and killed seven hundred of them
without a single loss to themselves." The reader scarcely
needs to be warned that there may be exaggeration in this
statement. After the city was freed, it was moved on October 6, 1541, to its present site in the Atemajac Valley.[15]

Viceroy Mendoza, now thoroughly aroused because of
the great proportions the revolt was assuming, determined to
take the field himself. He assembled a force of four hundred and fifty Spaniards, and thirty thousand (?) Tlascaltec
and Aztec allies. Against this powerful array the rebels
could no longer offer effective resistance. Successively, in a
series of short sieges and assaults, Mendoza captured the
native fortresses of Coyna, Nochistlán, and Mixton. With
the loss of the last-named *peñol,* the back-bone of the revolt
was broken. Having crushed all serious resistance north of
the Río Tololotlán, Mendoza crossed to the south. There
the rebels submitted without a blow, and quiet was restored.

[15] H. H. Bancroft, *The History of Mexico,* San Francisco, 1883, II.
546.

Thousands of natives had been killed in battle; thousands more had been enslaved, and many escaped to the mountains. Thus ended the last desperate struggle of the natives of New Spain to expel the Europeans and regain their ancient liberties.[16]

Spanish expansion to the north was profoundly affected by the Mixton War, for the uprising in Nueva Galicia not only checked advance in that direction, but even caused a temporary contraction of the frontiers. Also, fantastic notions of great wonders in the far north had been exploded. The Spanish frontiersmen were willing now to fall back upon the established outposts and expand by a more gradual and sensible movement. In other words, a definite phase of exploration on the northwestern frontier of New Spain had drawn to a close with the Mixton War; following it came a new phase of colonial expansion, a period extending to the end of the century and witnessing the advance of the frontiers from Guadalajara to central Chihuahua and Sonora.

The history of Nueva Galicia in the decade following the Mixton War was characterized by settlement and organization within the natural limits which had been so prematurely overstepped by Guzmán and his successors.[17] In February, 1542, the cabildo of Guadalajara was formally established and the following municipal officers appointed: alcaldes, Fernando Flores and Pedro Placencia; regidores, Miguel Ibarra and Juan Zubia.[18] Due to its ideal situation both in soil and in climate, Guadalajara soon became a place of importance and attracted most of the settlers who entered Nueva Galicia. These accessions were won principally at the expense of Compostela, which continued for a while

[16] Obregón relates Mendoza's campaigns in great detail.
[17] Cf. p. 25.
[18] Bancroft, *Mexico*, II. 546.

longer to be the capital of Nueva Galicia, though in other respects it declined in importance.

In January, 1543, the cabildo of Guadalajara, associated with the municipal councils of Compostela, La Purificación, and San Miguel de Culiacán, petitioned for royal authorization to incorporate the pueblos of the province of Ávalos into Nueva Galicia. They asked also that lands lost in the Mixton War be repartitioned among the conquerors and that they be permitted to make war upon and enslave the Zacatecos, marauding natives who lived north of Guadalajara.

According to Tello, the Indian tribes in Zacatecas before the conquest were: Zacatecos, Caxcanes, Chichimecos, Guachichiles or Nayaritos, and Tecuexes.[19] These requests were granted by the audiencia of Mexico, excepting the one to exterminate or enslave the natives. On the contrary, the Viceroy ordered the subjugation of the Indians by peaceful means. The man entrusted with this delicate task was Cristóbal de Oñate, who, after the return of Coronado, acted as his lieutenant-governor of Nueva Galicia. Oñate's methods, which were not absolutely pacific, were relatively effective, and temporary quiet was restored among the native population. In fact, the peace which reigned in Nueva Galicia permitted Oñate to turn his attention to prospecting for minerals. In 1543 he discovered the rich mines of Espíritu Santo and Xaltepec near Compostela; also, farther to the east, the mines of Xocotlán, Huachinango, and Etzatlán.[20]

The discoveries made by Cristóbal de Oñate attracted more Spaniards to Nueva Galicia to be added to those who were already working the rich soil of its fertile valleys. The Spanish population of Nueva Galicia, however, was not

[19] Elias Amador, *Bosquejo histórico de Zacatecas*, Zacatecas, 1892, p. 181; J. A. Tello, *Libro segundo de la crónica miscelanea . . . de Xalisco*, CCLXIV. 776.

[20] Amador, *Zacatecas*, p. 182; Mota Padilla, *Nueva Galicia*, pp. 193-194.

great, for at no time during the sixteenth century did it exceed five hundred families. The native neophytes, who were to be numbered by the thousands, formed the bulk of the Christian population. When the number of inhabitants was regarded as being sufficient, at the instance of Charles V, Pope Paul III issued a bull creating the diocese of Nueva Galicia with the episcopal seat at Compostela.[21] The actual establishment of the bishopric was somewhat retarded because of the difficulty of finding a man to occupy the new episcopal seat. Fray Antonio Ciudad Rodrigo was nominated, but he declined. Juan de Barrios was appointed, but died before he could assume his benefice. Finally, the presbyter Pedro Gómez de Maraver, dean of the chapter of the cathedral of Oaxaca, was selected. He assumed his office in 1547. Bishop Maraver, "the Apostle of Nueva Galicia," never resided in Compostela, but, being a very pious, energetic, and restless man, he moved about continually from one place to another in his diocese. In so far as he had an episcopal seat, it was located in Guadalajara.[22]

In August, 1544, Lorenzo de Tejada, oidor of the audiencia of Mexico, arrived in Guadalajara and instituted a general residencia or rigid inquest, which was usually held at the conclusion of a term of office. Numerous accusations of general neglect of duty, favoritism, cruelty to the native element, and immorality were brought against Coronado. Since he was not able to refute the charges, he was fined and deprived of his office.[23] For a time Nueva Galicia ceased to

[21] Amador, *Zacatecas*, pp. 182-183; Bancroft (*Mexico*, II. 549) says, "The Bishopric of Nueva Galicia was erected at Compostela in 1544." This may have been the date when the bull was issued, but the order was not actually enacted until 1547, and even then Compostela never became the actual seat of the bishopric.

[22] Mota Padilla, *Nueva Galicia*, p. 198; Riva Palacio, *México á través de los siglos*, II. 351.

[23] A. S. Aiton, "The Later Career of Coronado," in *The American Historical Review*, XXX. 298-304.

be a province and became an alcaldía mayor subject to the
audiencia of Mexico. Baltasar Gallegos was the first alcalde
mayor. In 1547 Gallegos was succeeded by Diego de
Guevara.[24]

The alcaldía mayor of Nueva Galicia was short-lived,
for, by royal cédula of February 15, 1548, there was ordered
established in Compostela an audiencia subordinate to that
of Mexico. The audiencia was composed of a president,
four oidores, and a fiscal. Though it had no military power,
and its functions in financial matters were strictly limited, it
was actually the governing body of Nueva Galicia. In short,
it substituted in an administrative way for a governor, but its
most important functions were judicial. It was assigned
first hearing of all cases within a radius of twenty-five miles
about Compostela and appeals from juezes ordinarios for
the remainder of Nueva Galicia. It had power to name
juezes de residencias, to send out special investigators, to
supervise inferior judges, to insure good treatment of the
Indians, to assume the rights and obligations of the royal
patronage and to judge all cases affecting the same; and
finally, to guard the royal prerogative. Appeals from the
decisions of the audiencia were to go to the audiencia of
Mexico.[25] The audiencia of Mexico also had the power to
consider controversies in Nueva Galicia between alcaldes
mayores and the oidores.[26] Subsequent royal decrees further
defined the relative positions of the two audiencias. In 1552
the audiencia of Mexico was ordered not to meddle in the
affairs of Nueva Galicia except when there were actual appeals. In 1555 it was ruled that during a vacancy in the

[24] Mota Padilla, *Nueva Galicia,* p. 193; Amador (*Zacatecas,* p. 183)
says that Gallegos was appointed by the Emperor Charles V.

[25] Mota Padilla, *Nueva Galicia,* p. 198; Riva Palacio, *México á
través de los siglos,* II. 351; C. H. Cunningham, *The Audiencia in the
Spanish Colonies,* Berkeley, 1919, pp. 22-25.

[26] Mota Padilla, *Nueva Galicia,* p. 199.

viceroyalty the audiencia of Mexico should govern all of New Spain and exercise viceregal authority over Nueva Galicia. The army and treasury were at all times under the viceroy's charge.

The territory over which the new audiencia was to have jurisdiction was vaguely defined in the *Recopilación de Indias* as, "on the east the audiencia of New Spain, on the south the South Sea, and on the north and west the unknown lands."[27] The extent of the audiencia is clearly illustrated by a map in Herrera's *Historia General* (I. 22) and is described as follows: "It borders the audiencia of Mexico near Puerto de Navidad and Lake Chapala, thence northwest, then north, and then somewhat to the west. Not all has been discovered [c. 1600]. The western boundary is the ocean."[28] This embraced all of Nueva Galicia and a strip along the coast including La Purificación, Navidad, and Zacatula. The audiencia was at this time divided into ten or twelve corregimientos and alcaldías mayores or districts under corregidores and alcaldes mayores. These provincial officials, appointed by the viceroy or the audiencia, resided in the chief towns (cabeceras) of their provinces and acted as judges, inspectors of tribute, and lieutenant-governors with authority of a military character. Of course, within the alcaldías mayores were numerous villas and partidos (Indian towns) under alcaldes, regidores, and alguaciles.[29]

[27] *Recopilación de leyes de los reynos de las Indias,* Madrid, 1841, I. 326-327.

[28] Antonio de Herrera, *Historia general de los Hechos de los Castellanos en las Islas y Tierra Firme del Mar Océano,* Madrid, 1730, I. 22.

[29] "In the Spanish colonies an *alcalde* was usually an ordinary judge, not always trained in the law to the extent of being a *letrado* or *togado*. An *alcalde ordinario* or an *alcalde de ayuntamiento* tried cases of first instance. An *alcalde mayor* or an *alcalde de partido* might try cases on appeal from these. Generally speaking *alcaldes ordinarios* were town judges, in contrast to *alcaldes mayores* who had provincial jurisdiction as well. *Alcaldes ordinarios* and *regidores* were members of the town *ayuntamiento* or *cabildo*. *Regidores* did not exercise judicial functions." Cunningham, *The Audiencia in the Spanish Colonies.* p. 10, note 3.

The partidos were generally under the direction of the encomenderos or of the religious.

The first oidores of the audiencia of Nueva Galicia were Hernando Martínez de la Marcha, Lorenzo Lebrón de Quiñones, Miguel de Contreras Guevara, and Juan de Oseguera. The last-named was appointed to take the place of Dr. Juan Meléndez de Sepulveda, who died en route to America. Though Quiñones was in Compostela by November 2, 1548,[30] and though he, Sepulveda, and Contreras had left Spain in May, 1548, not until January 21, 1549, were all the officials of the new audiencia in Compostela,[31] and thus the official inauguration of the audiencia should date from that time. One of the initial acts of the oidores was to petition that the seat of the audiencia be moved from Compostela to Guadalajara.[32] Not until several years later did this petition and many others of a like tenor receive favorable consideration.

Since the visit of Guzmán's captains in 1530, no white men had penetrated into the interior north of Nochistlán and Juchipila. The Indians of that region, the Cascanes, Zacatecos, and other savages called collectively Chichimecos, had, as we have seen, caused considerable trouble even after the Mixton War. Cristóbal de Oñate and other officers made several attempts to subdue them, but with only temporary success, for the Indians would flee to the mountains

[30] *Colección de documentos inéditos relativos al descubrimiento, conquista y colonización de las posesiones españolas en América y Oceania, sacados, en su mayor parte, del Real Archivo de Indias,* Madrid, 1861-1879, X. 52-56. Quiñones made recommendations to Charles V concerning the proper course to pursue in the administration of justice in Nueva Galicia.

[31] Mota Padilla, *Nueva Galicia,* pp. 198-199; Riva Palacio, *México á través de los siglos,* II. 351; Bancroft, *Mexico,* II. 547. Cristóbal de Oñate was suggested at this time for appointment as governor and captain-general of all Nueva Galicia to act jointly with the audiencia (A. G. I., 67-1-18, Los oidores de Galicia al Rey, Compostela, primero de noviembre, 1549); Valencia, "Carta al Emp.," in *Cartas de India,* Madrid, 1877, pp. 110-111.

[32] Mota Padilla, *Nueva Galicia,* p. 199.

on the approach of the Spaniards.[33]　The first of these attempts of which we have much information was that of Juan de Tolosa, who had been commissioned by Oñate to lead an expedition into the Zacatecos' country.　The object of this expedition was two-fold: first, to pacify the Cascanes, who had incited the Indians of Juchipila to hostilities during the Mixton War; and second, and perhaps more important, to prospect for mines reported to be located in that country.[34]

Juan de Tolosa was a Basque "of noble parentage," and was married to Doña Leonor Cortés Montezuma, the eldest daughter of Hernando Cortés and Doña Isabel Montezuma, daughter of the Aztec ruler.　Issues of this union were Juan Cortés Tolosa Montezuma, Isabel Cortés Montezuma, and Leonor Cortés Montezuma.　Leonor, the second daughter of Juan de Tolosa, married Cristóbal de Zaldívar, son of Vicente de Zaldívar, who was teniente de capitán-general under Viceroy Enríquez.　Doña Isabel married Juan de Oñate, son of Cristóbal de Oñate and conquistador of New Mexico.[35]　Tolosa had been active in the conquest of Nueva Galicia and had fought in the Mixton War and at other times against rebellious natives.　On one of these occasions he had marched beyond the pueblo of Nochistlán into the mountains of Suchipila and Tepesa and there heard of very rich

[33] "Ibarra and Camino led several small parties into the Nochistlán region to tranquilize it by arms and reforms in the encomendero management" (Bancroft, *Mexico,* II. 552, note 40).

[34] Amador, *Zacatecas,* p. 186; Mota Padilla, *Nueva Galicia,* p. 194; Frejes (*Historia breve,* p. 207), says that the governor and royal audiencia of Guadalajara sent Tolosa in 1546 to conquer Zacatecas.　This was an error, as the audiencia was not established until 1548 in Compostela; Riva Palacio (II. 363) says, "After the pacification of Nueva Galicia, Juan de Tolosa, with the knowledge of Cristóbal de Oñate, went by way of Juchipila in search of mines and with the intention of punishing the Cascanes of Zacatecas whom Oñate accused of being prime instigators of the Mixton War."

[35] A. G. I., 1-3-27/18, Información de Juannes de Tolosa, Guadalajara, 2 de mayo de 1594; A. G. I., 1-3-27/18, Información de Juan Cortés Tolosa de Montezuma, Guadalajara, 12 de mayo de 1574.

mineral deposits about eleven days' journey to the north. It was to test these reports that the new expedition was organized.

The explorers left Guadalajara in August, 1546. Tolosa was accompanied by several Spanish soldiers, four Franciscan friars, and Indian auxiliaries of Tlaxomulco. The expedition was outfitted by Miguel de Ibarra. But since Tolosa also contributed towards the expenses of the enterprise, all of these men seem to have had a joint interest in it.[36] The names of the friars are not known to us, though one was said to be Fray Gerónimo de Mendoza, the viceroy's nephew. These friars proved to be of great assistance later, as they soon learned the Zacateco idiom and acted as interpreters for the Spaniards.[37] The explorers marched by way of Juchipila, where more Indian allies were recruited. These Indians understood the language of the Zacatecos, and for that reason were particularly valuable. The Zacatecos, on witnessing the approach of the Spaniards, feared that this was a punitive expedition directed against them because of the assistance they had given the Cascanes during the Mixton War, and some fled to the mountains, while others withdrew farther north to the Sombrerete region.[38] On the Eve of the Nativity of the Blessed Virgin, September 8, 1546, Tolosa pitched camp at the base of the *peñol*, La Sierra de Bufa, the site of the modern Capilla de Bracho in the city of Zacatecas. He then began to negotiate with the natives who had sought refuge on top of the Bufa. With the Juchipila Indians acting as intermediaries, he gave

[36] A. G. I., 1-3-27/18, Información de Juannes de Tolosa. This información made by Tolosa's descendants claimed that, while he was in the pueblo of Quitanaque, he heard of mines eleven days to the north. Then, presumably without reinforcements, he discovered Zacatecas "alone with some of his servants and at his own cost."

[37] Arlégui, *Chrónica de la Provincia de S. Francisco de Zacatecas,* p. 22.

[38] Mota Padilla, *Nueva Galicia,* p. 194; Amador, *Zacatecas,* p. 186.

them presents to win their confidence and protested his peaceful intentions. The best evidence of this was the presence of the Juchipilas themselves. The Zacatecos were finally reassured and consented to descend from the Bufa; then, being grateful to Tolosa for his kindness and generosity, they directed him to some very rich silver deposits. In this manner Juan de Tolosa discovered the mines of Zacatecas, destined to become among the most famous in the world.[39]

Immediately after the discovery of the mines, Tolosa took three or four mule-loads of sample ore to Nochistlán, where he showed it to Captain Miguel de Ibarra and Diego de Ibarra. There the ore was assayed, and, to the surprise and pleasure of the discoverers, its extreme richness was attested. Thereupon Tolosa and three other men, Cristóbal de Oñate, Diego de Ibarra, and Baltasar Temiño de Bañuelos, entered into a formal agreement to exploit the mines and found a town near them.

Both Bañuelos and Ibarra, like their two partners, were scions of old Spanish nobility. Bañuelos was a member of the Temiño family of Burebe in Old Castile. Concerning his early life nothing is known. He was married and had a daughter, Doña Ana Temiño, who married a Rodrigo Pacho.[40] Concerning Diego de Ibarra, the uncle of Francisco de Ibarra, a very considerable amount is known. He was a native of the village of Ybar in Guipúzcoa and came to the New World in 1540. Shortly after his arrival in Mexico, the Mixton War broke out, and he joined Viceroy Mendoza in going to the assistance of Nueva Galicia. In that war he served under his uncle, Captain Miguel de Ibarra,

---

[39] Mota Padilla, *Nueva Galicia*, pp. 194-195; Bancroft, *Mexico*, II. 584; Riva Palacio, *México á través de los siglos*, II. 363; A. G. I., 1-3-27/18, Información de Juannes de Tolosa; A. G. I., 1-3-27/18, Información de Juan Cortés Tolosa de Montezuma.

[40] Mota Padilla, *Nueva Galicia*, p. 197; Trinidad García, *Los Mineros Mexicanos*, Mexico, 1895, p. 117.

and participated in the capture of Nochistlán, Coyna, Acatic, Mixton, and other *peñoles*. In these encounters he was wounded several times, once so seriously in the leg that it had to be amputated. After the Mixton War, Ibarra, now a knight of the Order of Santiago, continued to reside on the frontier and became actively interested in mining and cattle-raising. He later married Doña Ana de Velasco, daughter of the second viceroy of New Spain, Luís de Velasco. The only issue of this union, a daughter, Mariana de Ibarra, married Francisco de Velasco, son of Viceroy Luís de Velasco II.[41]

A few days after the assay of the silver ore brought from Zacatecas, Juan de Tolosa and a few settlers returned to the mines from Nochistlán.[42] The establishment of a settlement near the mines was not accomplished without difficulties and setbacks, for it was bitter cold at that time of the year, and, to make matters worse, supplies were short. Even more serious was the constant danger of attack by the Indians, which necessitated constant vigilance by day and by night. There is no evidence that the mines were worked extensively or that a villa was founded until over a year later. Tolosa left Diego de Ibarra in charge of the settlers and explored around Zacatecas. Aided by the Franciscan friars, he attempted to settle the Indians in pueblos. In the *tierra de guerra*, fifty miles from Zacatecas, the old saline known as Santa María was discovered. This saline proved to be most productive and soon yielded thirty thousand fanegas of salt annually. Without this it would have been difficult to reduce

[41] A. G. I., 87-5-1, Información de conquistadores; A. G. I., 58-2-18, Doña Mariana de Ibarra Velasco, 16 de septiembre de 1614; A. G. I., 87-5-1, Diego de Ibarra, Servicios, 2 de abril de 1593; A. G. I., 87-5-1, El Rey á Diego de Ibarra, Madrid, 20 de agosto de 1600; A. G. I., 87-5-1, Mariana de Ibarra; A. G. I., 1-1-3/22, Obregón, Crónica.

[42] This was also attested by Juan de Torres, a witness for Tolosa. He said, "Juan de Tolosa and Diego de Ibarra had gone to settle the mines" (A. G. I., 1-3-27/18, Información de Juannes de Tolosa).

the silver ore of the surrounding region, for the mines were situated almost two hundred miles from the sea.[43]

While Tolosa was looking for mineral prospects in the Tepecala mountains, the Guachichiles, who lived farther to the east, went on the war-path and attacked the natives of Tepecala, who were friendly to Tolosa. Tolosa assisted in repelling the invading Guachichiles, and afterward was able to proceed for a time with his explorations. But soon word was brought that the people whom he had left in Zacatecas were deserting the mines because of fear of the Indians. He set out to intercept the fleeing inhabitants and overtook them on the road to Jalpa, fifty miles from Zacatecas. A cart with supplies arrived opportunely from Nochistlán, so Tolosa could offer material inducement to the refugees to return to Zacatecas.[44] He also argued that the natives were not so dangerous, for two of the Negro slaves on horseback had made some of the Indians flee in terror. On the following day Tolosa, Diego de Ibarra, and the others returned to Zacatecas and started to build terraced-houses to afford greater protection against attack.

On January 29, 1548, the four "discoverers" were together in Zacatecas for the first time.[45] To them the town of Zacatecas, which was founded soon afterward, owed its

[43] A. G. I., 1-3-27/18, Información de Juannes de Tolosa; A. G. I., 1-3-27/18, Información de Juan Cortés Tolosa de Montezuma; Mota Padilla, *Nueva Galicia*, p. 195.

[44] Another witness for Tolosa said that Diego de Ibarra had sent Tolosa to Nochistlán for supplies, and that the refugees met Tolosa with arms and horses at Mocotavasco. Tolosa is mentioned by another witness as having gone to Guadalajara, Tlatenango, and Teul for supplies, "all of which were furnished at his own cost (A. G. I., 1-3-27/18, Información de Juan Cortés Tolosa de Montezuma).

[45] Mota Padilla, *Nueva Galicia*, p. 195; Frejes, *Historia breve*, p. 296; José de Rivera Bernárdez says in his *Descripción breve de la muy noble y leal ciudad de Zacatecas* (cited in Amador, *Zacatecas*, pp. 188-189) that in his time there existed on the Altar de los Reyes in the Iglesia Parroquial, an inscription which read, "Año de 1546, día de la Natividad de Nuestra Señora, á 8 de septiembre, entré en estas minas yo Joannes de Tolosa, y año de 1548, día del Señor San Sebastián, á 20 de enero, entré yo Baltasar Temiño de Bañuelos en estas minas."

origin, government, and prosperity. Curiously enough, each of the four "discoverers" later claimed in personal informaciones de méritos, or attested records of services, that he was the one most instrumental in the discovery. Diego de Ibarra claimed that he was the principal discoverer, "after God Himself," of the mines of Zacatecas. Baltasar de Bañuelos asserted that he was the first discoverer and settler of Zacatecas. In the interrogatorio, or list of questions to be answered by witnesses for the información of Cristóbal de Oñate, it was stated that "Cristóbal de Oñate went prospecting for mines and was the principal discoverer of the mines of Zacatecas." Extracts from Tolosa's información read: "Juan de Tolosa was the first to come to the mines (Zacatecas)," and "Juan de Tolosa in 1546 was the first to found an hacienda and extract silver at Zacatecas." That Diego de Ibarra and Juan de Tolosa preceded the other two "discoverers" to the mines was attested by Oñate himself, for, in 1550, when giving testimony for an información being prepared by Diego de Ibarra, he said, "He had heard that Diego de Ibarra and Juan de Tolosa were the first discoverers of the mines of Zacatecas." Since the weight of evidence in support of Tolosa's claims is so overwhelming, he can be accepted unqualifiedly as the man most instrumental in the discovery of the mines and settlement of the villa.[46]

The town of Zacatecas was first founded near the mines north of its present site; there a church was built. The settlement was moved later to its present location. As September 8, 1546, the Nativity of the Blessed Virgin, was the date when Juan de Tolosa made his camp at the foot of the Bufa, the Virgin was made the patron of the new town,

[46] A. G. I., 58-2-18, Diego de Ibarra, Servicios; A. G. I., 67-1-2, Información de Baltasar de Bañuelos, Zacatecas, 5 de octubre de 1587; A. G. I., 1-3-22/13, Información de Cristóbal de Oñate; A. G. I., 1-3-27/18, Información de Juannes de Tolosa; A. G. I., 1-3-27/18, Información de Juan Cortés de Montezuma.

which was given the name of Nuestra Señora de las Zacatecas.[47]   It was constituted an alcaldía mayor in the newly-
formed audiencia of Nueva Galicia.   Zacatecas remained an
alcaldía mayor until 1580, when it was created a corregi-
miento.   On October 8, 1585, Zacatecas was granted the
title of *ciudad;* and, on July 20, 1588, in recognition of the
services of the city in the wars against the Chichimecos and
for the working of the silver mines from which great riches
accrued to the royal treasury, it was granted a coat of arms
with the portraits of its first four founders; it was also
awarded the title of "muy noble y leal."[48]

The growth of Zacatecas was phenomenal.   The news of
the rich discoveries spread rapidly, and soon the region was
crowded with treasure seekers.   At the same time other parts
of Nueva Galicia were almost depopulated.   At the end of
two years forty-five reduction works were in operation in
Zacatecas.   During the year of the founding of Zacatecas,
the four discoverers opened up many more mines in its
vicinity.   The mines of Albarrada or San Benito on the
Veta Grande, San Bernabé, and Pánuco were discovered
respectively on March 1, June 11, and November 1, 1548.[49]
These mines were so productive that up to 1643 the royal
fifths alone amounted to twenty-nine million pesos.   From
1548 to 1810 Zacatecas produced in silver five hundred and
eighty-eight million dollars.   The total production to date
exceeds a billion dollars.   The average yield per ton since

[47] Mota Padilla, *Nueva Galicia*, p. 195; Amador, *Zacatecas*, p. 210.
In 1559 by a ruling of the cabildo of Zacatecas the town was named
Nuestra Señora de los Remedios, but later it became Nuestra Señora de
las Zacatecas.

[48] Bancroft, Mexico, II. 761; A. G. I., 1-3-27/18, Cristóbal de Zaldívar; A. G. I., 66-6-19, Escudo de armas de la ciudad de Zacatecas, 1588.
There is in the last-named legajo an original copy, in colors, of the coat
of arms granted the city.

[49] Amador, *Zacatecas*, p. 191; Mota Padilla, *Nueva Galicia*, p. 195;
Tello, *Crónica Miscelanea*, 161, p. 534; Bancroft, *Mexico*, II. 554; *North
Mexican States and Texas*, I. 99.

the date of discovery has been about seventy dollars, although some ores produced as high as a thousand dollars per ton.[50]

It was not long before the four impresarios became the wealthiest men in the Americas. But, if we are to believe petitions presented by them in later life or by their heirs, the discoverers of Zacatecas did not succeed in retaining their wealth; each and every one died on the verge of bankruptcy. The heirs of Cristóbal de Oñate claimed that, though he extracted a million and a half pesos from the mines and was the richest man in Nueva Galicia, he expended all in war or in the peaceful service of the king. Some of the most noteworthy of these deeds for which his heirs claimed recompense were: important military services in the Mixton War; preparations made at great personal expense for the relief expedition to Peru at the time of the Pizarro rebellion, though this expedition was never sent; the maintenance at his own expense of the villa of Compostela and many other places in Nueva Galicia; and, finally, his service in discovering many rich mines, including Zacatecas, all of which increased the royal revenues very considerably. In brief, they claimed that their ancestor had won and sustained Nueva Galicia and that the only recompense he had ever received were two encomiendas. The date of Oñate's death is not at hand. Tello says that he died in Zacatecas in 1547 and was buried in that place.[51] This date is definitely disproved by the fact that, on March 22, 1550, Cristóbal de Oñate testified in Zacatecas in support of an información presented by Diego de Ibarra. At that time Oñate was forty-five years old. It is certain then that he died after 1550. At the time of his death he left his six minor children an estate valued at one

[50] C. B. Dahlgren, *Historic Mines of Mexico,* New York, 1883, pp. 44-55.

[51] Tello, *Crónica Miscelanea,* p. 531.

hundred thousand ducats, but it was encumbered by debts exceeding its actual value.[52]

Baltasar Temiño de Bañuelos also complained, a quarter of a century after the founding of Zacatecas, of being in want. After the discovery of the mines Bañuelos resided in Zacatecas. In 1572 he was commissioned by Viceroy Enríquez as captain-general of Nueva Galicia to wage war on the Chichimecos and the Guachichiles. Since he had to use his own money to equip and pay his men, he was finally forced to relinquish his commission because his funds were exhausted. After that he held official positions in Zacatecas such as receiver, deputy (1581-1582), and solicitor (1585-1587). Several serious charges were brought against Bañuelos in his residencia as solicitor, but he was found to be innocent. We then hear of him in 1587 petitioning to be appointed regidor of Zacatecas. He died in 1600.[53]

Diego de Ibarra and Juan de Tolosa were as improvident and ill-starred as their partners. In later life Ibarra complained that his many undertakings had so depleted his fortune that, after having been one of the richest men in the New World, his wealth decreased to almost nothing. His heaviest drain was incurred in financing the expeditions of Francisco de Ibarra, which cost him two hundred thousand pesos. Since he never received any recompense for these expenditures, he petitioned the king in 1593 for ten thousand pesos de minas in rents. He also asked that he be granted the title of count or marquis as being commensurate to the great services he had performed. Only a fraction of

[52] A. G. I., 67-1-18, Los oidores de Galicia al Rey; A. G. I., 67-1-14, Información de Cristóbal de Oñate, 18 de noviembre de 1578; A. G. I., 1-3-25/16, Probanza de los méritos y servicios de Cristóbal de Oñate, México, 23 de enero de 1584; A. G. I., 87-5-1, Informes de conquistadores; Mota Padilla (*Nueva Galicia*, p. 196) gives an interesting sidelight on Cristóbal de Oñate's hospitality: "He had a bell which each day was rung to summon to his table all who wished to eat. This custom he maintained throughout his life."

[53] Mota Padilla, *Nueva Galicia*, p. 197; A. G. I., 67-1-2, Información de Baltasar de Bañuelos.

his demands were granted; he was given an income of two thousand pesos in Indian tributes, payable when a vacancy should occur, and the title of adelantado. Since it was impossible to enjoy the Indian rents for some time to come because of prior claims, and since the title of adelantado could not be transmitted to his heirs, he petitioned once more for an equivalent of the tribute from the royal treasury for a period of four years or until his death (for he was then ninety years old), and he requested a title that was inheritable.[54] This last petition was not granted, for Doña Mariana Ibarra de Velasco, Diego's daughter, presented similar claims as late as 1614. That Diego de Ibarra was not penniless when he died in 1600 is proved by his will. The principal items mentioned, which were bequeathed to his daughter, were: a farm named Truxillo, three cattle ranches, and one mule-raising farm—all in the jurisdiction of Sombrerete and Fresnillo in Nueva Galicia. He also left some mines and other ranches said to be uninhabited and worthless. The annual income from the estate was six thousand pesos, and it was valued at eighty thousand pesos.[55]

As for Juan de Tolosa, excepting his participation in a few more exploring enterprises which will be considered later, our information concerning his last days is more meager. With advancing years his fortunes continued to decline, and finally he died with an estate heavily burdened by debts. These obligations were left for his heirs to liquidate, but their inability to do so led them to petition the Council of the Indies for aid and recompense in return for the signal services of their ancestor.[56] The financial straits

[54] A. G. I., 58-5-12, Audiencia de México al Rey, 10 de marzo de 1600; A. G. I., 58-2-18, El Rey á Diego de Ibarra, Madrid, 20 de agosto de 1600; A. G. I., 58-2-18, Diego de Ibarra al Rey, México, 25 de febrero de 1596; A. G. I., 58-2-18, Diego de Ibarra, Servicios.

[55] A. G. I., 58-2-18, Mariana de Ibarra; A. G. I., 67-1-16, Información de Doña Mariana de Ibarra Viuda, 1610.

[56] A. G. I., 1-3-27/18, Información de Juannes de Tolosa; A. G. I., 1-3-27/18, Información de Juan Cortés Tolosa de Montezuma.

of the four founders of Zacatecas were probably not so bad as they were represented, the exaggeration being due to their habit of measuring necessities according to their social stations. But it is true that the bulk of their fortunes had melted away, a fact ascribable in large part to unprofitable exploring enterprises.

Soon after the founding of Zacatecas, the great mines of Guanajuato were discovered. One of the convoys bound for Zacatecas heard about some mineral prospects, and, turning off its road, discovered the mine of San Bernabé. The discovery of this famous vein was followed by many other important "finds," which culminated in 1558 in the discovery of the Veta Madre. For three centuries the Veta Madre of Guanajuato was the richest in the world.

The mining population of Guanajuato increased so rapidly that Viceroy Velasco, in 1554, bestowed upon it the title of "Real de Minas de Santa Fé de Guanajuato." It was elevated to the rank of *villa* in 1619 and was finally made a *ciudad* in 1741. From 1548 to 1803 Guanajuato produced $520,750,000 in silver, and, together with Zacatecas, it produced half of all the silver extracted in Mexico.[57]

The status of Nueva Galicia in 1550 is clearly set forth in the report of a visita, or general inspection, conducted by Hernán Martínez de la Marcha, oidor of the audiencia of Nueva Galicia. Shortly after his arrival in Compostela, la Marcha received royal authorization to conduct a general inquest of all Nueva Galicia with particular reference to the conduct of officials who had held office in the period between Tejada's residencia and the establishment of the audiencia. The visita extended from December 3, 1549, to December 7, 1550, during which time la Marcha inspected to the farthermost confines of Nueva Galicia.

[57] García, *Los Mineros Mexicanos*, pp. 186-188; Dahlgren, *Historic Mines of Mexico*, p. 55.

La Marcha first went to Guadalajara, where he examined the records of the royal and municipal officials. Books of accounts, judgments, and processes were carefully examined; cédulas granting encomiendas were scrutinized to see if the encomenderos were exceeding their grants; the usurpation of the common lands of Guadalajara, as well as the assignment of lots in the same city, was investigated; and thirty cases were instituted against particular persons named in residencias, secret inquiries, and informaciones. Diego de Guevara and Baltasar de Gallegos, one-time alcaldes mayores of Nueva Galicia, had procesos instituted against them.[58] At the instance of the cabildo of Guadalajara, la Marcha drew up informaciones petitioning the removal of the seats of the audiencia and of the bishopric from Compostela to Guadalajara. The visitor also undertook material improvements, such as the repairing of roads and construction of bridges. He even introduced the pear and vine from Michoacán into the province of Guadalajara and took steps to introduce the pomegranate, quince, fig, and peach. Because of the high prices of maize and wheat, he encouraged increased production of those grains.

La Marcha left Guadalajara in March, 1550, and visited the pueblos down the Río Grande de Tololotlán as far as Copalá; then he turned north and visited Teul, Tipichan, and Talthenango. In the vicinity of the last-named pueblo, some mines were being worked by Toribio de Bolaños and Ginés de Mercado. These men disputed possession of the Indians on the Río de Tepic with Diego de Proaño and Hernando

[58] Other officials of Nueva Galicia, prior to the audiencia, whose terms of office were investigated were: Julian de Hojeda, Diego Hurtado, Juan Sánchez de Olea, Francisco Cornejo, Hernán Flores, and Diego de Orozco. Also mentioned in the procesos were: Cristóbal Romero, Martín de Contreras, Juan Michel, Pedro de Planencia, Diego de Colio, and Diego Vásquez (A. G. I., 66-5-14, Relación sacada en suma de visita general hecha por el señor Ldo. Hernán Martínez de la Marcha, Zacatecas, 19 de abril de 1550).

Martel. The controversy was settled by la Marcha in favor of Proaño and Martel. On the two banks of the Río de Tepic, in rugged mountain strongholds, lived two tribes of troublesome Indians. La Marcha endeavored to negotiate with them, but failed to arrive at any agreement. He accordingly prepared an información which explained the dangerous situation in Tepic and advised that these Indians be subdued, since settlement in that region would be precarious as long as they remained unpunished. From Tepic, la Marcha returned to Talthenango and then went to Zacatecas, visiting Indian pueblos on the way. At the various pueblos he inquired if the natives were paying more than they were assessed, if they had religious instruction, and if they were well treated; in short, he inquired into everything making for good government and good treatment of the Indians.

In Zacatecas the same kind of inquest was conducted as in Guadalajara. Ordinances designed for miners were published, and an información was made requesting the establishment of a caja real, or royal strong-box, in Zacatecas because of the inconvenience of sending silver to Compostela. La Marcha, realizing the urgency of the petition, established a caja real in Zacatecas under Alonso de Roa and two assistants. The new treasury officials were to remit the royal revenues to Compostela every six months. As at Guadalajara, the visitor tried to stimulate an increased production of foodstuffs, for prohibitive prices were causing the mining settlements to decrease in population.

La Marcha then ordered the alguacil mayor to take a census of all the mines, mills, and residences in Zacatecas. The census, taken in April, 1550, revealed the fact that there were in and around Zacatecas nearly fifty reduction works, foundries, and refineries; over two thousand households of Negro slaves; five churches; and an unestimated number of houses in which the Spaniards lived. Some of the greatest property holders were: Cristobál de Oñate, Juan de Zaldívar, Diego de Proaño, Baltasar de Bañuelos, Baltasar de Gallegos, Juan de Tolosa, Hernán Martel, Alonzo Martín, and Juan Martín. Two religious, Padre Luís Ponce and Padre Melo, were mentioned as possessing households of slaves. Various tradespeople and artisans were also mentioned. It is evident that Zacatecas was a populous, thriving, rich settlement in 1550. After making plans for a new church and some public buildings, la Marcha left Zacatecas and returned to Guadalajara by way of Jalpa and Juchipila.

One June 18, he went to the eastern frontiers of the audiencia, to Tetlan and Tonalá, and thence north of the Tololotlán to the district of Nochistlán. After settling a dispute between rival caciques of Nochistlán, he retraced his steps and visited the Chapala district. Next he visited the country west of Guadalajara, where there were numerous pueblos of Indians held in encomienda. Still farther to the west was the country of the warlike, cannibalistic and idolatrous Tecoles. These savages preyed upon the settlements of the peaceful Indians and at times even attacked the outlying Spanish haciendas. It was impossible to subdue them, because they lived in the inaccessible sierras. On this tour la Marcha went as far west as the coast near the Mascota River.

The district of La Purificación was inspected next. An earlier visit had been delayed by the heavy rains, and even in October (October 15, 1550) access was difficult because of the flooded condition of the country. Tlaxomulco and other pueblos were examined on the way, and then all the pueblos in the neighborhood of La Purificación. In the villa of La Purificación, residencias of all the officials were taken; informaciones were made concerning treatment of the natives; and official records of the past seven years were examined.

After the visitation of La Purificación, la Marcha returned to Compostela. The capital of Nueva Galicia was in a very decadent condition. When founded by Guzmán in 1531 it was thought to possess an ideal central location, and it had in its environs many rich mines and prosperous pueblos. But time had altered conditions; the center of population had shifted, leaving Compostela "at the end of the world," as its thirty vecinos complained. The few Indians who remained in that section were poor physical specimens and totally unsuited for exploitation either in the mines or on the farms. Also, because of the extreme heat and the unhealthy nature of that region, most of the Spaniards had deserted it and had moved north to Guadalajara and Zacatecas. The few who remained petitioned their king for assistance lest they also be forced to abandon Compostela.[59] The province of Culiacán was not visited by la Marcha because of the great distance which isolated it from the rest of Nueva Galicia. La Marcha reported that communication between Compostela and Culiacán was imperiled by warlike natives who lived between the two places. He followed up his report of the visita with a personal letter to the king in which he summarized his findings. He placed particular stress upon the Indian situation and advocated protective measures. He also mentioned a Dominican friar, Gregorio de Beteta, who had left the mines of Tepic on February 15, 1551, to work among the Indians of the interior.[60] The visitation of the oidor la Marcha, presented above, gives a good detailed picture of northwestern New Spain in the middle of the sixteenth century when Francisco de Ibarra took up his labors.

[59] A. G. I., 66-5-14, Visita general hecha por la Marcha; A. G. I., 67-1-18, Los oidores de Galicia al Rey, Compostela, primero de noviembre de 1549.

[60] A. G. I., 67-1-18, Carta sobre la visita del Ldo. de la Marcha á S. M., Compostela, 18 de febrero de 1551.

The work of one more individual needs to be related before we introduce Francisco de Ibarra. After the settlement of Zacatecas, the oidores of the audiencia of Nueva Galicia, suspecting the location of rich minerals farther north in Sinaloa and Durango, resolved to undertake the conquest of the whole region. They entrusted this task to Ginés Vázquez de Mercado, commissioned him captain-general with ample powers, and instructed him to subdue the district of Jacotlán (Tlacotlán). Mercado, a native of Valvera in Old Castile, was a vain, headstrong person. By marriage to the daughter of Bernardino Vázquez de Tápia, the conquistador, he acquired the rich silver mines in Tepic. In addition to his wealth, Mercado had considerable experience in exploration to justify his appointment. On one occasion he had led a party of fifteen horsemen on a nine days' journey north of Tepic, discovered the pueblo of Guazamota, and opened communication over the mountains with Culiacán.[61]

N = Cerro del Mercado in 1552 discovered

Mercado accepted with alacrity the chief command of the expedition, because it offered an opportunity to distinguish himself. When all arrangements for the expedition, which cost Mercado fifty thousand pesos, were completed, he left Guadalajara in 1552 for Jacotlán with a retinue of one hundred men. The main object of the enterprise, the conquest of the Indians of Jacotlán, was accomplished with ease. Shortly thereafter Mercado heard about a mountain of solid silver located farther inland. He determined to find this mountain, and hastened north across the mountains near Valparaiso. Between that place and Chalchihuites he found more silver prospects, probably those later known as Chacuaco. But he did not stop, so anxious was he to discover the mountain of solid silver. He pushed on by way of Chalchihuites, San Martín, and Sombrerete, and, finally, near the end of 1552,

---

[61] *Ibid.;* A. G. I., 87-5-1, Informes de Conquistadores; Mota Padilla, *Nueva Galicia,* p. 202.

he came in sight of a mountain which he took to be his goal. On this occasion Mota Padilla ascribes to Mercado these words: "This is the treasure, for so great difficulties would have fatigued the first explorers; this is that for which the Viceroy Don Antonio de Mendoza sent expeditions in search of by land and by sea; this is the mountain which Coronado could not find, for God willed that Mercado should find it."[62] But when the Spaniards got close to the mountain they saw that they had been deceived; instead of being a mountain of silver, it was a mountain of iron. This famous mountain near the city of Durango, called *El Cerro del Mercado* after its discoverer, is six hundred and forty feet high and contains over three thousand tons of solid iron ore down to the level of the plain; below, to an unknown depth, the average is seventy per cent. iron.[63]

Discouraged and sore at heart, they began to retrace their steps. Mercado was doubly disappointed because he had neglected so many alluring mineral prospects in his haste to find the silver mountain. Moreover, the prime motive of the expedition, the pacification of the natives, had been undertaken in a desultory manner, and the task had by no means been completed. One night while the explorers were near the subsequent site of Sombrerete, some Indians of the ranchería of Sain attacked them when they were off guard, killed two soldiers, and wounded several others, including Mercado. The return march was continued with difficulty as far as Teul, which was an encomienda of Juan Delgado, a relative of Mercado. There the fortune-hunter

---

[62] Mota Padilla, *Nueva Galicia*, p. 202.

[63] The fame of El Cerro del Mercado came to the ears of Guzmán when he entered Nueva Galicia. He ordered Chirinos to make an expedition to the mountain, but he was unsuccessful in his quest; the attempts of Captains Angulo and Oñate also ended in failure (García, *Los Mineros Mexicanos*, pp. 126-128).

was left to die of grief and his wounds. He was buried in the Convent of San Francisco de Juchipila.[64]

Such was the miserable failure of the audiencia's first attempt to penetrate the northern hinterland. All idea of conquest was abandoned for a time, mainly because royal authorization was now necessary for any exploring project. Excepting isolated, illegal raiding excursions, no Spaniard ventured far beyond Zacatecas.

[64] Amador, *Zacatecas,* pp. 192-193; Bancroft (*Mexico,* II. 550, note 34) states erroneously that Mercado died in 1558. The date of Mercado's death was near the end of 1552, or in the beginning of 1553.

CHAPTER III

FRANCISCO DE IBARRA AND THE EXTENSION OF
THE FRONTIERS (1554-1562)

Two years after the ill-fated Mercado expedition, Viceroy Velasco sought and received royal authorization to renew the exploration of the northern interior. His specific purpose was "to explore those lands which Coronado had scarcely seen, to locate sites for towns, and to search for mines."[1] Francisco de Ibarra, nephew of Diego de Ibarra, Velasco's son-in-law, was put in charge of the enterprise. When he entered upon his arduous duties as a conquistador, Francisco was a mere stripling of about sixteen years of age.[2] The appointment of mere boys to such responsible positions was not uncommon in those days; the most essential qualifications were birth and wealth. Moreover, it must be noted that Spanish youths mature rapidly, being perhaps two or three years ahead of the boys of northern Europe. The amount of real responsibility vested in Francisco is another matter, and regarding this our evidence is inadequate, but it is to be presumed that the opinions of his officers carried great weight in councils. Also, as will be pointed out later, Juan de Tolosa took unto himself most of the credit for the expeditions in which he was associated

[1] Herrera, *Historia General*, p. 247; Riva Palacio, *México á través de los siglos,* II. 364-365.

[2] A. G. I., 66-6-17, Información de Diego de Ibarra; A. G. I., 1-1-/20, Memorial con documentos del Lcdo. Juan de Ybarra gobernador de la Nueva Vizcaya, junio de 1575. In Ibarra's información (A. G. I., 1-3-20/11, Francisco de Ybarra, Información de méritos) various witnesses testified concerning his age in 1554 as follows: Pedro López del Peral, twenty years; Martín de Carraga, eighteen to nineteen years; Miguel de Castro, Pedro de Hermosillo, and Alonso de León, sixteen to seventeen years; and Miguel Ruiz de Giral, eighteen to nineteen years. The interrogatorio of the same información says, "When he made the first entrada he was fifteen to sixteen years old."

with Francisco de Ibarra. From the standpoint of actual direction, as opposed to honorary authority, Tolosa was probably justified in his pretensions.

The youthful conquistador took the field in 1554, and for the next twenty years he dominated the history of the vast region in northwestern New Spain comprising the present states of Sonora, Sinaloa, Chihuahua, and Durango. The public career of "the phoenix of the explorers," as he has been called, extending over the years 1554-1575, can be divided into two phases: first, 1554-1562, preliminary explorations; and, second, 1563-1575, major explorations and the organization of Nueva Vizcaya. The account of Ibarra's preliminary work, because of the scarcity of records, must necessarily be somewhat fragmentary and certainly less detailed than the account of his governorship. But what little is contributed in the present chapter constitutes new material and serves to fill what was hitherto an utter void in our knowledge of the founder of Nueva Vizcaya.

After the viceroy had appointed him captain of the projected expedition, Francisco lost no time in making preparations. He established headquarters in Zacatecas, and there he organized his following. When preparations were completed he set out from Zacatecas in September, 1554. He was accompanied by a small company variously estimated as numbering between twenty-four and thirty.[3] One of these was Juan de Tolosa. The exact nature of the authority, if any, exercised by Tolosa is uncertain, there being contradictory evidence that he was the leader of the expedition,[4] that

---

[3] Miguel Ruiz de Giral testified that there were thirty soldiers; Martín de Carraga said that there were twenty-five, and Miguel de Castro said there were twenty-four soldiers in the party. All three witnesses were members of the expedition. A. G. I., 1-3-20/11, Francisco de Ibarra, Información de méritos; *Col. Doc. Inéd., XIV.* 463.

[4] "In 1554 Francisco de Ibarra left Zacatecas to discover mines by order of Juan de Tolosa" (Amador, *Zacatecas,* p. 212).

he was a coequal with Ibarra,[5] and that he occupied a subordinate position.[6] Informaciones presented by Ibarra and similar testimonials of the heirs of Juan de Tolosa are so partisan as to be valueless on this point, for it was generally true that in presenting an información de servicios the deeds of the petitioner would be stressed to the disadvantage or to the utter disregard of his superiors, colleagues, and subordinates. This, then, accounts for the failure of the Tolosa informaciones to mention Francisco de Ibarra in a single instance, though it is certain that Tolosa and Ibarra were associated on at least one entrada.　It is also certain that Tolosa made an expedition in 1556 or 1557 with Luís Cortés, and, though he mentions this expedition, the name of Cortés is omitted.[7] A careful examination of the evidence leads to the conclusion that Juan de Tolosa occupied a prominent position in Ibarra's company, because of his rank and experience and because his name is so often selected and coupled with that of Ibarra's.　But he was not the official leader of the expedition.　Perhaps on account of his intimate relations with the Ibarra family and his wide experience as an explorer, he consented to accompany the youthful captain in the capacity of maestro de campo, or first lieutenant.[8]　The names of a few more of Ibarra's men besides Tolosa have been preserved.

[5] Martín de Rentería, Martín Oñez, and Juliano Tufino merely say that Ibarra, with Juan de Tolosa, and other soldiers, left to discover new lands.　Martín Pérez says, "Francisco de Ibarra and Juan de Tolosa discovered mines," etc.　(A. G. I., 1-3-20/11, Francisco de Ybarra, Información de méritos).

[6] "By command of Francisco de Ibarra, who was the leader of all, this witness (Miguel Ruiz de Giral), Juan de Tolosa, and others, went to the said mines of San Martín" (Ibid).

[7] A. G. I., 1-3-27/18, Información de Juannes de Tolosa; A. G. I., 1-3-27/18, Información de Juan Cortés Tolosa de Montezuma; A. G. I., 59-4-3, Toribio de Bolaños al Rey, México, 20 de abril de 1557.

[8] A. G. I., 1-3-27/18, Información de Juannes de Tolosa.　Tolosa's first expedition to Zacatecas was with some men supplied by Miguel de Ibarra, uncle of Diego de Ibarra.　Immediately after the discovery of the mines of Zacatecas, Diego de Ibarra was given a share in the enterprise.

They were: Pedro de Hermosillo, Miguel de Castro, Martín de Carraga, Pedro López del Peral, Miguel Ruiz Giral, Martín de Rentería, Juan de García, and Domingo de Villabona. The party was supplied with arms, horses, cattle, Negro slaves, Indians, and sixty-two mules loaded with food and munitions. The total expense of the expedition was paid out of Ibarra's personal fortune, for the expenditure of royal revenue to assist exploration was prohibited.[9] But it is to be presumed that Diego de Ibarra assisted in this as well as in his nephew's later enterprises.

Ibarra and his companions directed their march to the north and west of Zacatecas into the uninhabited country, for in 1554 Zacatecas was the Spanish outpost on the northern frontier. Although they passed the site of Fresnillo and discovered near that place some mineral deposits,[10] they did not stop to work them, but continued to the Río de Nieves, or the Río Grande, as it was called. After crossing the river with some difficulty on account of its swollen condition due to the heavy rains, they followed down its opposite bank for a short distance to the pueblo of Cein or Sain, probably located near the present Cein Alto. Farther on they came to another settlement whose inhabitants had fled to the mountains.[11] Ibarra and a few soldiers pursued the Indians and succeeded by peaceful entreaty in persuading them to return to their pueblo. Altogether there were about two hundred natives. By means of an interpreter the licentiate Juan de García preached to the Indians and baptized a number of

[9] A. G. I., 1-3-20/11, Francisco de Ybarra, Información de méritos; *Col. Doc. Inéd.*, XIV. 464.

[10] *Ibid.*, XIV. 464-466; A. G. I., 1-3-20/11, Francisco de Ybarra, Información de méritos; Amador, *Zacatecas*, pp. 195-196, 212; García (*Los Mineros Mexicanos*, pp. 151-152) relates how Tolosa left Zacatecas at the end of 1554, and a few days later arrived at Fresnillo where he left Captain Francisco de Ibarra with some Spaniards and Indians. Ibarra made an effort to establish a settlement at Fresnillo, following instructions of Tolosa, but the attempt was unsuccessful.

[11] A. G. I., 1-3-20/11, Francisco de Ybarra, Información de méritos.

them, while Francisco de Ibarra stood sponsor for the neophytes. The Indians promised to live peaceful lives, and in truth this pledge was remarkably well kept, for on his later entradas Ibarra was always well received by them. Because of their evangelical success in this pueblo, the Spaniards named it El Baptismo.

These Indians living near the Río de Nieves were called Chichimecos. But Chichimeco was a general term meaning "without abode" or "peregrinating," and was used to designate a multitude of tribes inhabiting the region north of Mexico. They possessed no civilization comparable to the more cultivated nations to the south, their main subsistence being dependent on the chase. According to Mota Padilla, "Under this name are found many nations with different languages such as the Pamies, Capuzes, Samies, Zancas, Maiolias, Guamares, Guachichiles, and others, all different, although similar in customs."[12] Rather closely related to the Guachichiles were the Zacatecos, for they, the Cazcanes, and the Guachichiles, were often spoken of simply as Chichimecos. The Indians of El Baptismo were in fact Zacatecos, for, according to Orozco y Berra, "The Zacatecos extended to the Río Nazas. Cuencamé, Cerro Gordo, San Juan del Río, and Nombre de Diós were located within their limits."[13] Furthermore, it appears that the Zacatecos also inhabited the greater part of northern Zacatecas and southern Durango, the area explored by Ibarra on his first entrada, for he mentions them on several occasions.

The Zacatecos were a tall, well-proportioned, muscular people, their strength being evidenced by the great burdens they carried for the Spaniards. But in facial appearance they were actually ugly, because of a peculiar cast of features —oval face, long black eyes wide apart, large mouth, thick

[12] Mota Padilla, *Nueva Galicia*, p. 44.
[13] Orozco y Berra, *Apuntes para la historia de la geografía*, p. 285.

lips, and small flat nose. Since they were thick-skinned, it was difficult to ascertain their expression of countenance, but it was generally one of melancholy.[14] As for dress, the Zacatecos were more naked than otherwise. Breech-cloth for the men and a short petticoat of skins or woven maguey for the women constituted their dress. Men and women went barefoot. It was a common practice among the natives to rub their bodies with clay of various colors and to paint reptiles and other ornaments on them. In addition to the artistic effect, the clay acted as a preventive against vermin and a protection against the sun's rays.[15]

Unlike the more nomadic Guachichiles, who lived farther to the east in Potosí and Coahuila, the Zacatecos had habitations of a more permanent character. Since they lived in the colder highlands, they needed more substantial houses, and also the fact that they cultivated the soil to a limited extent tended to make their settlements more fixed. Their houses, when located near the wooded sierras, were generally made of trunks of trees; the walls were plastered with mud and clay, and a flat roof of split timber was kept in place with stones. The majority of their rancherías, however, were located on the plains, where there was a scarcity of trees. There their houses were constructed of adobe or sun-dried bricks and stones. They were one story high and had but one room. A few stones placed in the middle of the floor served as a fireplace where food was cooked. Household furniture and implements were few and simple. They had no beds but slept on the floor; likewise there was an absence of benches and tables. They possessed a few unglazed earthenware vessels, but such articles as bottles, bowls, and cups were made from gourds. Where maize was

[14] Bernardino de Sahagun, *Historia General de las Cosas de Nueva España,* Mexico, 1829, III. 133.

[15] *Ibid.,* pp. 123-134; Herrera, *Historia General,* Dec. LV, Lib. VIII, Cap. I.

grown the metate was an indispensable article. This was an oblong stone, twelve by eighteen inches in size and smooth on one side, which was used with a stone roller for rubbing down the maize.

For food the Zacatecos trusted chiefly to the natural productions of the soil, such as roots, herbs, and a variety of wild fruits, and to game, such as rabbits, deer, birds, moles, rats, and reptiles. They cultivated to a very limited degree maize, beans, and other vegetables. They made a tortilla or cake from the pulp of the maguey, which was first boiled with lime, then washed and boiled again in pure water, after which it was squeezed dry and made into cakes. The tribes of Durango hunted human beings for food as they hunted deer and other game. The flesh of brave foes they ate, thinking thereby to augment their own bravery.[16]

The Zacatecos were very warlike, for to them war was a normal state. Whenever war broke out between them, each side endeavored to secure the assistance of its neighbors. Their method of fighting and treatment of captives are vividly described by Bancroft:

A council is held, and the assault planned, care being taken to secure places suitable for an ambuscade and stones for the slingers. A regular organization of forces is observed and every effort made to outflank the enemy. Archers and slingers march to an attack in single file, always occupying the van, while warriors armed with clubs and lances are drawn up in the rear; the assault is commenced by the former, accompanied with furious shouts and yells. During the period of their wars against the Spaniards, they often expended much time and labor in the fortification of heights by means of tree-trunks, and large rocks, which were so arranged, one on top of another, that at a given signal they might be loosened, and let fall on their assailants. The chiefs of the Tepecanos and contiguous tribes carried no weapons during the action, but had rods with which they chastised those who exhibited symptoms of cowardice, or became disorderly in the ranks. The slain were scalped or their heads cut off, and the prisoners were treated with the utmost barbarity, ending invariably in the death of the unfortunates; often

[16] Mota Padilla, *Nueva Galicia,* p. 80; Arlégui, *Chrónica de Zacatecas,* p. 175.

were they scalped while yet alive, and the bloody trophy placed upon the heads of their tormentors. The heads of the slain were placed on poles and paraded through their villages in token of victory, the inhabitants meanwhile dancing round them. Young children were sometimes spared, and reared to fight in the ranks of their conquerors; and in order to brutalize their youthful minds and eradicate all feelings of affection toward their own kindred, the youthful captives were given to drink the brains and blood of their murdered parents.[17]

The Zacatecos married young; seldom did girls over fifteen years of age remain single. The consent of parents was absolutely necessary to marriage, and any infraction of this custom meant the death penalty. The marriage ceremony, although itself a very solemn affair, was always followed by riotous feasting and dancing. Monogamy was the general practice, but husbands could repudiate their wives on the slightest cause and then take another. Many had concubines. The wives were kept under the subjection of their husbands, performed arduous menial tasks, and, in short, their position was little better than that of slaves. The pious Spanish chroniclers remark at length about the unparalleled immorality and prostitution that existed among these Indians.[18]

In character the Zacateco was enigmatical. He was generally courageous, yet at times cowardly; extremely ignorant and expressionless, yet keen and receptive to new ideas; unambitious and lazy, yet capable of long hours of toilsome labor in the mines, in the fields, and on the march. "The wild tribes of the north," says Bancroft, "are rude, revengeful, dull, irreligious, lazy, and given to robbery, plunder and murder. Such are the characteristics attributed to them under the name of Chichimecs by old Spanish authorities and others. Indeed, the only creditable traits they were allowed

[17] Bancroft, *Native Races*, I. 628-629.
[18] *Ibid.*, p. 635.

to possess, were, in certain parts courage and an independent spirit."[19]

From El Baptismo, Ibarra and his companions marched in a northerly direction until they came to another native settlement which they called San Miguel, since they arrived there on Michaelmas (September 29th). Between four and five hundred Zacateco warriors from San Miguel greeted the Spaniards. The latter were able to carry on friendly intercourse with the natives, thanks to a cacique of Sain who understood the Spanish language. Presents were given the Indians, and the Spaniards were allowed to enter the pueblo in peace. Then Juan de García explained the mysteries of Christianity, exhorted the natives to lead peaceful lives, and baptized many of them. While in San Miguel the Spaniards heard for the first time about the mines of San Martín. The Indians mentioned the mines and, upon inquiry, agreed to lead the Spaniards to them. Francisco de Ibarra, being the leader of the expedition, ordered Juan de Tolosa, Miguel Ruiz de Giral, and four others to accompany an Indian guide to the mineral deposits. They found them without difficulty, and, since four of the six soldiers bore the name of Martín, the mines were named Las Minas de San Martín. "This," says Ibarra, "constituted the discovery of the mines."[20] After extracting some sample ore, Tolosa and his companions returned to San Miguel, where Ibarra had remained with the other members of the party.

The line of march taken by the party after leaving San Miguel is uncertain. Eight of the nine witnesses who testified for Ibarra in 1569, when he was making an información of this, his first entrada, declared that he went direct to Aviño from either San Martín or San Miguel. But the testimony of Miguel Ruiz de Giral, which is much more

[19] Bancroft, *Native Races,* p. 643.
[20] A. G. I., 1-3-20/11, Francisco de Ybarra, Información de méritos.

detailed than the rest, tells of a side expedition in the direction of Mazapil before the mines of Aviño were discovered. According to Giral:

From San Miguel they went in the direction of Mazapil, where are at present certain settled mines, and they discovered three more pueblos with about three hundred inhabitants. The natives received the Spaniards peaceably, for the governor (Ibarra) sent messengers ahead to tell them that they meant no harm. He gave them many presents, and at his order the said licentiate (García) baptized them. From there they went east and recrossed the same river (Río Grande) in which some horses and mules were drowned. For four or five days they could not find water, and for that reason they turned to the northwest. While searching for water they marched eight days and finally discovered a native settlement called Aviño.[21]

It will be noted that Giral does not say that they went as far as Mazapil; the pueblos they discovered were *west* of the Río Grande, but he is curiously negligent about mentioning a recrossing of the river when the explorers turned to the northwest. The fact that Giral stands alone in his account of the activities east of the river seems to indicate that he had his facts confused; perhaps the circumstances he relates appertain to a subsequent expedition, for it is to be noted that he calls Ibarra *governor*, a title he did not bear until after 1562.

It can be assumed with some degree of certainty that Aviño was the next place of importance, after San Martín, that was discovered by Ibarra. As was his custom, he sent messengers ahead to notify the natives of his coming and to allay their fears. In Aviño over two hundred were baptized. The Spaniards were told that there was in Aviño an Indian woman who had fled with her husband and son from Suchipila and Nochistlán when Nuño de Guzmán was in Nueva Galicia. The natives of Aviño had killed her husband and her son, but her life was spared. At Ibarra's request she was turned over to him, since she understood

[21] *Ibid.*

several Indian languages.　He thus acquired a "Doña Marina," who proved to be invaluable to him as an interpreter.　Near the Indian pueblo of Aviño some mines were discovered.　Ibarra, Tolosa, and their companions were thus the discoverers of the famous mines of Aviño.　They did not attempt to work the mines, but merely extracted some sample ore and moved on.　At Aviño they heard about the fabulously rich province of Copalá, and, therefore, they made that mysterious land their next goal.　North of Aviño they discovered San Juan Valley, in which there were three pueblos.　It appears that this valley was erroneously named Copalá because one of the pueblos was called Copale. On the approach of the Spaniards, the inhabitants fled into the mountains near by, and though they strove by peaceful persuasion to induce the Indians to return, they were not successful.　Not desiring to use force, they gave up their efforts and continued their march to the mines of San Lucas.[22]

From San Lucas the explorers pursued a southerly course passing through Laguna del Valle, or Guatimape, to the valley of Guadiana, where they found various Indian pueblos.　The inhabitants had fled into the mountains, but Ibarra determined to bring them back and ordered camp pitched while he went after the natives.　With about a dozen soldiers he followed the Indians into the sierras and tried to persuade them to return to their pueblos, but he was unsuccessful, for, instead of submitting quietly, the Indians launched a fierce attack.　In the encounter, which lasted almost three hours, several of the soldiers were severely wounded (all were wounded according to Giral) and one, Domingo de Villabona, was killed.　Even Ibarra did not escape injury, for he was severely wounded in the leg

[22] A. G. I., 1-3-20/11, Francisco de Ybarra, Información de méritos. Once again Giral is the sole authority for the account of the discovery of the valley of San Juan, on this, Ibarra's first entrada.

by an arrow and was many days in recovering. This fight seems to have taken place outside Guadiana Valley proper, for the Spaniards are said to have discovered the valley later. But there is ample evidence to prove that the scene of the conflict was in Guadiana. We may take this to signify solely that there was disagreement concerning the exact boundaries of the valley. This contradictory evidence is not serious, for it is important only to know that Ibarra and his companions spent some time in Guadiana Valley and explored it thoroughly. Giral says that Ibarra and his companions remained in Guadiana for about six months, but there is good reason to believe that they did not remain that long. While in Guadiana, Ibarra sent to Zacatecas for supplies, but before they were received he decided to return because food was running short. Their return was uneventful, and the route is not known. The party arrived in Zacatecas in November or December, 1554, after an absence of about three months.[23]

On this entrada Francisco de Ibarra and his men traversed the territory extending between Zacatecas and the Río Nazas, and from the Río de Nieves to the valley of San Juan. In addition to the places already mentioned, other discoveries in the district of San Martín attributed to this entrada are Sombrerete, Ranchos, Chalchihuites, and Nieves.[24] Strictly speaking, the states of Zacatecas and Durango were not discovered by Francisco de Ibarra; he

[23] Lorenzo de Ureta says that they returned in the same year, 1554, after an absence of three months. Diego de Colio's account of a journey (A. G. I., 67-1-18, El Alcalde Mayor de Nueva Galicia, Diego de Colio al Consejo de Indias, Minas de San Martín, 15 de febrero de 1570) from Zacatecas in 1553 or 1554, which was undoubtedly Ibarra's first expedition, was as follows: "About sixteen years ago (i.e. 1553 or 1554), certain Spaniards, residents of Zacatecas, set out to discover mines. In the lands beyond Zacatecas they found many rancherías of bellicose Indians called Chichimecos. There they found a mineral ore which they brought back with them, and found it to contain silver."

[24] Col. Doc. Inéd., XIV. 464.

merely rediscovered and made known lands previously
visited by the captains of Guzmán and by Ginés Vázquez de
Mercado. But these prior expeditions bore no fruit, whereas
the return of Ibarra to Zacatecas with the news of his discoveries inaugurated extensive exploration and settlement of
the territory he had visited. Between 1555 and 1563, or the
interval between Ibarra's first expedition and his appointment as governor, several other entradas, civil and ecclesiastical, were made into the above-mentioned region, but it is
not known that any of these went beyond the limits outlined
by the expedition of 1554.

An expedition of great promise, which actually achieved,
however, no known tangible result, was that conducted by
Juan de Tolosa and Luís Cortés, son of the conquistador.
Tolosa and Cortés left Zacatecas in December, 1556, with
about fifty Spaniards and a number of Indian allies. They
marched north for a considerable distance, going in search
of minerals.[25] This was probably the same journey of discovery mentioned by Tolosa in his información, on which he
and forty men traveled inland from Zacatecas for a distance of about forty leagues and discovered the mines of
Sombrerete, San Martín, Aviño, and others.[26] Tolosa and
Cortés, however, did no more than retrace the steps of
Francisco de Ibarra, though they did succeed in arousing a
hostile attitude on the part of the natives, who had been
friendly toward the Spaniards. The report which the explorers sent the viceroy was filled with the grossest exaggerations concerning the great wealth and numerous inhabi-

---

[25] A. G. I., 59-4-3, Toribio de Bolaños al Rey, 29 de abril de 1557.
[26] A. G. I., 1-3-27/18, Información de Juannes de Tolosa; A. G. I.,
1-3-27/18, Información de Juan Cortés Tolosa de Montezuma; Mota
Padilla, *Nueva Galicia,* p. 196; Amador, *Zacatecas,* p. 196; Arlégui
(cited by Amador, *Zacatecas,* p. 198) says, "Sombrerete was discovered
by General Juan de Tolosa; also Aviño and other places in 1558; and
our convent was erected in 1567 with royal and ecclesiastical sanction."

tants of a land which was in reality poverty stricken and which had few natives living in settled habitations.[27]

The first important Spanish settlement made within the newly-discovered region was San Martín. Two or three years after the return of Ibarra and his followers, some thirty Spaniards, including a friar, set out from Zacatecas to make a settlement and to work the mines.[28] This group of settlers bears such marked resemblance to a party led into this region at about the same time by a certain Martín Pérez that it is presumed they were one and the same. Both expeditions had as their starting place Zacatecas; both followed the same course of march; there was one friar in each group; and resulting from each expedition arose identical claims on the part of Zacatecas over the whole region.

[27] A. G. I., 67-1-18, Morones al Rey, Compostela, 8 de octubre de 1559; A. G. I., 59-4-3, Toribio de Bolaños al Rey, 29 de abril de 1557; Obregón (A. G. I., 1-1-3/22, Obregón, Crónica) has a different version of the expedition: Velasco's interest in discovery having been aroused by Mendoza's instructions on exploration to his successor, and also by reports brought back from the frontiers by various individuals, he commissioned Luís Cortés to head an exploring expedition. Cortés went north from Mexico along the path of the early captains for about two hundred leagues. He found the land sparsely settled by a naked and savage people. While he was en route, Velasco and the audiencia of Mexico sent Juan de Cueva, secretario mayor, after Cortés to advise him of a royal order prohibiting the execution of the journey, and to order him to return because of the great excitement created among the Spanish settlers of New Spain who were desirous of going with him. Obregón adds that if Cortés had been allowed to continue his journey he would have discovered New Mexico.

[28] Bancroft, *Mexico,* II. 761-762; Colio (A. G. I., 67-1-18, Diego de Colio al Consejo, 15 de febrero de 1570) states that it was in 1556 when San Martín was settled. Other references are vague, some stating "a short time," and others "two and three years after." Mota Padilla (*Nueva Galicia,* p. 203) says Pérez discovered San Martín in 1558. Amador (*Zacatecas,* p. 201) states that Pérez left Zacatecas in November, 1554, and that this was during the alcaldía of Tápia, who held office until 1557. But on the same page Amador says that Pérez left Zacatecas when Morones was juez de residencia, which was not until 1557. Frejes (*Historia breve,* pp. 209-215) places the Pérez expedition at about ten years after the founding of Zacatecas, or about 1557 or 1558. The probable date was therefore 1557 or 1558; evidence presented below concerning Aviño bears out this assumption. The date 1556, from Colio, is irreconcilable with one important fact, that is, the date of the Morones residencia.

The interest of Martín Pérez, an alcalde of Zacatecas, was
so greatly aroused when some Indians showed him some
specimens of rich silver ore that he determined to go in
search of the deposits.[29] Although his expedition had the
sanction of the alcalde mayor of Zacatecas, it was undertaken without the knowledge of the audiencia of Nueva
Galicia.[30] It was not difficult for Pérez to recruit a following,
for there were in Zacatecas at that time many Spaniards
who had fled from the severe residencia which was being
conducted at that time by Doctor Morones in Compostela
and Guadalajara. Fray Gerónimo de Mendoza, then residing in Zacatecas, offered to accompany Pérez.

Mendoza, a native of Vitoria, in Castile, was a nephew
of Viceroy Antonio de Mendoza, and he came to New Spain
with the latter. He served for a time as captain of the
viceregal guards and then forsook worldly affairs for the
Franciscan habit. He appeared on the frontier for the first
time in 1546, when he accompanied Juan de Tolosa on an
expedition into the Zacatecos country. In 1553 Fray Mendoza was sent to Zacatecas to quell some disturbance.[31] The
nature of the trouble is not known, but it is presumed that
it related to forced Indian labor in the mines. Fray Mendoza, by employing great tact and wisdom, reconciled the

[29] Amador, *Zacatecas*, pp. 200-201. This incident does not seem plaus-
ible to Amador since the mines of San Martín had already been discovered by Ibarra and Tolosa. Nor does it seem reasonable to him that
the Indians who were said to have revealed the mineral deposits of San
Martín should have preferred to go all the distance to Zacatecas with
that object when they could have told the Spaniards at Sombrerete and
Chalchihuites. But as a matter of fact those places had not been settled
by that time; therefore the impossibility of the Indians seeing the Spaniards without going to Zacatecas.

[30] Bancroft (*Mexico,* II. 597) is in error on this point; he says that
Pérez was sent by the audiencia of Nueva Galicia.

[31] Cf. p. 41; Bancroft, *North Mexican States and Texas,* I. 102;
Arlégui (*Chrónica de Zacatecas,* pp. 257-264) states that Viceroy Mendoza sent his nephew in 1553. This was an error, for the viceroy died in
Peru in 1552. Cf. Amador, *Zacatecas,* p. 201; Tello, *Crónica Miscelanea.*
pp. 182, 572-573; Arlégui, *Chrónica de Zacatecas,* pp. 22, 257-264; Bancroft, *North Mexican States and Texas,* I. 102.

disputing miners and reassured the natives who had fled from the mines. It was on this occasion that the Zacatecos gave Martín Pérez presents of silver purporting to have come from the San Martín region. Mendoza was preparing to return to Mexico after the successful conclusion of his mission, when Martín Pérez, excited by the gifts of the Indians, began preparations for his expedition. Influenced by the fine opportunity to convert the natives, the friar joined Pérez.

Pérez and his companions left Zacatecas in 1557 or in 1558, and, guided by the Indians, they discovered some very rich silver veins from which the Indians had extracted the specimen ore. This constituted the rediscovery of the mines of San Martín. Pérez sent samples of the ore to Zacatecas to be tested and then undertook to make a settlement near the mines. For this purpose he had brought a number of Negro slaves from Zacatecas. He also explored in the environs of San Martín, and thus to him has been attributed the discovery of the mines of Fresnillo, Ranchos, Chalchihuites, Sombrerete, Santiago, and Nieves.[32] These, however, were not original discoveries, for all this region had been explored previously by the captains of Nuño de Guzmán, by Mercado, and by Ibarra and Tolosa. But Pérez may be accorded credit for rediscovering those mines and for founding settlements at San Martín and other places in its vicinity. The greater importance of the work of Martín Pérez lies in the fact that he strengthened the claims of the audiencia of Nueva Galicia to that territory.

While Pérez and his companions were exploring and making settlements in the San Martín country, Fray Men-

---

[32] Frejes, *Historia breve*, pp. 209-215; M. E. G. Tarayre, *Exploration Minéralogique des Régions Mexicaines suivie de notes archéologiques et ethnographiques*, Paris, 1859, pp. 185-186; Mota Padilla (*Nueva Galicia*, p. 203) is authority for the statement that these discoveries occurred in 1558.

doza did not neglect his opportunity to preach to the natives. With one soldier and a Mexican neophyte he went north from San Martín and tramped over the country known today as Calabazal in the direction of Río del Súchil. On the banks of that stream he found a great number of Zacatecos, who received him kindly.[33] From Súchil, now accompanied by some Zacatecos, Mendoza went to a place afterwards named Ojo de Agua de los Berros. This place, where there were a great number of Zacatecos settled in an extensive ranchería, was a sort of outpost against the Tepehuanes, a savage tribe that inhabited the territory to the north.[34] Arlégui piously assures us that Mendoza's great zeal had such good effect that the Indians immediately abandoned their barbarous customs. For several months the faithful padre looked after the spiritual welfare of the Spaniards in San Martín as well as of the Indians in the surrounding rancherías. Since his labors were great and increased daily, he sent a request to his provincial, Fray Francisco de Bustamante, in Mexico, asking that some friars be sent to assist him. While Mendoza was waiting for aid from Mexico, he persuaded the remaining Zacatecos who were living in the mountains to come down to the plains. When they finally consented, he had them settle in a place named San Francisco del Nombre de Diós. There he erected a small temporary church.[35] To Fray Mendoza, therefore, belongs the honor of making the first settlement in Nombre de Diós. As will be shown later, there is reason to believe that this attempt was abortive and had no other affinity to the eventual Nombre de Diós than its name.

[33] Amador, *Zacatecas*, p. 203; Bancroft, *North Mexican States and Texas*, I. 100.

[34] Tarayre, *Exploration Minéralogique*, p. 271.

[35] "The date of the erection of the church in Nombre de Díos was 1555" (*ibid.*). This obviously is a mistake, since Mendoza did not leave Pérez until later.

Viceroy Velasco's interest in the northern frontier had been reawakened by the extravagant reports brought back by Luís Cortés, Juan de Tolosa, and others.[36] Since he was in receipt of a royal cédula dated December 29, 1557, enabling him to reëmbark upon discoveries and to establish settlements, he made plans to dispatch a great expedition to New Mexico, or Copalá, as it was called.[37] On September 30, 1558, Velasco reported to the king that the project had to be postponed because of the great urgency of dispatching an expedition of thirteen vessels and about fifteen hundred soldiers under command of Tristán de Luna to Santa Elena in Florida. In the meantime, he stated, he had sent three friars to San Martín to assist Fray Mendoza in his missionary work. They were also instructed to investigate conditions and to prepare the field, it being his intention to supplement their work by an expedition, equipped at small expense to the king, to search for the elusive Copalá. Although Francisco de Ibarra was not mentioned in the communication, it appears that he was empowered to accompany the friars and to explore in the northern interior, for Velasco, in issuing Ibarra his commission as governor of Nueva Vizcaya (July 24, 1562), said, "I granted a commission to Francisco de Ibarra in order that with certain religious men of the Order of St. Francis, and Spaniards who go in his company, they might enter the land beyond San Martín and Aviño and discover the settlements that are said to be in those parts." It is remarkable that Ibarra in his información and in his letters did not see fit to mention the vice-

[36] Luís Cortés and Juan de Tolosa were later accused by Morones, the visitador, of wilful exaggeration which deceived the viceroy (A. G. I., 67-1-18, Morones al Rey, 8 de octubre de 1559); A. G. I., 59-4-3, Toribio de Bolaños al Rey, 29 de abril de 1557.

[37] A. G. I., 58-3-8, El traslado de la comisión que dió don Luís de Velasco á Francisco de Ybarra para su gobernador é capitán-general, México, 24 de julio de 1562.

regal permission to accompany the friars, but there can be little doubt that such consent had been given.[38]

The comisario general of the Franciscans in Mexico City coöperated with the viceroy in answering Fray Mendoza's appeal by sending him three Franciscan friars and a native donado or lay-brother;[39] namely, Pedro de Espinareda, Diego de la Cadena, Jacinto de San Francisco (known both as Cintos and Cantos), and the donado Lucas.[40] Pedro de Espinareda was originally a member of the Provincia de Santiago in Spain and was one of the first twelve friars sent by his province to Mexico. In the first six years of his missionary activity he is said to have baptized fifteen thousand natives. After the retirement of Fray Mendoza, to be noted later, Espinareda assumed charge of the work on the frontier and on one occasion made a journey to Mexico to get additional assistance. He became guardian of the monastery at Nombre de Diós and later was made custodian of the convent at Zacatecas. He was the author of a vocabulary of the Zacateco language, which is mentioned in the Boletín de Geografía y Estadística and in many other places. After thirty years of service among the Indians he died in October, 1586, and was buried in Zacatecas.[41]

[38] A. G. I., 58-3-8, El Virrey Velasco al Rey, México, 30 de septiembre de 1558.

[39] Ibid.; the interrogatorio of Ibarra's información (A. G. I., 1-3-20/11, Francisco de Ybarra, Información de méritos) states that it was nine or ten years prior to December 31, 1569, that the padres arrived in San Martín. Amador (Zacatecas, p. 205) says, "The three friars and the donado left Mexico at the end of 1555, and arrived in Nombre de Diós on January 11, 1556."

[40] Bancroft, North Mexican States and Texas, I. 101, 116; Riva Palacio (México á través de los siglos, II. 385), in naming the friars confuses them with those who went on Ibarra's expedition of 1563; he says, "These, according to Mendieta, were Azevedo and Herrera, and two other religious unnamed."

[41] Juan de Torquemada, Monarquía Indiana, Madrid, 1723, III. 344; Amador, Zacatecas, p. 207; Bancroft, North Mexican States and Texas, I. 116, note 45; A. G. I., 1-3-20/11, Francisco de Ybarra, Información de méritos.

Jacinto de San Francisco had served as one of Cortés' soldiers in the conquest of Mexico. As a reward for his services he received valuable encomiendas, but, tiring of worldly goods, he decided to forego all and to enter the Franciscan Order. Later, in 1566 Father Cintos accompanied Espinareda from San Martín to Pánuco and back to Nombre de Diós. The object of this long and arduous march was to find a large lake and some extensive Indian settlements, but the quest was unsuccessful. No other details of Cintos' activities in Durango are known, except that he was extremely zealous and was popular with the natives. Torquemada is authority for the statement that when Cintos died in 1566 he was buried in Nombre de Diós, where for many years his grave was decorated daily with flowers. Concerning Diego de la Cadena very little is known. After thirty years of service among the Zacatecos he died in 1586 and was buried in Durango.[42]

The lay-brother Lucas was a Michoacán neophyte who played a very important rôle in missionary activities. It was quite customary for the early padres in New Spain to be assisted by native converts in the capacity of donados. Among these were two brothers from the Province of Michoacán, one named Sebastián and the other Lucas. These two, though not friars, performed the religious offices as if they were professed friars. Lucas is said to have performed miracles like the padres. He was a most valuable linguist, for he could preach in the Tarascan, Mexican, and Chichimeco languages. The two donados accompanied Coronado on his expedition to New Mexico, but, when the adelantado returned to Mexico, they remained behind with two padres, Juan de Padilla and Juan de la Cruz. When Fray Padilla heard about some Indians who might be converted, he, with the two donados and a soldier, who had

[42] Bancroft, *North Mexican States and Texas*, I. 116, note 45.

remained with them, left the other friar; but soon afterward they were set upon by the natives, and Padilla was killed. The donados managed to escape, and, after many marvelous adventures, succeeded in reaching their native Michoacán. Sebastián died soon after because of the hardships he had suffered, but Lucas continued his missionary activities for many more years.[43]

The three friars, Lucas, and some soldiers who accompanied them were given a viceregal commission conferring upon them permission to enter the lands beyond San Martín, to convert the natives, and to found a villa.[44] When the padres arrived in San Martín, and Francisco de Ibarra, who was at San Martín at that time, heard of their intentions, he offered to accompany them and to afford what protection he could. According to his información, "Ibarra, knowing the great danger the religious and their soldiers would run in that land, it being undiscovered and the Indians at war, joined them with a certain number of soldiers equipped at his own expense." This would seem to indicate that the viceregal permit enabling Ibarra to accompany the friars came subsequent to the appearance of the friars in San Martín. The proffered assistance was accepted, and the padres, Ibarra, and some soldiers variously estimated as being between twenty and forty in number,[45] started for the interior. Fray Gerónimo de Mendoza also accompanied his newly-arrived brothers on the entrada.[46]

[43] Torquemada, *Monarquía Indiana*, III. 610.
[44] Herrera, *Historia General*, p. 247; *Col. Doc. Inéd.*, XIV. 466; A. G. I., 1-3-20/11, Francisco de Ybarra, Información de méritos.
[45] There is disagreement regarding the number of soldiers, as will be exhibited from the following excerpts from Ibarra's información (*ibid.*): "Ibarra took with him at his own cost twenty-two soldiers, which was the largest part of them (the religious therefore had soldiers of their own). . . . Ibarra joined them with about twenty soldiers. . . . This witness and eight other soldiers went with Ibarra and the religious. . . . In June, 1562, Francisco de Ibarra, this witness, and thirty to forty soldiers left San Martín and went to the place where they founded the villa of Nombre de Diós."
[46] *Ibid; Col. Doc. Inéd.* XIV. 553.

From San Martín they went by way of the valley of Guadiana to Aviño, where there was a Spanish settlement. From Aviño they continued to Peñol Blanco, San Juan Valley, and Río Nazas and discovered some Indian settlements in El Mesquital.[47] At about this time (c. 1560) Fray Mendoza left his companions and returned to Mexico in answer to a summons from his comisario general, Fray Francisco de Bustamante. The summons had been brought to Mendoza by the three padres, but, contrary to the fact that he was ordered to return immediately, it is clear from evidence at hand that he accompanied his brother friars and Ibarra on a portion of the entrada. He abandoned his missionary work with great reluctance, for, notwithstanding the fact that he had been alone for so long, he had great success in converting the natives; and now with assistance at hand he probably realized with regret how much more he could accomplish. The Indians also, because of their confidence in him, were reluctant to see him go. But, as an obedient soldier of Christ, Fray Mendoza obeyed the orders of his superior and returned to Mexico by way of San Martín and Zacatecas. He returned to Spain as Bustamante's companion and never again visited the New World; he died in Madrid.[48] Mendoza carried to Spain a memorial

---

[47] Francisco de Sosa was alcalde mayor of Aviño at the time of Ibarra's first entrada, and he testified that he saw Ibarra, his soldiers, and the religious. He declared specifically that there was no settlement at Nombre de Diós at that time. The religious with Ibarra, he said, were Fray Cantos and Fray Francisco de Guzmán. This is our only mention of the latter padre. Since Francisco de Ibarra made several expeditions with and without the padres, and since the accounts are scattered and fragmentary, the difficulty and near-futility of accounting for his early career becomes apparent (A. G. I., 1-3-20/11, Francisco de Ybarra, Información de méritos).

[48] Torquemada (*Monarquía Indiana*, III. 371-374) and Mendieta (Gerónimo de Mendieta, *Historia Eclesiastica Indiana*, Mexico, 1870, pp. 540-543) state that Francisco de Bustamante was custodio from 1555 to 1567. Therefore it must have been at the expiration of his term when he returned to Spain, and not in 1556, as claimed by Amador (*Zacatecas*, p. 207) ; Bancroft, *North Mexican States and Texas*, I. 102, note 3; Arlégui, *Chrónica de Zacatecas*, 22, pp. 257-264.

containing an account of all the missionary and exploring activities on the northern frontier up to the time when he gave up his work. Unfortunately, the memorial has not come to light, for undoubtedly it would constitute an invaluable addition to our documentary evidence relating to the history of the northern frontier of New Spain.[49]

After the departure of Mendoza, Ibarra and the remaining padres continued their work of exploration in the Río Nazas region. On one occasion they went far to the north of Aviño in search of Copalá. An account of this entrada was written by Francisco de Ibarra to his uncle Diego. It was dated in Aviño, June 6, 1562, and was as follows:

Most Illustrious Sir:

I did not wish to write an account of Copalá to Your Most Illustrious Lordship until I had sufficient information concerning it, and after I had seen it with my own eyes; and so I left the mines of San Martín with Fray Cintos and another friar and a few soldiers, in order to give to Your Lordship a full account. Our Divine Lord willed that on the day when we left, the horses should be mired in a swamp. For days it rained excessively, and finally it was necessary to turn back. Remarkable results could not be expected, since we were without horses, the land was unsubdued, and we lacked the soldiers that were required for such a journey, in view of the great number of natives who were reported to be in those lands. The expedition, however, accomplished a great deal, because that which was not attained in the eight years spent in that enterprise, the Lord willed to bring to light. And so, without any guide, and with the assistance of Our Divine Lord, I dared to go to the native settlements within five days after I left these mines [San Martín or Avino?] with the few companions who proved to be sufficient in spite of the lack of horses. This brief entrada was the only one made into that land. What I very much desire of Your Lordship, since much of the difficulty has been removed and nothing remains to be done but to go to that land and settle it (for it is suitable for that purpose and it can be done with ease), is that Your Lordship assist the first ones who go there in order that they can be sustained in that land; and this without His Majesty spending anything from his royal hacienda. There are people in these parts who are desirous of going, and I on my part will assist in guiding them. To best serve His Majesty and Your Lordship, at least one hundred

[49] A. G. I., 1-3-20/11, Francisco de Ybarra, Información de méritos; Col. Doc. Inéd., XIV. 467.

Spaniards will be necessary for this journey because of the reported number of natives in that land. They ought to be assembled in these mines by the end of September, because then the conditions of travel will be better, and there ought to be on hand a sufficient supply of food for those who go, and to supply them afterwards in case of necessity. Thus, there can result great service to Our Divine Lord and to His Majesty, a service to many, and a loss to none. And since from Your Lordship can proceed so much good, I implore Your Lordship as a true [Christian] to complete this journey so that they [the friars] can undertake the work of saving the souls of the numerous ones who are wandering lost in that region. And Your Lordship ought to assist the first to enter and to go on the discovery of that land, for it is a thing which reacts to the service of Our Divine Lord and of His Majesty. They [the settlers] have gone to much trouble and expense to accompany the friars, but by this means they have secured the land. Since Your Lordship will act as Christianity dictates, no additional information is necessary other than that the land is very populous with clothed people who have much food and live in adobe and stone houses. We have discovered a valley one hundred leagues from these mines of Aviño, the best that I have seen in all of New Spain, inhabited by a great number of people, with much food, and as skilful in the cultivation of their fields and in the irrigation of them as one can find in the world. We have learned, with God's assistance, that there is corn in abundance throughout that district, which has been discovered, which will be quite valuable to the settlers of these mines and San Lucas. We left the religious congregating the people, for they are peaceable, and it is true that they are a good people, and great results can be accomplished there. I expect to visit them often while they [the religious] remain there. Our Divine Savior, etc. Aviño, June 6, 1562. I kiss the hands of Your Lordship.

Francisco de Ibarra.[50]

Since the padres bore a commission to establish a villa, they searched on their return journey for a suitable site. The place selected was the present location of Nombre de Diós. It is not known definitely whether this was the same site selected by Fray Mendoza for his chapel; but that is not probable, for Alonso García, as witness for Ibarra's *información*, states emphatically that, when they went to the Río Nazas, the villa of Nombre de Diós was not settled *or even started*. About two months later the padres under-

---

[50] *Ibid.,* A. G. I., 58-3-8, Copia de la que me escrivió Francisco de Ybarra de las minas de abiño en seis de junio de 1562 sobre lo de Copalá.

took to found the villa, and at that time there was no settlement of Indians or Spaniards on or near the site of Nombre de Diós.

The Indians of the valley of San Juan and its vicinity rebelled some time afterward and killed several Spaniards. Among them were Pedro Gonzalez de León, Juan Rodríguez de Venbrive, and Hernando de Arenalo.[51] So menacing were the natives and so great was the damage wrought by them, even in the inhabited districts, that Francisco de Ibarra, who was in San Martín at the time, organized a force to subdue the rebels. Among those Ibarra had with him were Alonso García, Hernando de Valderama, and Juan Gómez de Salazar. As a fine example of contradictory evidence and the necessity of caution in accepting the testimony of witnesses in the informaciones, Juan Gómez de Salazar testified several years later that Alonso García was with the padres at the time of the outbreak, whereas García himself tells how he joined Ibarra at San Martín.[52] With about thirty soldiers and one friar Ibarra went to San Juan. There, solely by peaceful means, he pacified the natives and secured their consent to live in settled communities. To effect this, he returned with many Indians and settled them in Nombre de Diós. From that time the natives of Nombre de Diós were remarkably peaceful and gave no more trouble.[53] After the Indians had been quieted down, more Spaniards moved into that district and settled in and around the new villa. Also, the officials and residents of Zacatecas and San Martín

[51] One of the witnesses testified that five of the Spaniards were killed (A. G. I., 1-3-20/11, Francisco de Ybarra, Información de méritos).

[52] Ibid.

[53] Francisco de Sosa testified that some years later when Fray Pedro de Espinareda was guardian of the Monastery of Nombre de Diós, he told Sosa that he was one of the friars who was in Nombre de Diós, and that Ibarra came with some soldiers to assist them in pacifying the natives and in settling them in pueblos (ibid.) ; Col. Doc. Inéd., XIV. 467.

aided Nombre de Diós by furnishing it with supplies and money.[54]

Father Espinareda, with wisdom and diligence continued the work so ably started by Father Mendoza and soon won the respect of all the natives. Because of his great desire to spread the faith, he was not content to remain in the territory which had been visited by Father Mendoza, but he insisted on carrying the Gospel to more distant places. On one of these missionary journeys, as has been noted above, he traveled as far as Pánuco on the Gulf Coast. Father Espinareda also ordered Father Diego de la Cadena to work among the Indians north of Nombre de Diós. The conversion of numerous Tepehuanes resulted from his efforts. Espinareda also started a mission community named San Juan de Analco in the Guadiana Valley. This later became the nucleus of the town of Durango which was founded by Francisco de Ibarra.[55]

Padre Pedro de Espinareda, feeling the urgent need of more help to convert the natives and to administer to the spiritual needs of the Spaniards, went to Mexico to secure more friars. Presumably Fray Bernardo de Cossin, who joined the missionary band at about this time, was one of the recruits. Cossin, a Frenchman from Aquitaine, came from the Convent of San Juan de la Luz near the Basque city of Fuenterrabia. On arrival in America, he joined Espinareda and was sent by him to join Cadena at Guadiana. Shortly after he arrived in Guadiana, he was attacked by the savages and was killed. Prior to this, Cossin, according to Torquemada,[56] was attacked while on his way to Guadiana,

---

[54] A. G. I., 67-1-18, Diego de Colio al Consejo, 15 de febrero de 1570.

[55] Arlégui (*Chrónica de Zacatecas,* p. 35) relates that Cadena founded Durango; on another page (58) he says that Juan de Tolosa was the founder of Durango. The time of Cadena's activities is not known; it was some time before 1562; Bancroft, *North Mexican States and Texas,* I. 102; Amador, *Zacatecas,* pp. 207-211.

[56] Torquemada, *Monarquía Indiana,* III. 612-613.

but the arrows of the Indians were turned back upon them, and not a thread of Cossin's garments was injured. Cossin was the first missionary to suffer martyrdom in Nueva Vizcaya.[57]

Fray Juan de Tápia of the Provincia de la Concepción de Valladolid was the next missionary to go to Guadiana, and, according to Torquemada, he arrived in better season than his predecessor Fray Cossin. The date of Tápia's arrival cannot be definitely placed, but since it is positively stated that it was after Fray Cossin's death, it was approximately 1558.[58] He did not go alone on this entrada, but had with him at least one companion, for in his *Quenta,* or relation, he speaks of his "padre compañero." Whether his companion was the donado Lucas, who accompanied him on his last expedition, is not known.

The territory traversed by Tápia was approximately the following: From Acaponita he crossed the mountains to the northeast and came to the Tepehuanes tribes. There, in the valley of Panaño, he baptized many natives, and then resumed his march until he came to a very fertile valley, which he named San Francisco. The Guadiana River flowed through this valley. Tápia was evidently in the vicinity of Durango, which was founded later, for he built a convent in that valley "three days' journey from San Martín and Aviño, and two to three days' to Copalá, where it was reported there was a great number of people." Guadiana was also mentioned by Tápia as the "gateway to the Plains of the Cows, and a good road to Florida." From Guadiana, Tápia returned to Acaponita, from whence he went to

[57] "The date of his death is not known," says Torquemada (*Monarquía Indiana,* III. 613). "It must have been after 1556," conjectures Arlégui (*Chrónica de Zacatecas,* pp. 35-37).

[58] Both Torquemada and Mendieta agree that Tápia went to Guadiana in 1556. Arlégui says that he mas martyred in 1557. The dates as given by the religious chroniclers are most untrustworthy.

Chiametla. From the latter place he continued to Mazatlán and up the coast of the South Sea for several days. He preached to the natives, baptized thousands of them, and built several churches.[59] Indian tribes visited by Tápia were: Xiximes, Otomies, Tepehuanes, and Acaxées. The Tepehuanes inhabited the mountains of southern Chihuahua and the northern portions of Durango. The Xiximes lived "in the heart of the mountains of San Ándres." The Acaxées inhabited the valleys of the mountain regions of Tôpia and San Ándres in Durango and Sinaloa.[60]

Father Tápia went as far north as Elotlán, near Culiacán, where he followed his customary procedure of baptizing the natives, erecting a church, and settling the converts in a pueblo. He then returned to the Convent of San Francisco in Guadalajara to render an account of his work to his padre superior. He reported that he had baptized ten thousand natives, "not counting women and children," and he asked for additional assistance to enable him to continue the work he had but started. The padre superior, being greatly impressed by Tápia's remarkable report, gave him permission to return to the northern lands to continue his work among the natives. But first he ordered the missionary to write an account of his evangelical activities, for it was his intention to send it to the king and the Council of the Indies to acquaint them with the extreme necessity of sending more religious to America.

Tápia set out a second time from Zacatecas to work among the natives of Guadiana. He was accompanied by the lay-brother, Lucas. According to Arlégui, they reached Guadiana, but later, when they were returning to Zacatecas, they were attacked and killed by the Guachichiles Indians

---

[59] A. G. I., 67-1-18, Quenta de Fray Juan de Tápia de la jornada q. hizo al Valle de Guadiana y los pueblos q. ajuntado.

[60] Arlégui, *Chrónica de Zacatecas*, pp. 187-188; Bancroft, *Native Races*, I. 613.

west of Zacatecas. Their bodies were recovered and were buried in the Convent of Zacatecas, which belonged to the Province of the Holy Evangel.[61] With the exception of two unnamed friars who were sent to work in Tôpia and were killed by the natives about 1562,[62] the above constitutes the known missionary activities in Nueva Vizcaya prior to the organization of that region under the governorship of Francisco de Ibarra.

After the settlement of San Martín, Gaspar de Tápia, the alcalde mayor of Zacatecas,[63] in following his policy of extending the limits of his jurisdiction, appointed for the new settlement an alcalde ordinario in the name of the king and of the audiencia of Nueva Galicia. The alcaldía of San Martín included the mines of Sombrerete, Chalchihuites, Ranchos, and San Martín. The next step was to make San Martín an alcaldía mayor. The man selected by the audiencia for the new position was Francisco de Sosa. The jurisdiction of San Martín extended far into Durango.[64]

[61] A. G. I., 67-1-18, Quenta de Fray Juan de Tápia; Amador, *Zacatecas*, p. 201; Mendieta, *Historia Eclesiastica*, p. 746; Torquemada (*Monarquía Indiana*, III. 611) says that Lucas died *de enfermedad* while going to convert the Chichimecos. This would imply that he did not meet a violent death at the hands of the natives; but evidence points to the contrary.

[62] Two Franciscans, one an old man and the other a young man, are said to have been sent (probably by Espinareda) to work in Tôpia, and after considerable success they met death at the hands of the Indians (Arlégui, *Chrónica de Zacatecas,* 65, pp. 222-225); Mendieta (p. 746) and Torquemada (III. 613) state that the friars were killed in 1555.

[63] According to Amador (*Zacatecas,* p. 201) Tápia was alcalde mayor of Zacatecas until 1557. It is not known when he assumed office, but it was probably about 1554. On another page (p. 213) Amador states that the alcalde mayor of Zacatecas, who took possession of San Martín, Sombrerete, Chalchihuites, Aviño, Santiago, and Ranchos, and who named a lieutenant to represent him in that territory, was alcalde mayor Maldonado, and that the date of this appointment was 1561. Ample internal evidence places the date of this act several years before 1561, and thus it falls quite logically in the alcaldía of Tápia.

[64] Mota Padilla, *Nueva Galicia,* p. 207; Amador believes that Ulloa, appointed by Morones, was the first alcalde mayor; he fails to mention Francisco de Sosa (Amador, *Zacatecas*, pp. 212-213); Bancroft, *Mexico,* II. 701-702; A. G. I., 67-1-18, Diego de Colio al Consejo, 15 de febrero de 1570.

In the meantime, occupation went on apace. Settlers arrived, worked the mines, started farms and cattle ranches, and founded pueblos. Francisco de Ibarra resided for some time in San Martín, and, though he was not the official head of the settlement, he was very active in encouraging its growth and prosperity. He supervised the working of several of his mines, explored the surrounding country, and protected the settlers from Indian depredations. On more than one occasion he recruited and equipped soldiers at his own expense and personally led them against rebellious natives. His generosity was noteworthy, for his house was always kept open to afford shelter and food to the needy, and before he allowed them to leave he supplied them with money and arms. Pedro López del Peral and Lorenzo de Ureta, two pioneer settlers of San Martín, testified in 1569 that it was an accepted fact at that time that Francisco de Ibarra was the discoverer of the mines of San Martín. In addition to his mines, Ibarra possessed in the San Martín-Zacatecas region several farms and cattle and sheep ranches.[65]

The Spanish settlement that was made at Aviño was a direct result of the initiative of Francisco de Ibarra. Two or three years after his discovery, in 1554, of the mines and Indian pueblo of Aviño, he undertook to plant a Spanish settlement at that place.[66] Juan de García, Gaspar de Mesa, Martín de Rentería, and other soldiers were sent to Aviño to locate a Spanish settlement and work the mines. Shortly after their arrival in Aviño, Ibarra joined them and assisted

[65] A. G. I., 1-3-20/11, Francisco de Ybarra, Información de méritos; *Col. Doc. Inéd.*, XIV. 465.

[66] Ibarra's interrogatorio on Aviño (A. G. I., 1-3-20/11, Francisco de Ybarra, Información de méritos) declares, "Desde a poco tpo. se comencaron á poblar las dhas. minas." According to Martín Oñez, a witness for Ibarra, it was two years after the discovery of the mines, or in 1557 or 1558, that Ibarra settled them. Juliano Tufino testified that it was in 1559 or 1560 that Ibarra went to the mines of Aviño to settle them. Gaspar de Mesa said that he went to the mines in 1558, which was three or four years after Ibarra and his soldiers had discovered them.

in the mines. He found his men on the verge of deserting their posts because that district, the most distant from Zacatecas, was menaced by hordes of warlike Indians. Perhaps the Spaniards were discouraged because the Indians refused to work in the mines. Also, supplies were short, and, because of the difficulty of obtaining them at that great distance, prices were almost prohibitive. Ibarra took the settlement under his personal care, for he was especially desirous of preventing its failure. He set about pacifying the natives and was able to settle them in fixed habitations near those of the Spaniards. Then he induced them to work in the mines. This service the Indians consented to do and they received pay in return. To encourage the miners of Aviño, Ibarra selected one of his richest mines, installed a complete equipment of mining machinery in it, and then turned it over to the residents of Aviño free of charge. This mine, named El Tajo, was given with the provision that the inhabitants maintain their residence at that place. This was to insure sufficient protection for the frontier. From El Tajo there was extracted about eight hundred thousand pesos of silver, and of this Francisco de Ibarra did not receive a single ounce. In supplying the settlers of Aviño with foodstuffs, in subduing the natives, and in buying machinery for the mine, Ibarra spent great sums of money in return for which he received no recompense whatsoever. The royal coffers benefitted greatly from these mines, for they were so rich that, within ten years after the founding of Aviño, between eight hundred and one thousand pesos of silver were produced weekly. Ibarra resided for some time in Aviño and urged responsible people to settle there.[67]

Coincident with the founding of Aviño, other settlements sprung up at Chalchihuites, Sombrerete, Fresnillo, Nieves,

[67] A. G. I., 1-3-20/11, Francisco de Ibarra, Información de méritos; Col. Doc. Inéd., XIV. 471-472; García, Los Mineros Mexicanos, p. 179.

Santiago, and Ranchos. Over all of these the alcalde mayor
of Zacatecas had jurisdiction, but this authority was later
transferred to the alcalde mayor of San Martín.[68] It is generally believed that most of the settlements owed their origin
to movements radiating from San Martín. The mines of
Chalchihuites, twenty miles from San Martín, were probably
settled after the latter place. There were no warlike tribes
to combat in that vicinity, and, equally important, they enjoyed a good supply of water, whereas the country surrounding San Martín was exceedingly dry. Bernárdez, author of
a history of Zacatecas and quoted by Amador (*Zacatecas,* p.
197), claims that Chalchihuites was founded in the years
1530-1531. He says, "The founding of Chalchihuites,
according to documents in the archive of Tonalá, a pueblo
which now forms a part of the villa of Chalchihuites, was
effected in the years 1530-1531 by a colony separating from
Guadalajara. Thus Chalchihuites was founded before
Zacatecas." Amador remarks that, if Chalchihuites was
founded in those years, it was by some Indians fleeing from
Guzmán, for he believes that these first settlers were not
Spaniards, since they left no trace of themselves.

The mines of Sombrerete, also located near San Martín,
were settled soon after the former place. Although they had
been discovered by Francisco de Ibarra, or Juan de Tolosa,
there is an account of a later discovery by a Juan Bautista
de Llerena: "In a very dry year the inhabitants of San
Martín, in searching for water discovered the Vetas de la
Cañada in Sombrerete." As these silver veins were very
rich, the discoverers, who were led by Juan de Llerena,
founded a settlement in that place. They named it "San
Juan Bautista de Llerena, Real y Minas de Sombrerete."
Whatever may be the authenticity of this discovery, it is

[68] Bancroft, *Mexico,* II. 597; A. G. I., 1-3-20/11, Francisco de Ybarra,
Información de méritos.

nevertheless true that Sombrerete was known as Villa de Llerena. In later days Sombrerete became populous because of the wealth of its mines, which were scarcely less rich than those of Zacatecas. In 1567 the Convent of San Mateo de Sombrerete was erected at that place, and in 1570 Sombrerete was made a villa.[69]

The exact time when the mines of Fresnillo were first worked is not known. Though the existence of the mines was noted by Ibarra on his first entrada, he did not attempt to work them. Their actual exploitation must have come soon after their discovery, since they were on the direct route from Zacatecas to Sombrerete and San Martín. The founding of the villa has been attributed to Antonio Maldonado, alcalde mayor of Zacatecas in 1561. A few years later, about 1568, under the viceroyalty of Enríquez, a body of troops was stationed at Fresnillo to guard caravans en route from Zacatecas to Sombrerete against attacks by the Guachichiles Indians. About 1570 the vein of Cerro de Proaño was discovered. So rapidly did Fresnillo grow that it was made an alcaldía in 1580.[70]

It is also futile to attempt to fix with precision the time when the mines of Santiago, Nieves, and Ranchos were first exploited.[71] All of these were being worked by 1563 and

[69] Amador, *Zacatecas*, pp. 196-198; Bancroft, *Mexico*, II. 762; García, *Los Mineros Mexicanos*, p. 155.

[70] Amador, *Zacatecas*, p. 212.

[71] It is interesting to note the variety of evidence and opinions regarding the probable dates of the discovery of the more important mines in this region. Tello (*Crónica Miscelanea*, 183, p. 573) says that the mines of San Martín were discovered in 1558, and after that the following mines were discovered: Ranchos, Sombrerete, Aviño, Santiago, and Nieves. Arlégui (*Chrónica de Zacatecas*, p. 41) quotes Torquemada, "After 1555 there were discovered by the religious of that custodio (Zacatecas) the mines of Sombrerete, Aviño, Arzate, Chalchihuites, Indé, Tôpia, Guanazevi, Santa Bárbara, Villa de Nombre de Diós, Durango, Peñol Blanco, Valle de San Bartolomé, and many other places up to 1564." As was so common in the religious orders, they claimed all achievement for themselves. According to Mota Padilla (*Nueva Galicia*, p. 201) the discoveries of Fresnillo, San Martín, Som-

were yielding their share of the one million pesos in royal fifths which was the amount of silver the royal treasury received from the mines opened up by Francisco de Ibarra.

Francisco de Sosa, the first alcalde mayor of San Martín, resigned his position after a brief incumbency, and the oidor Morones appointed as his successor Juan Vázquez de Ulloa. The definite date is not known, but was probably 1559. Ulloa was later accused of being a person of rude character, violent, and headstrong. His hasty temper is said on one occasion to have caused him to fight with some Spaniards, and in the brawl he was badly wounded in the throat by an arcabus shot.[72] However true that might have been, it was certainly true that Ulloa was a weak administrator, for he was unable to keep the Indians in subjection. They rebelled and not only caused great property damage, but even killed some Spaniards. To suppress the rebellion, the audiencia of Nueva Galicia dispatched to San Martín as juez de comisión one Pedro de Ahumada. Ahumada was successful in dislodging the rebellious natives from their fortified positions. He then set about putting in order the whole countryside from Guadiana and the valley of San Juan to Aviño, Peñol Blanco, and San Lucas. After the successful conclusion of his mission, Pedro de Ahumada returned to Zacatecas. A short time after that the three friars and the donado, who were sent by Velasco and Fray Bustamante to assist Fray Mendoza, arrived in San Martín.[73]

brerete, and Nieves were made from Zacatecas. Finally in Orozco y Berra (*Apuntes para la historia de la geografía*, 10, p. 1038) we learn that "Sombrerete was known as a mine ever since 1555, and the same was true of Chalchihuites, and Nieves was not known as such until four years later, or in 1559."

[72] A. G. I., 67-1-18, Diego de Colio al Consejo, 15 de febrero de 1570; Amador, *Zacatecas*, pp. 212-213.

[73] *Ibid.* It is probable that Ahumada's expedition was the one said to have been led by Ibarra (to be noted later) in which the natives were brought to Nombre de Diós. But most of the evidence points to two separate expeditions.

After an incumbency of two and a half years, Juan Vázquez de Ulloa resigned his position as alcalde mayor of San Martín. The audiencia of Nueva Galicia appointed as his successor Captain Diego García de Colio; he was given the added authority of taking Ulloa's residencia. Colio arrived in San Martín in 1562. He found Ulloa guilty of several grave offenses and ordered him sent to Guadalajara; from there he was sent to Mexico, where he died.[74] Two days after his arrival in San Martín, Colio received an urgent letter from the friars of Nombre de Diós appealing for assistance against a threatened Indian attack, for they had heard that the Indians were planning to attack them on a certain night. In answer to the appeal Colio sent eight soldiers to Nombre de Díos, where their presence discouraged attack. This seems to have been the expedition under the leadership of Francisco de Ibarra which was noted above.[75]

Since Colio possessed a commission to conduct a visita of the alcaldía mayor, he set out immediately after he had completed the residencia. From San Martín he visited Ranchos, Chalchihuites, and the valley of Súchil. At all three places Spaniards were working the mines, and there were numerous ranches and farms. The mines of Santiago were also registered by this time. Colio then went to Nombre de Diós. He summoned before him all of the natives who were settled there and exhorted them to continue to lead peaceful lives. Then he took formal possession of Nombre de Diós in the name of the king and of the audiencia of Nueva Galicia.[76] Since the friars insisted that Colio should appoint a justice for Nombre de Diós to act

[74] Amador, *Zacatecas*, p. 213; Bancroft, *Mexico*, II. 597.

[75] Cf. p. 82.

[76] According to Mota Padilla (*Nueva Galicia*, p. 207), "The audiencia of Nueva Galicia named Diego de Colio as first alcalde mayor of San Martín, and ordered him to found a villa where he deemed it best. This he did and founded Nombre de Diós in 1562, and incorporated it into his alcaldía mayor."

as protector of the Indians against the Spaniards and as judge in disputes between the Spaniards, he appointed as alcalde ordinario for Nombre de Diós Alonso de García, a resident of that place. Colio was successful in pacifying the frontiers of his alcaldía mayor and enabled the vecinos to follow their customary pursuits, some in the mines and others on their farms. In the opinion of Bancroft, these acts of Colio should constitute him, or Martín Pérez, the true founder of Nombre de Diós. Official sanction of Colio's acts seems to have been lacking, which made it possible for Ibarra a year later to found the city "officially."[77]

Before entering upon a discussion of the career of Francisco de Ibarra as governor of Nueva Vizcaya, it seems necessary to consider some important political developments in the audiencia of Nueva Galicia. In 1557 Dr. Morones arrived in Compostela to succeed Hernán Martínez de la Marcha as oidor and to take the residencias of the oidores, alcaldes mayores, and royal officials of Nueva Galicia. Morones was granted the title of oidor and alcalde mayor of Nueva Galicia by royal order dated in Valladolid on February 26, 1556. By order of the same date he was appointed visitador. He had served as fiscal in the audiencia of Mexico for about five years and as oidor of the same audiencia for one year. During the time that he was taking the residencia, the results of which were to be sent to the audiencia of Mexico within ninety days, Morones suspended all of the oidores and assumed the administration of the audiencia himself.

The investigation affected only those oidores whom Morones had suspended: Lebrón, Contreras, and Oseguera. De la Marcha was not examined, for he had already relinquished his office. Against Lebrón de Quiñones Morones conducted his strictest inquiry, and he sustained all charges

[77] Bancroft, *North Mexican States and Texas,* I. 104.

brought against the oidor. Indeed, Morones contended that he could have proved much more had he had more time. An enumeration of Lebrón's offenses is lacking, though it is known that he was charged with being a poor Christian, a corruptor of the natives, and of having improper relations with married women, in particular with the wife of Alonso López, a resident of Guadalajara. While acting as visitador of Nueva Galicia, Lebrón was accused of collecting more than twelve thousand pesos in salary for four years, in which time he occupied himself mostly in fiestas, bull-fights, games, and banquets. He was also accused of evading the residencia by secreting his goods in a monastery, by neglecting to pay fines imposed upon him, by failing to furnish bail, and by intimidating witnesses.[78] In short, Morones decided that Lebrón was a person "mentally incapable of holding the office of oidor and visitador," and should be fined and removed from office. Morones also contended that Lebrón should not be allowed to resume his office, for he was a vindictive person and had sworn to get revenge upon those who had humbled him.[79]

Contreras was also subjected to a very severe examination, for he worked hand in glove with Lebrón, or to quote Morones, "they voted as one." Morones said that Contreras had a very hasty temper, was abusive, and was very little thought of in Nueva Galicia. The most serious charge against Contreras was that of rape, the girl in question being María Caramillo, daughter of Alonso López, resident of Guadalajara. As was true in Lebrón's case, all of the witnesses appearing for the oidor were persons of small fortune, poor birth, and questionable reputation, in whom little credence could be placed. Contreras had also threat-

[78] A. G. I., 103-3-1, Registros de Oficio, 1554 á 1671; A. G. I., 67-1-18, Ldo, Morones al consejo, Compostela, 17 de agosto de 1557; A. G. I., 67-1-18, Morones al Rey, Compostela, 18 de septiembre de 1557.
[79] A. G. I., 67-1-18, Morones al Consejo, 17 de agosto de 1557.

ened to reap revenge when he was returned to office, so, "to avoid scandal," the visitador decided not to give him or Lebrón an opportunity.

The licentiate Oseguera was acquitted of the various accusations brought against him. Morones was not entirely satisfied as to his innocence, but felt that it was necessary to free him and restore him to office because of insufficient time which prevented the collection of additional evidence. Subsequently Oseguera made a splendid record, and by 1563 he became the president of the audiencia of Nueva Galicia with Morones and Alarcón as his associates. He was later promoted to the audiencia of Mexico.[80]

While Dr. Morones was conducting the residencia, the advisability of reconquering Chiametla was brought to his attention. The rehabilitation of that west coast province was absolutely necessary if the Spaniards wished to retain their outposts in Culiacán, which was fast becoming depopulated, since the roads leading to it were continually harassed by natives. The trails through that country were also closed six months out of the year because of the rains and the swollen streams. Chiametla had been settled by Guzmán both to afford protection to travel between Compostela and Culiacán, and also because of the great attraction of its fertile valleys and its mountains rich in gold and silver. But, notwithstanding its intrinsic value, the difficulties of maintaining settlements in Chiametla became too great, and it lost most of its Spanish inhabitants. There had been twenty-three repartimientos in Chiametla, but in 1557 most of them were deserted, for the natives refused to pay tribute and fled into the mountains. There they lapsed into barbarism and made frequent raids upon convoys moving between

[80] *Ibid;* Morones was succeeded by Mendiola, and he in turn by Orozco, brother of the oidor of Mexico. Quinoñes was reinstated later, but died while on his way to Guadalajara (Bancroft, *Mexico,* II. 549, note 31).

Compostela and Culiacán. Morones recognized the necessity of pacifying these natives and of reconverting them to Christianity, and he petitioned the king to be entrusted with that task.[81]

Morones was not the first man to see in Chiametla a fertile field for the advancement of the king's interests as well as those of the petitioner. In November, 1555, Alonso Valiente,[82] a resident of Los Angeles (Puebla) and one of the companions of Cortés in the conquest, petitioned the king for permission "to settle and pacify the province of Chiametla and Guazamota, and all the mountains to the north coast"; that is, all lands extending between the limits of Compostela and Culiacán, and east to the mines of Jacotlán.[83] He promised to effect the subjugation of the natives with the least possible effusion of blood, and, to insure this, he promised to take some friars with him to act as witnesses who could report to the viceroy. Certain concessions were demanded by Valiente: he asked to be commissioned captaingeneral and justicia mayor of the new provinces for twenty years; to be granted power to apportion repartimientos; and to be allowed to acquire encomiendas for himself in return for expenses incurred. Whether Valiente's proposal was inopportune, or whether his demands were too exorbitant, is not known; at any rate his requests were not granted.

[81] A. G. I., 67-1-18, Morones al Consejo, 15 de agosto de 1557; A. G. I., 59-4-3, Manuel Valiente á S. M., Los Angeles, 18 de mayo de 1556.

[82] Alonso Valiente, a native of Medina de las Torres came to Española in 1517, and arrived in Mexico four months after the conquest of the city. He served in the conquest of Michoacán, and then went to Honduras with Cortés. He claims to have discovered the entrance to the Bahama Channel. Cortés granted him, in encomienda, the pueblo of Tecamachalco (ibid.; A. G. I., 87-5-1, Informes de conquistadores). While la Marcha was on his visita in Tepeque, he heard that "an Alonso Valiente, resident of Los Angeles, with companions, had sent there for sale a quadrilla of negroes, and among them were thirteen free Indian women who had been taken by treachery" (A. G. I., 66-5-14, La visita general hecha por de la Marcha).

[83] A. G. I., 59-4-3, Capitulación de Alonso Valiente para con S. M. en lo de Chiametla.

Morones' proposal received more favor in the Spanish court. By royal cédula, dated in Toledo, March 11, 1560, he was granted permission to undertake the conquest and settlement of Chiametla, but he was ordered to defray his own expenses and not to call on the king for assistance. If he found that he could not finance the expedition himself, then he was to propose some alternative.[84] Neglecting to heed the royal warning regarding the financing of the expedition, Morones undertook the enterprise. In January, 1561, he reported that preparations were being made for the expedition. Although many "persons of quality" had consented to accompany him, their combined fortunes were not sufficient to defray the expenses, and he requested permission to draw on the royal treasury to the extent of twenty thousand pesos. The expedition was delayed not only by the lack of funds, but also because Morones was unwilling to leave in charge of the audiencia the oidor Oseguera, whom he did not trust. Oseguera had written to the king advising against the Chiametla adventure. Although he admitted that the settlement of the territory between Compostela and Culiacán was very necessary, he denied the advisability of such an undertaking at that time. He believed that mines in that direction would continue to be discovered, and gradually that territory would be settled. Any other method he said was "doubtful of success, and if his Majesty put money into it, he would surely lose it." Naturally the opposition of Oseguera was instilled because of Morones' residencia. As another oidor was being sent to Nueva Galicia, Morones hoped he would arrive soon, for then he could start on the entrada.

[84] A. G. I., 67-1-18, Morones al Rey, Guadalajara, 15 de mayo de 1563; A. G. I., 67-1-18, Morones al Rey, Guadalajara, 2 de enero de 1561. The bishop of Nueva Galicia wrote that the conquest of Chiametla by Morones would be very beneficial and pleasing to every one. Furthermore, he suggested that a new bishopric be erected in Chiametla and Culiacán (A. G. I., 67-1-18, El Obispo de Nueva Galicia, 27 de enero de 1561) ; A. G. I., 67-1-18, Ldo. Seguro al Rey, Guadalajara, 6 de enero de 1561.

The request of Morones that royal assistance be extended to him received no response; the proposed expedition to Chiametla, therefore, continued to be postponed. As late as May, 1563, Morones begged for aid "to save his honor," and to extricate him from a most embarrassing position, for he had just received word that Francisco de Ibarra was usurping his rights in Chiametla.[85] He died in the same year without having undertaken the conquest of Chiametla, and he left his claims to the audiencia of Nueva Galicia to press against Ibarra.

While acting as visitador to Nueva Galicia, Morones petitioned the king on several occasions to order the transfer of the audiencia from Compostela to Guadalajara. He declared that Compostela was not suited to be the seat of the audiencia because of its unhealthy situation, poor lands, scarcity of food, and few Indians. It had but twenty Spanish families, no stores, no doctor, no druggist, and no barber. He declared that Guadalajara was much more suitable, because it enjoyed good climate, fertile soil, abundant game and fish, good roads, and a great number of natives.[86]

The innumerable petitions requesting the removal of the audiencia were finally acted upon on June 6, 1557, when, by royal cédula, the audiencia of Nueva Galicia was ordered to submit informaciones relating to the advisability of moving the episcopal chair, the audiencia, and the caja real of Nueva Galicia from Compostela to Guadalajara.[87] The informaciones were written in great detail and submitted to the king on September 26, 1559. By royal cédula, dated in Toledo, May 10, 1560, the audiencia and the caja real were ordered

---

[85] A. G. I., 67-1-18, Morones al Rey, 15 de mayo de 1563; Obregón (A. G. I., 1-1-3/22, Obregón, Crónica) says that the king finally granted Morones fifty thousand pesos, but the oidor, fearing the expenses of an expedition and the labor it entailed, did not dare to undertake it.

[86] A. G. I., 67-1-18, Morones al Rey, 15 de agosto de 1557.

[87] Since Morones' petition was dated August 15, 1557, it will be noted that his letter was not the cause of the issuance of the royal cédula.

transferred to Guadalajara. Upon receipt of the order, November 15, 1560, the oidores and the royal officials started to move immediately; the transfer was completed by December 10. Sites about the plaza of Guadalajara were selected with great care for the audiencia building, for the casa de fundición, the caja real, and homes for the oidores and the officials of the real hacienda.[88]

Prior to the transfer of the audiencia, the episcopal seat of Nueva Galicia was located in Guadalajara, though it had never been legally transferred from Compostela. As has been noted above, Bishop Maraver never resided in Compostela, but continually moved about his diocese. His successor, Pedro de Ayala, a Franciscan and a native of Guadalajara in Spain,[89] who took possession of his office in November, 1559, refused to reside in Compostela and established himself in Guadalajara. When the audiencia was ordered to move to Guadalajara, it was understood that the episcopal capital should continue at Compostela. This anomalous situation was remedied by a royal cédula of May 18, 1561, which declared that the bishop should henceforth reside in Guadalajara and that a cathedral church should be built in that place.

As it was impossible for the Spanish residents of Nueva Galicia to keep in subjection the Chichimecos who continually harassed the roads to Zacatecas and made possession of the mines extremely difficult, the viceroy decided to take the protection of that region into his hands. Action became imperative when a serious disaster befell the Spaniards. In the mountains of Zacatecas the Indians ambushed a large Spanish convoy of thirty carts and killed most of its guard. This attack alarmed Velasco, and, to protect the road to

---

[88] A. G. I., 67-1-18, Los oidores de Nueva Galicia al Rey, 30 de enero de 1561; A. G. I., 67-1-18, Los Oidores de Nueva Galicia al Rey, 4 de enero de 1561; A. G. I., 67-1-18, Morones al Rey, 8 de octubre de 1559.

[89] Mota Padilla, *Nueva Galicia*, p. 203.

Zacatecas, he ordered forts established along the route and founded two Spanish military colonies, San Miguel el Grande and San Felipe.[90] These garrisoned places were useful in affording protection to travelers, and they also led to the discovery of more mines and the foundation of other Spanish settlements to the south and east of Zacatecas. The most important of these were Queretaro and Guanajuato.

In 1570, when Viceroy Enríquez was informed by his provincial officers that the Chichimecos were still attacking the Zacatecas convoys, he ordered more presidios established. This order was executed, and the settlements of Ojuelos and Portizuelos came into being. But it seems that these measures were not attended by the satisfactory results the viceroy anticipated, for the Chichimecos continued to make incursions as far as Guanajuato, destroying haciendas and robbing and killing the Spaniards. To protect the isolated settlements and especially to give security to the convoys, Enríquez dispatched to that region Juan Torres de Lagunas. Lagunas was a man of considerable experience in fighting the Indians, and, in the war against the Chichimecos, he justified his appointment. He followed the Indians into their mountain retreats and dislodged them from their fortified *peñoles*. Those who escaped were pursued far into the interior, from whence they did not dare to return. By these means order and security were brought to the region between Guanajuato and Zacatecas. For the able assistance afforded Lagunas in the campaign, the settlement of San Felipe was given the title of villa.[91]

[90] San Felipe was founded by the viceroy's brother as a frontier post against the Indians. With the pacification of the Chichimecos, San Felipe declined (*Col. Doc. Inéd.*, XV. 247). According to Beaumont (*Crónica de Michoacán*, XXIII, 2d. part) Fray Juan de San Miguel founded the villa of San Miguel el Grande in 1549.

[91] García, *Los Mineros Mexicanos*, pp. 166-168.

CHAPTER IV

THE FOUNDING OF NUEVA VIZCAYA

The conquest of Copalá, the fabulously rich and populous kingdom which was reported to be located north of San Martín and Aviño, had been interrupted in 1558, but not abandoned. Indeed, Ibarra, the Franciscan fathers, and the few Spaniards who had been sent by Viceroy Velasco into the northern borderlands "to pave the way for the settlers" were making good progress in exploring the new lands and in establishing friendly relations with the natives. The Viceroy's interest in exploration was reawakened by the letter concerning Copalá which had been written by Francisco de Ibarra to his uncle Diego in June, 1562,[1] and which had been sent by Diego to Velasco. The letter was accompanied by a petition in which Diego de Ibarra requested permission to undertake at his own expense the conquest of Copalá. He specified, however, that he be allowed to put his nephew, Francisco, in charge of the expedition. We must recall that Diego was a cripple, and for that reason we do not find him entering actively upon the work of exploration. Undoubtedly the explorer's letter had a considerable influence on the Viceroy, for statements found in the letter are encountered almost verbatim in the Viceroy's commission to Francisco de Ibarra.

In proposing Francisco's name, Diego acknowledged the youth of his nephew, for at that time he was only about twenty-five years of age. Several letters passed between Velasco and Diego. Although the latter recognized the importance and seriousness of the undertaking as one demanding maturity and wide experience, he nevertheless felt

[1] Cf. p. 80.

that the experience, prudence, and ability of his nephew were far beyond his years. Furthermore, he promised to stand by ready to render every assistance within his power. This, to the great credit of Diego, he fulfilled in good faith throughout the life of his nephew.

Velasco determined, after discussing the matter with the oidores of the audiencia of Mexico and with other persons of note, "to bring the new provinces to peace and to a knowledge of God by dispatching an expedition under a competent leader who should be granted the authority of a governor."[2] Francisco de Ibarra was not originally selected for the position, for the Viceroy first appointed Dr. Corita, oidor of Mexico, as governor and captain-general of Copalá. But Corita was not able to accept the commission on account of insufficient funds; and thus, as second choice, Ibarra was selected for the position.[3]

On July 24, 1562, Francisco de Ibarra was clothed with the authority of a governor and captain-general for the purpose of undertaking the exploration, conquest, and settlement of the unknown lands extending to the north of San Martín and Aviño. His commission read as follows:

I, Don Luís de Velasco, viceroy, governor, and captain-general for His Majesty in this New Spain, and president of the royal audiencia which is located in the same place:

Inasmuch as His Majesty by royal provision, signed by Her Most Serene Highness, the Princess Governess of the kingdoms of Castile and the Indies, and dated in Valladolid on December 29, 1557, has granted me license and authority to do what seems to me to be best, proper, and convenient in making new discoveries, and in founding settlements in this land and in other provinces, and with the object of accomplishing that purpose, has given authority to appoint persons who seem to me to be most fit according to the provisions and instructions which were conveyed to me and whose tenor is as follows: Don Felipe, by grace of God, King of Castile, León, Aragon, England, France, the Two Sicilies, Jerusalem, Navarre, Granada, Toledo, Valencia, Galicia, Majorca, Sevilla,

[2] A. G. I., 58-3-8, Comisión de Francisco de Ibarra.
[3] A. G. I., 1-1-1/20, Memorial del Lcdo. Juan de Ybarra.

Córdova, Corsica, Murcia, Jáen, the Algarves, Algeciras, Gibraltar, the Canary Islands, the Indies, Islands and Tierra Firme of the Ocean Sea, Count of Barcelona, Lord of Vizcaya and of Molina, Duke of Athens, Count of Roussillon and of Cerdagne, Marquis of Oristan and of Gociano, Archduke of Austria, Duke of Burgundy, of Brabant, and of Milan, Count of Flanders and of the Tyrol, etc.

. . . To you, Don Luís de Velasco, our viceroy and captain-general of New Spain, and president of the royal audiencia which is located in the same place. . . . Whereas it was provisioned and ordered by us that you could not dispatch expeditions or make new discoveries and settlements, or appoint governors for them without our license and special order; and, since we, desiring greatly that that land and provinces subject to that audiencia and La Florida should be peopled and placed in good order, both for the good of the natives who should be instructed and enlightened in matters of Holy Faith, and for the good of the Spaniards who reside in those lands, and for the benefit of those who pass through them, in order that they might profit and be given security in establishing abodes and in prosecuting their affairs, it was deemed advisable to issue an order concerning the said settlements; and because of the great confidence which we have in your person and in your wisdom, we have agreed to discharge you of this, in order that you as the person who has the thing in mind [best qualified] may decide what ought to be done, and thus for the service of God and of ourselves, and for the good of the land, you will provide there what seems fitting to you: . . . Therefore, for the present we give you license and authority so that when you consider the time proper you can dispatch [expeditions] to make the aforementioned new discoveries and settlements in accordance with the [enclosed] instructions which we command you to observe wholly as stipulated; and to the persons whom you send to the said lands and new discoveries, you and the oidores of that audiencia will grant the necessary warrants conforming to the mentioned instructions so that by those means there will be avoided the damage and disorders which up to the present time have occurred in new discoveries; and always be careful to keep informed how the provisions and instructions are being fulfilled, and how the natives are being treated. Given in the city of Valladolid, the 29th of December, 1557. The Princess, etc.

And since, during the past few years I have learned that beyond the mines of San Martín and Aviño, which are past the mines of Zacatecas, there are certain settlements of Indians and rich provinces, like one named Copalá, and others which up to now have not been discovered by Spaniards, and since the natives of those places were without the light of our Holy Catholic Faith, I granted a commission to Francisco de Ibarra, in order that, with certain religious of the Order of St. Francis, and Spaniards who went in his company, they might enter the country beyond the mines of San Martín and Aviño, to discover the settlements that were reported to be in that region; and, concerning what they might see, discover, or hear, they were ordered to report to me in order that provision convenient to the service of God and of His Majesty might be made; and also they were ordered to bring in peace and to the royal dominion the said natives; and since, at the present time, according to letters from the said Francisco de Ibarra, and a report of the said religious, I learned that in prosecuting the entrada and discovery they went on some journeys inland beyond the mines of San Martín and Aviño, and discovered certain valleys and good irrigated lands, and some settlements which up to that time had never been seen, and that there they heard that farther on there were great settlements of people who wore clothes, but who were without a knowledge of Christian Doctrine; and because it conforms to the will and desires of His Majesty, after discussing the matter with the royal audiencia and with persons of importance and experience regarding what should be done to bring the natives of the said lands to peace and to a knowledge of God Our Lord in order that they might be saved, for they were without the light of Faith, it was decided that some Spanish people should be dispatched under the leadership of a person with complete authority to govern them; and since you, the said Francisco de Ibarra, in order to serve God Our Lord and His Majesty, volunteered to go with some Spanish horsemen to discover and treat with the said peoples, we acquired great confidence in you, and believe you to be a person of trust, quality, and ability such as is required of one to perform well and faithfully the charge which I herewith commit and entrust to you:

In the name of His Majesty and by virtue of royal authorization hereinbefore incorporated, I charge, command and empower you, Francisco de Ibarra, that, with as many as one hundred horsemen, whom you shall select, and religious of the Order of St. Francis who choose to accompany you, to enter freely on the discovery of lands and settlements said to be located beyond the mines of San Martín and Aviño, excepting those which are in the province of Chiametla, for its discovery has been entrusted by His Majesty to Doctor Morones, oidor and alcalde mayor of the royal audiencia of the New Kingdom of Galicia. In order that the above may be best pursued, in the name of His Majesty, I name and appoint you captain and governor of the people whom you shall lead, and I grant you license and power to undertake the said discovery by all ways and means deemed necessary to bring in peace to our Catholic Faith, and to obedience to His Majesty, the natives of those said lands. And you shall see that the religious shall not be hindered in pacifying them by preaching the Holy Gospel. You shall be empowered to make settlements where you deem best, according to the location, fertility of the soil, and quality of the site. Concerning this you shall render me accounts in order that provision may be made for their perpetuity, and if the said natives resist the preaching of the said religious and the entrada, your people shall not harm them, nor use force, but shall take all possible care to win a free entry.

Concerning this and all else which you shall have to do, you will follow the list of instructions enclosed,[4] signed by my hand, and by the oidores of this royal audiencia. You will keep them and fulfill them, for they contain, without change, the duties of a governor and captain-general which are similar to yours. By them you are to be guided in the administration of justice, and in all cases and causes, civil and criminal, which might occur. In all this I grant you complete authority and command all persons who accompany you to obey you as their governor and captain, and to fulfill your commands and heed your call, and to obey you without excuse or reservation, subject to whatever penalty you desire to impose upon them. Since in the said list of instructions are declared and specified all that pertains to the exercise of your office, and since much of this is not incorporated in this commission, you must adhere to the instructions as if they were herein contained. Dated in Mexico, the 24th of July, 1562. (Rubric) Don Luís de Velasco.[5]

In the absence of the list of instructions, what were the powers and duties of Francisco de Ibarra as governor and captain-general of the new lands he was to conquer and settle? Unfortunately the *Ordenanzas sobre descubrimiento nuevo é población,* issued by Philip II in 1563, came one year too late to solve this question for us; after that date all the capitulations, or contracts, were drawn up in uniform style. They enumerated concisely and minutely all the customary obligations, duties, and privileges of persons entering into contracts with the crown for the purpose of making discoveries and founding settlements and receiving therefor the title and office of adelantado, alcalde mayor, or whatever office was being conferred.[6] It is possible, however, to detect in the "list of instructions" which Velasco gave Ibarra, defining his powers and duties as governor and captain-general, something quite analogous to provisions of the *Ordenanzas* of 1563. The object of the crown in issuing the general ordinance was to standardize the duties and powers of the conquistadores and thus to avoid confusion and conflict of authority. The same motive was in the mind of the

[4] These supplementary instructions have been lost.
[5] A. G. I., 58-3-8, Comisión de Francisco de Ibarra.
[6] *Col. Doc. Inéd.,* VIII. 484-537.

king in 1557, for, in commanding Velasco to reëmbark upon
the work of exploration and founding of settlements, he said,
"You and the oidores of that audiencia will grant the necessary warrants conforming to the aforementioned instructions
so that by those means there will be avoided the damage and
disorders which up to the present time have occurred in new
discoveries."[7] Thus it is possible that the king's instructions
became the basis of the *Ordenanzas* of 1563, and if this be
true, the powers and duties which were bestowed upon Francisco de Ibarra can be read in a general way in the *Ordenanzas*. Fragmentary statements of this and that privilege
granted Ibarra as governor and captain-general of Nueva
Vizcaya serve to reinforce the assumption that the general
nature of his authority can be read in the *Ordenanzas*.

When referring to the Indies the word "governor" had various
accepted meanings according to the territory to which it was applied. . . . More concretely it designated those high officials of
certain provinces like La Plata, Chile, Antillas, etc., which did not
have at their head viceroys. These governors enjoyed very ample
authority similar to that of the viceroys, although not so extensive,
and maintained in their respective audiencias a relation equal to that
of those we have described. . . . In a stricter adaptation, the
word "governor" was applied to officials of the smaller jurisdictions
placed in the cities and places which were at the head of a province,
or where they seemed necessary as delegates of the central power.
In this sense the denomination was equivalent to the corregidor
(used in Peru) and to the alcaldes mayores (frequent in Mexico and
also in Peru). In Cuba, Don Luís Colon had a lieutenant-governor,
and when the authority of the island was elevated to the state of a
captain-general, there were governors in the cities of Matanzas,
Trinidad, and Fernandina.[8]

Dismissing the governorship of the first category as named
above, let us examine the nature of the office when considered in a stricter sense. The governor was the administrative, legislative, and judicial head of a division of a viceroyalty called a gobierno, which ordinarily included several

[7] A. G. I., 58-3-8, Comisión de Francisco de Ibarra.
[8] Rafael Altamira y Crevea, *Historia de España y de la civilización
española*, Barcelona, 1913, III, par. 695.

regions denominated provinces. "These governors, corregidores, or alcaldes mayores called together or presided at the
cabildo meeting; intervened in the public works by lending
money for their construction, forced expropriations, etc.;
watched over the buenas costumbres, being able to impose
penalties on those who broke them, as they did respectively
in several cities, etc."[9]   Also, the governor was the superior
judicial officer of the gobierno; to him came the appeals
from the decisions of the lesser judges like the alcaldes ordinarios and the alcaldes mayores.   Ordinarily the governor
exercised military authority over his jurisdiction, but this
was by virtue of his being captain-general or alcalde mayor.
Generally his military authority was conveyed in the same
patent of governorship.   Finally, the governor was entrusted
with the enactment of royal decrees, the oversight and maintenance of good government, and the protection of the royal
prerogative.[10]

Francisco de Ibarra was clothed with these ordinary
powers of a governor and captain-general, but since he was
commissioned to explore and settle "unoccupied" lands, and
since the enterprise was to be undertaken at his own expense,
he was obviously granted privileges and exemptions not
enjoyed by the governor of a settled province.   The nature
of his authority as deduced from scattered references was
the following: He was granted the title of governor and
captain-general for the duration of his life and the life of an
heir whom he should name.   He was empowered to explore
and settle the lands beyond the settled Spanish frontier and
to "bring into his government all the towns that were not
provided with a church and a missionary"; but this work
was to be undertaken without governmental support, and
furthermore he was to receive no salary.   It was not until

---

[9] Altamira y Crevea, *loc. cit.*

[10] For the office of governor, cf. the *Recopilación de leyes,* and Juan
de Solórzano y Pereyra, *Política Indiana,* Madrid, 1776.

1574 that the king conferred upon Ibarra an annual salary
of two thousand ducats.[11]   Up to that time he received no
recompense whatsoever and no title other than that of governor and captain-general.   Francisco de Ibarra was never
given the title of adelantado, and though his successor, Juan
de Ibarra, petitioned for that honor, his plea remained unanswered; but the third governor of Nueva Vizcaya, Diego de
Ibarra, was rewarded with the title of adelantado, although
he had asked for something grander, namely, a marquisate.[12]

Among Ibarra's administrative functions was that of
granting the Indians in encomienda for the purpose of exploiting their labor and giving them religious instruction.[13]
He also was granted authority to appoint lesser officials. We
shall find that one of the governor's first acts after he
arrived within the limits of his new jurisdiction was to
appoint his provincial officials.   Then, when municipalities
were founded, he filled the first offices by appointment.   A
suitable salary had to be provided by him for his officials.[14]
The legislative power of the governor included the making
of ordinances for the government of his province; this power
was restricted only by the provision that these decrees must
not be contrary to justice and royal orders.   His judicial
authority consisted of his ability to hear appeals from the
decisions of his lesser officials.   In matters of superior control he was subject to the audiencia of Mexico.   Therefore,
appeals from the decisions of the governor were to be taken

[11] A. G. I., 1-1-1/20, Memorial del Lcdo. Juan de Ybarra.

[12] Bolton and Marshall (*Colonization of North America,* p. 541)
mention Francisco de Ibarra and Luís de Carabajal as *adelantados,* but
this title was never conferred upon either of them. Mr. R. R. Hill, in his
article "The Office of Adelantado," in the *Political Science Quarterly,*
XXVIII. 656, lists the men who were given the title of adelantado.
This list is not exact, however, for we note the absence of the name of
Diego de Ibarra, who was created adelantado in 1583.

[13] A. G. I., 1-1-3/22, Obregón, Crónica; A. G. I., 1-3-20/11, Francisco
de Ibarra, Información de méritos.

[14] A. G. I., 1-1-3/22, Obregón, Crónica; A. G. I., 67-1-3, Información
de Nombre de Diós, 1608.

direct to Mexico. The royal tribute was also to be sent to the caja real in Mexico City.[15]

As captain-general for the purpose of exploring and subjugating new provinces, Ibarra was vested with considerable military authority. In fact, his office should be considered very largely as a military one; that at least was its nature until the time when his gobierno was pacified and settled with Spanish pobladores. All men who joined the expedition were charged to obey the governor and not to desert under pain of death. Ibarra was also commissioned alguacil mayor, or high sheriff. The most important power which this office carried with it was that of appointing the ordinary sheriffs and bailiffs.[16]

In addition to the considerable privilege of granting encomiendas, Ibarra enjoyed certain exemptions. He and his followers were excused from the alcabala, or sales tax, for a period of twenty years. Also, in lieu of the customary payment of the royal fifth of all gold or precious metals mined or found by other means, the founders of Nueva Vizcaya were to pay the royal treasury but one-twentieth. The mines of Nueva Vizcaya, however, did not pay any royal tribute whatsoever until after the discovery of the mines of Indé and Santa Bárbara in 1567; and then the salaries of the royal officials, which Ibarra had paid for the prior four years, were deducted from the king's tribute.[17]

It is said that Francisco de Ibarra was very doubtful whether to accept the commission which bestowed upon him the great authority and privileges of a provincial governor. His knowledge, based on personal experience, of conditions on the frontier and the well-nigh insuperable obstacles which would confront the new governor caused him to hesitate,

---

[15] A. G. I., 67-1-18, Audiencia de Nueva Galicia al Rey, 18 de abril de 1563.

[16] A. G. I., 1-3-20/11, Francisco de Ibarra, Información de méritos.

[17] A. G. I., 67-1-18, Diego de Colio al Consejo.

and he modestly accused himself of lack of experience and of immaturity. But finally, being greatly influenced by the fact that Velasco had selected him for the high honor and that upon his uncle depended the fulfillment of the enterprise, he accepted the office. "The commission granted Ibarra," says Baltasar de Obregón, the chronicler of the expedition, "was deserved; he proved himself a gentleman, capable, honest, and prudent; his deeds, his life, his habits, vindicated his appointment."[18]

The most complete, and in many respects, the most trustworthy account of the expeditions of Francisco de Ibarra as governor of Nueva Vizcaya is that written by Baltasar de Obregón. His narrative entitled, *Chronicle, Commentary or Narrative of Ancient and Modern Discoveries in New Spain and in New Mexico,* has only recently been discovered in the Archivo General de Indias at Seville.[19] It contains thirty-seven chapters, or two hundred and forty-four folio sheets, bound in parchment and accompanied by two letters dedicating the work to the king. It was completed in Mexico in April, 1584. Because of our dependence on Obregón's *Chronicle* for much of our information regarding the early history of Nueva Vizcaya, and since Obregón was one of Ibarra's companions on many of his entradas, it seems proper to discuss the man and his work in so far as available evidence permits.

Baltasar de Obregón was a member of one of the leading families in New Spain; his father and both grandfathers played important rôles in the conquest and settlement of the

---

[18] A. G. I., 1-1-3/22, Obregón, *Crónica.* In his report to the king (*Col. Doc. Inéd.,* XIV. 553-555) the viceroy mentions Ibarra as "un hombre virtuoso y bastante."

[19] There is a transcript of Obregón's *Chronicle* in the Bancroft Library, University of California, and another in the Ayer Collection in the Newberry Library, Chicago. It has recently (1924) been printed by the Secretaría de Educación of Mexico under the editorship of Mariano Cuevas.

Indies and of the City of Mexico. Not only did Obregón belong to one of the leading families of the New World, but he was fortunate in forming a marriage union with a lady of importance, Doña Mariana de Luna, grand-daughter of Antonio de Caricedo, one of the original conquerors.

When he was nineteen years of age, Baltasar "started out to emulate the worthy deeds of his forefathers." He entered the services of Governor Francisco de Ibarra when the latter was in Sinaloa, and served under him in his subsequent entradas. The *Chronicle,* therefore, has the value of being a first-hand account of those expeditions; but at the same time it suffers the disadvantage of having been written several years after the occurrence of the events narrated. Notwithstanding the prominence of his family connections and his services in Nueva Vizcaya, Obregón was forced in 1584, on account of the poverty of his encomienda in the Mizteca Baja, to petition the king for relief. It was specifically for this purpose that he wrote his *Chronicle* and prepared an información de méritos to accompany it. The informacion is concerned solely with Obregón's family tree and tells us practically nothing about his personal activities. But in his *Chronicle* he aimed to set forth the complete story of the discovery and exploration of northwestern New Spain, from the earliest time through the expedition of Antonio de Espejo to New Mexico in 1584. His ostensible purpose in writing the *Chronicle,* as stated by himself, was, "that by this account his Majesty may be served by an increase of many provinces, cities, and royal fifths; for his captains, being informed of things that will be of value on such journeys, will be able to avoid trials that the first discoverers had to experience due to a lack of information." He then begged the king to examine the *Chronicle* carefully so that he might be fully informed regarding what was most necessary for the advancement of the royal service. Because of his experience in exploration,

and "the example of the good and Christian methods which
Francisco de Ibarra was accustomed to practice on his discoveries," he felt qualified to act as a lieutenant or as a captain of any expedition which the king might care to send to
New Mexico. Thus, Obregón's true object in writing his
history was his desire to be "commissioned to one of those
positions which are wont to be granted to others, not because
of their having served Your Majesty, but because of the
influence which they bring to bear."[20] The name of Baltasar
de Obregón is to be added to the long list of applicants for
the position which was finally awarded Juan de Oñate.

Francisco de Ibarra received news of his appointment in
July, 1562. At that time he was in the vicinity of San Martín, whither he had gone to settle some mining districts for
his uncle. When he received his commission, he immediately
returned to Zacatecas and there began recruiting men for
his entrada. A short time before Christmas, he and his
recruits marched to San Martín, where the final organization
took place. Arms, munitions, horses, clothing, and supplies
were issued to one and all. Diego de Ibarra was present to
offer encouragement, and he gave his nephew a gorgeous
standard of damask-blue embroidered in gold and silver and
with the images of Christ and the Virgin upon it. The flag
was taken to the church of San Martín where it was blessed;
it was then entrusted to the high constable, or alguacil mayor,
Martín de Rentería.[21]

"One hundred and seventy men,"[22] says Obregón, "were
assembled for the entrada, the greater part of whom were

[20] A. G. I., 1-1-3/22, Obregón, Crónica; A. G. I., 87-5-1, Informes de
conquistadores; A. G. I., 59-6-23, Información de Baltasar de Obregón.
México, 12 de abril de 1584.

[21] A. G. I., 1-1-1/20, Memorial del Lcdo. Juan de Ybarra; Amador,
Zacatecas, p. 213.

[22] There is disagreement regarding the number of men who accompanied Ibarra on this entrada. The number varies from 110 to 170.
Cf. A. G. I., 1-3-20/11, Francisco de Ybarra, Información de méritos,
and Col. Doc. Inéd., XIV. 554.

Basques, a carefully selected . . . body of men." All were well equipped with horses, arms, coats of mail, and munitions. Three missionaries, Father Pablo Azevedo, Brother Juan de Herrera, and a third whose name is not known, accompanied Ibarra. Azevedo was a Portuguese who had taken religious orders in the Province of Santa Cruz in Santo Domingo. He went to the northern frontier soon after his arrival in Mexico. Juan de Herrera, a lay-brother, arrived in New Spain in 1541. Prior to his arrival in Nueva Galicia, he had worked for some time in Yucatan.[23] The remainder of the personnel was made up of a great number of Negro slaves and Indian auxiliaries. Among the latter were some Aztecs.[24]

After the distribution of the arms and supplies and the completion of preliminary organization, written instructions from the Viceroy were read by Ibarra to his men. These instructions enumerated the purpose of the expedition, the nature of the authority vested in the governor, and the duties and obligations of the men who were to accompany him. It was the governor's desire that the men should know what was expected of them, so that they would not be remiss in their duties.

On January 24, 1563, after a stay of over forty days in San Martín, Ibarra departed for the lands over which he was to be governor.[25] "Diego and Francisco de Ibarra," says Obregón, "took leave of each other in San Martín with evidences of deep affection. Diego gave advice to his nephew and his soldiers, and assured them of aid throughout

[23] Mendieta (*Historia Eclesiastica*, pp. 759-761), Bancroft (*North Mexican States and Texas*, I. 103), and Amador (*Zacatecas*, p. 214) state that Ibarra was accompanied by four Franciscans.

[24] Expedición de la Nueva Vizcaya, 1563, MS 13, Bancroft Library. This is an account in Aztec with a Spanish translation by Professor Jalicia.

[25] A. G. I., 67-1-18, Diego de Colio al Consejo; Obregón gives the date of the departure from San Martín as April, 1564, which is obviously an error; Amador, *Zacatecas*, p. 214.

the entire journey." The alcalde mayor, Diego de Colio, and the inhabitants of San Martín, gave the explorers a farewell celebration consisting of a great banquet and a bull-fight. But if one is to believe Colio's own account of Ibarra's sojourn in San Martín,[26] this celebration was quite as much in the nature of a public thanksgiving for good riddance of unwelcome and troublesome guests. Colio accused Ibarra of having recruited his following from the riff-raff of the frontier; men whose licentious habits he was either unable or unwilling to curb. Left to their own resources and unrestrained, they robbed and maltreated the inhabitants of San Martín with impunity. Even Colio did not escape, for "on one occasion he was assaulted and narrowly escaped death at the hands of this murderous crew." When the explorers left San Martín, complained Colio, they took with them not only many horses and mules belonging to the citizens of the villa, but even their Indian servants. To all the protests of the alcalde mayor, Ibarra turned a deaf ear, and wrongs were not adjusted. Needless to say, Colio undoubtedly magnified the indignities and injuries suffered by the inhabitants of San Martín, but one may venture the opinion that there was some basis for complaint and that Ibarra and his men were not over-considerate of the rights of others.

From San Martín the explorers marched by way of Nombre de Diós, where, Colio declared, he himself had preceded Ibarra by two months and seventeen days. At Nombre de Diós the ambitious conquistador revealed his intention not to be too strictly bound by the terms of his commission, for he forced Colio's lieutenant in Nombre de Diós, Alonso García, to acknowledge his superior authority. This was certainly a contravention of his commission, for he was explicitly authorized to assume authority over the *unoccu-*

[26] A. G. I., 67-1-18, Diego de Colio al Consejo; A. G. I., 66-5-14, Averiguaciones de Contreras, 1569.

pied lands. From Nombre de Diós the explorers went to Aviño, where the inhabitants were maltreated in the same manner as they had been in San Martín. There also the alcalde was coerced to acknowledge the authority of the governor of Nueva Vizcaya. Colio accused Ibarra of applying these same illegal methods in San Lucas, San Juan Valley, Peñol Blanco, and Guadiana, places which he claimed were within the jurisdiction of Nueva Galicia. It is undeniable that Ibarra transgressed his commission in that he appropriated places actually settled by Spaniards. For these reasons Colio's protests were legitimate, but, as we shall see, they were without avail.

From Aviño the explorers marched north until they reached the lands over which Ibarra was to have authority, i.e., the unoccupied lands. There he ordered a halt, and mass was celebrated. All prayed for strength, divine assistance, and guidance in the exploration and subjugation of those unknown lands. After mass Ibarra took possession of his new gobierno in the name of the king. Then, in an address to his men, he exhorted them to coöperate with him "loyally, bravely, and piously," in the service of God and their king. "This necessary obedience and loyalty was promised by all like good Christians and loyal soldiers of his Majesty."[27] After these formalities, they continued their march to the north and established a camp at a place which was named San Juan and which was probably located near the present San Juan del Río. San Juan served as headquarters for future expeditions.[28]

At San Juan Ibarra took advantage of the delay occasioned by heavy rains to reorganize his following. First, he selected the men who were to assist him in official capacities.

[27] A. G. I., 1-1-3/22, Obregón, Crónica.
[28] A. G. I., 1-3-20/11, Francisco de Ybarra, Información de méritos; Bancroft (*North Mexican States and Texas,* I. 103) says that Ibarra arrived in San Juan Valley in June, 1562, which is certainly an error.

They were: Martín de Gamon as maestro de campo, or first
lieutenant; Martín de Rentería as alguacil mayor, or high
constable; Pedro de Quesada, Ándres de Ibarra, and Martín
de Araña as captains; Martín López de Ibarra (Francisco's
nephew), Bartolomé de Arriola, and Julio de Heredía as
officials of the royal treasury; Sebastián Quiros and Lerma
as secretaries; and Alonso de la Marcha as alferez, or en-
sign. These appointments were made on March 5, 1563.[29]
To San Juan, while they were waiting, were brought numerous cartloads of flour, maize, biscuits, bacon, cheese, and
other foodstuffs. By command of the governor these were
arranged in great piles, and then each man was allowed to
select what he needed. An inventory showed that the traveling commissary consisted of four hundred cows, one
thousand sheep, and as many goats.[30]

Early in March, 1563, when the heavy rains had sub-
sided, the governor and his followers left San Juan bent on
the conquest of Copalá and Tôpia. The latter place was
said to be located in the mountains to the northwest.[31] About
eighty miles inland they discovered a very fertile valley with
a large river flowing through it. It was surrounded on all
sides by heavily forested mountains in which they found
numerous favorable mineral traces. This valley, which was
named San Josepe, was probably the upper Nazas, for they
would pass through that region on their way to Indé, which
was discovered on this entrada.[32] Suspecting that their

[29] A. G. I., 59-6-15, Información de Bartolomé de Arriola, Indehe, 11
de marzo de 1570.

[30] *Col. Doc. Inéd.*, XIV. 476.

[31] *Ibid.*, 553-554; A. G. I., 1-3-20/11, Francisco de Ybarra, Información
de méritos.

[32] Arriola, in his información (A. G. I., 59-6-15), states that he was
with Ibarra on his *first* expedition when the mines of Indé and San
Julian were discovered. Because of the rain they returned after three
months, and established camp in San Juan. According to Herrera (p.
248), Pacheco, after the settlement of Durango, set out with 130 men
and discovered Indé and San Juan. The weight of evidence supports

guides were trying to lead them astray into the rugged country for the purpose of entrapping them, Ibarra ordered a halt and determined to reconnoiter. He decided to go back to San Josepe with the main body of his following, while Martín de Rentería, with twenty soldiers and five Indian guides, continued the search for Tôpia. The guides were told to lead Rentería to the settlements they had spoken about in such glowing terms, "in order that their veracity might be proved." After an absence of six days, Rentería returned and reported that he had traveled about ninety miles through an exceedingly rough country and "found nothing but mountains and more mountains."

Obregón states that other scouting parties were dispatched by Ibarra at this time. One composed of four soldiers under the command of Salvador Ponce was sent in search of Tôpia. After many hardships they sighted Tôpia from a distance, and then they returned to Ibarra with the news. The governor immediately ordered Gamon and twenty soldiers to go to Tôpia for additional information. Gamon had several native guides with him who promised to take him to Tôpia in ten days; but, after many more days of travel through extremely rugged country, Gamon became convinced that he was being misled and so determined to punish the guides. They were hung from a tree which was in full bloom, but, according to Obregón, in condemnation of the unjust death of the Indians, the tree immediately wilted and died! Regarding the alleged trip of Ponce and his four companions, we have no other authority than Obregón, and Obregón himself states later that Salvador Ponce joined Ibarra's expedition after its return from San Juan. Thus, it is very doubtful whether this journey ever took place, at least on this particular entrada. As for

the conclusion that Indé was discovered by Ibarra on his first expedition (A. G. I., 1-3-20/11, Francisco de Ybarra, Información de méritos, 1574; *Col. Doc. Inéd.*, XIV. 476).

the reconnoitering trip made by Gamon, there is every reason
to believe that it was the same one which was headed by
Martín de Rentería, for it had the same number of men and
was prevented from reaching its goal because of the sus-
pected treason of the guides.[33]

After the return of Rentería, Ibarra and his men turned
back and followed substantially the same route which they
had taken on the outward journey. While returning they
discovered some mineral veins in a valley which they named
San Gerónimo, for, to appease his men, who were greatly
disappointed because of their lack of success in the search
for Tôpia, the governor allowed them to prospect for minerals. When they approached Guatimape, located near Ayala,
an Indian woman told Ibarra that he had been deceived by
his guides, for she herself knew the way to Tôpia. To consider this matter a general council was called, and it was
agreed that the governor and about forty chosen men should
go in search of Tôpia while the rest of the expedition returned
to San Juan.[34]

Ibarra and his forty companions departed on April 15,
1563, and, guided by the Indian woman, they marched for
eight days in the same general direction which Rentería had
taken. In fact, only twenty-five miles farther to the north
from the place where Rentería had stopped,[35] they looked
down from the summit of a lofty range upon the settlement
of Tôpia. Because of their small number, they did not let
themselves be seen, but merely examined the settlement from
a distance. It seemed to be a comparatively large village,

[33] A. G. I., 1-1-3/22, Obregón, Crónica.

[34] *Col. Doc. Inéd.*, XIV. 556-557; the number of men who accompanied
Ibarra to Tôpia is variously estimated as being between twenty and
forty (Herrera, *Historia General*, I. 248; A. G. I., 1-3-20/11, Francisco
de Ybarra, Información de méritos).

[35] In his letter to Diego de Ibarra, May 2, 1563 (*Col. Doc. Inéd.*,
XIV. 559), Francisco said, "If Martín de Rentería had gone four
leagues farther, today our camp would be in that land."

with many white, several-storied, flat-roofed houses. The inhabitants were clothed, and indeed the whole settlement impressed the observers as being another Tenochtitlán. At night they ventured near the village and could hear the Indians playing the Aztec "teponaztli," or drum. Enthusiastic in their belief that a province of fabulous wealth had been discovered, Ibarra and his men hastened to rejoin their companions at San Juan. In recrossing the mountains they underwent great hardships; since their supplies were exhausted, they were compelled to sustain themselves on horse-flesh. They rejoined their camp at San Juan early in May.[36]

Immediately after his arrival in San Juan, Ibarra reported his achievements in glowing words to Diego de Ibarra and through him to the viceroy and the king. In his hasty and distant examination of Tôpia he may have been sincerely convinced of its wealth and advanced civilization. On the other hand, he may have intentionally exaggerated to insure support for future expeditions. Whatever was his real motive, it is certainly true that he reported the wealth and possibilities of the province of Copalá in no modest terms, but rather with gross exaggeration. The incident is strongly reminiscent of Friar Marcos and the Seven Cities.

When the governor rejoined his camp at San Juan, he found that a mutiny had broken out among some of his followers. The ringleader was the maestro de campo, Martín de Gamon, whom Obregón said was the bravest man in the expedition. But, notwithstanding his courage, he was exceedingly proud and headstrong, and when Ibarra appointed Martín de Araña as his lieutenant while he went on the journey to Tôpia, Gamon's pride was greatly hurt, and he was "submerged in an abyss of envy." It also seems that

[36] A. G. I., 1-3-20/11, Francisco de Ybarra, Información de méritos; Col. Doc. Inéd., XIV. 554, 557-558, 476-477.

Gamon was opposed to such a hasty return to San Juan. He therefore tried to get revenge by discrediting the expedition. He placed himself at the head of a few turbulent Basques, among them being Pedro de Quesada and Ándres de Ibarra, and planned to make an expedition on his own account. Martín de Araña, in attempting to quell the disorder, seized the royal standard and summoned all the loyal servants of the king to step forward. Martín de Gamon, Pedro de Quesada, and Ándres de Ibarra not only refused to step forward, but added to their offense by insulting words. At this dangerous juncture, the governor made an opportune appearance and immediately jailed or expelled the guilty ones. Gamon escaped to San Martín, but Ibarra followed him there and arrested him in the house of the alcalde mayor, notwithstanding the protests of Colio. Gamon was brought back to San Juan for trial, was condemned to death, and was executed. "This grieved the governor and the camp greatly, for Gamon was a brave soldier."[37]

In a general council of war Antonio de Betanco, who had recently arrived from Mexico, was selected to succeed Gamon as maestro de campo. Obregón characterized Betanco as "a gentleman in whom were combined the qualities and merits necessary for such an enterprise, and an efficiency in war." With Betanco there also arrived in San Juan, Rodrigo del Río, Salvador Ponce, Hernando Ramon, and other men who were to distinguish themselves in subsequent entradas.[30]

[37] A. G. I., 1-1-3/22, Obregón, Crónica; A. G. I., 66-5-14, Averiguaciones de Contreras; Amador (*Zacatecas,* pp. 214-215) and Bancroft (*North Mexican States and Texas,* I. 103) follow Tello's version that Gamon and his twelve companions, who were a turbulent lot of Basques, rebelled and attempted to make an expedition on their own account. Ibarra accused Gamon to the viceroy, who ordered him arrested. The governor arrested Gamon in the house of the alcalde mayor of San Martín where he had sought refuge. Gamon was taken back to Nueva Vizcaya and was executed.

[38] A. G. I., 1-3-20/11, Francisco de Ybarra, Información de méritos.

For about seven months Ibarra maintained headquarters in San Juan, but he did not remain inactive by any means. It was during this time that Nombre de Díos and Durango were formally founded.[39] There is a great confusion of evidence regarding the founding of Nombre de Díos. It has been noted above[40] that the padres, Espinareda, Cintos, and Cadena, who had been sent to the frontier by Velasco in 1558, possessed a commission to found a villa. By virtue of this authority they selected a site at or near the Nombre de Díos which had been established by Fray Gerónimo de Mendoza, and there they erected a chapel and gathered the Indians into a settled community. In these activities they were assisted by Francisco de Ibarra. The settlement, probably because of the name applied by Mendoza, was called Nombre de Díos. On October 6, 1563, the viceroy granted Fray Espinareda "a license to found a villa and a monastery to be named Nombre de Díos on a site to be selected between the Río Santiago and the Río Grande which empties into the Guadiana."[41] Obviously we are confronted by contradictions; a license had been granted to found a town which in reality had been founded four or five years prior to that time. Since it is incontrovertible that there was a settlement of some sort at Nombre de Díos prior to 1563, it can only be surmised that the commission granted Pedro de Espinareda, probably on the occasion of his visit to Mexico, was for the specific purpose of establishing a municipal government in the already-existent settlement of Nombre de Díos.

When Ibarra heard about the viceregal commission, he declared that, since the proposed villa was to be located within his jurisdiction, he should have the right to name the

---

[39] "While passing the rainy season in San Juan, the governor built a house. Then with certain soldiers he went to found the city of Durango. He also went to found the city of Nombre de Díos" (A. G. I., 59-6-15, Información de Bartolomé de Arriola).

[40] Cf. p. 78.

[41] A. G. I., 67-1-3, Información de Nombre de Díos, 1608.

municipal officials. Accordingly, on November 6, 1563, the limits of the city were outlined, repartimientos were assigned, and the municipal officials were appointed.[42] Viceroy Enríquez, at a later date, in referring to the founding of Nombre de Diós, said, "The first villa which Francisco de Ibarra founded in Nueva Vizcaya was Nombre de Diós, in which as first founder, he elected alcaldes and officials of the regimiento; he also traced the limits of the said villa, and performed the other duties of a governor in the same villa."[43] Ibarra himself informs us that the friars, some Spaniards, and Indians had settled the villa of Nombre de Diós and that he went to the settlement, officially registered it, appointed alcaldes, and outlined its jurisdiction and limits.[44] The first alcaldes ordinarios of Nombre de Diós were Alonso García and Sánchez Jiménez; the first regidores were Gaspar de Torres and Francisco Gonzales. They were to assume office on January 1, 1564.[45]

Nombre de Diós, situated in the heart of a fertile valley which was well adapted to the cultivation of wheat and maize, soon became the granary of not only the settlements near by, but of Sombrerete, Fresnillo, and Zacatecas as well. Within a short time the annual production of corn and wheat was twenty and thirty thousand fanegas respectively. Because of the increased production of foodstuffs, prices became lower, thereby encouraging an increase in population and a consequent increase in the yield of the mines. The excellent grazing lands were particularly suited to

---

[42] The Información of Nombre de Diós (*ibid.*) refutes statements found in: A. G. I., 1-3-20/11, Francisco de Ybarra, Información de méritos; A. G. I., 1-1-1/20, Memorial del Lcdo. Juan de Ybarra; *Col. Doc. Inéd.*, XIV. 466-469; and Herrera, *Historia General,* I. 247, to the effect that immediately after the granting of his commission as governor, Ibarra went to Nombre de Diós and then to Durango. Both of these places were founded after the return from Tôpia.

[43] A. G. I., 139-1-2, El Rey al Virrey Enríquez, 31 de marzo de 1576.

[44] A. G. I., 1-3-20/11, Francisco de Ybarra, Información de méritos.

[45] A. G. I., 67-1-3, Información de Nombre de Diós.

cattle and sheep raising, and within six years the Nombre de Diós district supported 250,000 head of cattle and sheep.[46] In the vicinity of Nombre de Diós were also some very productive silver mines, the most noted of these being Santiago and San Buena Ventura.[47]

The city of Durango was also founded by Francisco de Ibarra some time after his return from Tôpia. According to his información, Durango was founded immediately after the villa of Nombre de Diós had been officially established. That being the case, it was founded in November or December, 1563.[48] While the Governor was in San Juan, in August, or September, he dispatched Captain Alonso Pacheco with some soldiers to Guadiana Valley to make preparations for the establishment of a city. Pacheco and his companions were supplied with live-stock, maize, flour, munitions, and other necessities to sustain them until they could raise their own foodstuffs. They were instructed to select a suitable site for a city and to outline its boundaries. Two or three months later Ibarra himself joined Pacheco on the site which had been selected near San Juan Bautista de Analco, a native settlement which owed its origins to Father Cadena.

Ibarra organized a municipal government for the new villa; appointed alcaldes, regidores, and other municipal officials; and apportioned the natives of the district among the Spaniards in encomiendas.[49] The city was named Du-

[46] A. G. I., 1-3-20/11, Francisco de Ybarra, Información de méritos; A. G. I., 1-1-1/20, Memorial del Lcdo. Juan de Ybarra.

[47] A. G. I., 1-3-20/11, Francisco de Ybarra, Información de méritos; Col. Doc. Inéd., XIV. 469.

[48] A. G. I., 1-1-1/20, Memorial del Lcdo. Juan de Ybarra; García (Los Mineros Mexicanos, p. 130) says that Durango was founded on July 8, 1563. Since Ibarra did not return to San Juan until about May 1, obviously then April 14, 1563, the date applied to the founding of Durango by Dos Republicos, February 8, 1879 (cited by Bancroft, North Mexican States and Texas, I. 104), is disproved.

[49] Col. Doc. Inéd., XIV. 472-473; A. G. I., 1-3-20/11, Francisco de Ybarra, Información de méritos.

rango after Durango in Vizcaya, but for some time it was better known as Guadiana. Solicitous care and numerous favors were bestowed upon the city, because it was Ibarra's intention to make it the capital city of his gobierno of Nueva Vizcaya.. He spent considerable sums of money from his private fortune in erecting fine public buildings because of his desire to beautify the city; and, to facilitate a rapid increase in its population, he ceded to its inhabitants in perpetuity one of his richest mines in Aviño with the sole provision that they build homes in Durango. He set an example by building a home for himself, but, as will be seen, the total time he spent in Durango was very short indeed.

Pacheco displayed good judgment in selecting a site for Durango, for the city was admirably located. Situated on a high plateau at an altitude of nearly seven thousand feet, Durango enjoyed a remarkably clear, dry, and cool atmosphere; the healthful qualities of the climate could hardly be surpassed. Surrounding the city were ample fertile lands where wheat and maize could be raised in abundance; but more widespread were the grassy plains where sheep and cattle could graze. The Indians of the vicinity were peaceful and worked for the Spaniards without protest. There was soon produced in Durango an abundance of maize and wheat, and, as was true of Nombre de Diós, this occasioned a drop in prices of foodstuffs and an attendant increase in population. During the lifetime of Ibarra the capital city of Nueva Vizcaya did not have more than five hundred settlers, but this number did not include the numerous ranchers and miners who resided in the surrounding country. The district of Durango, as a matter of fact, became quite populous.[50] After the founding of the municipality, Ibarra

[50] A. G. I., 1-1-1/20, Memorial del Lcdo. Juan de Ybarra; *Col. Doc. Inéd.*, XIV, 473-474.

returned to San Juan. Bartolomé de Arriola was left in Durango as lieutenant-governor. He was succeeded in 1565 by Martín López de Ibarra, who became both lieutenant-governor and treasurer of real hacienda.[51]

To make his camp in San Juan more secure against native attack, Ibarra constructed a stockade and assembled all of his following within it. There they remained for seven months, and during that time the governor furnished all his men with supplies which had been brought from San Martín. But, notwithstanding their precautions, the Indians on one occasion stole or killed between two and four hundred horses. This outrage the governor determined should not go unavenged; so, after he had recruited more soldiers, he set out to punish the natives.[52]

The Indians were finally located in Guatimape Valley, but even then they eluded the Spanish sentinels and stole some horses. Ibarra left Betanco in charge of the camp while he followed the culprits into the mountains. There he easily defeated them in a light encounter, but he was not able to recover the horses which the Indians had hidden. He then dispatched Betanco, Rodrigo del Río, Salvador Ponce, and a few more men to locate the horses. In an extremely rocky and forbidding place in the mountains, which could only be reached on foot, the horses were found; but the Indians would not give them up until the Spaniards threatened to use force. A truce was arranged between the explorers and the Indians, but it was short-lived, for the Indians were naturally treacherous and bellicose, and their depredations forced the governor to send the maestro de campo, and Fray Pablo de Azevedo, Salvador Ponce, and a number of soldiers to subdue them. On this occasion an

[51] Bancroft, *North Mexican States and Texas,* I. 104; A. G. I., 59-6-20, Información de Martín López de Ibarra, México, 21 de octubre de 1577.
[52] *Col. Doc. Inéd.,* XIV. 476, 479; A. G. I., 1-3-20/11, Francisco de Ybarra, Información de méritos; A. G. I., 1-1-3/22, Obregón, Crónica.

Indian village was discovered but it was deserted by all of the inhabitants, who had sought shelter in the mountains. A considerable store of maize was discovered near by and was appropriated by the Spaniards. The natives were not willing to surrender the maize without a struggle and were advancing in great numbers upon the maestro de campo and his men, when Ibarra arrived at a most opportune moment with reinforcements. By means of interpreters he was able to conciliate the natives and so avoided a battle. When the Indians started to withdraw, the Spaniards began to load the corn preparatory to taking it away to their camp. This unpardonable duplicity embittered the natives very greatly, and their trust in the word of the Spaniards was destroyed.[53]

These Indians, who gave Ibarra so much trouble, belonged to the Tepehuane nation. They inhabited the mountains of southern Chihuahua and the northern portions of Durango, a district commonly called the "partido de Tepehuanes." They were particularly savage and warlike, and it seemed that their animosity toward the whites was perpetual. Although they cultivated the soil and raised maize and beans, they nevertheless relied chiefly upon the chase for subsistence. Their habitations were generally on top of almost inaccessible crags.

Christmas, 1563, was spent in camp in Guatimape Valley. A few days later, after his men had sufficiently recuperated from their encounters with the natives, the governor decided to go once more in search of Tôpia. His implicit belief in the great wealth and advanced culture of that province and his expectation that its conquest would eclipse that of Mexico inclines us to exonerate him from the charge of wilfully exaggerating the wealth of Tôpia in his reports to the viceroy and the king.[54] The route taken by Ibarra to Tôpia can

[53] A. G. I., 1-1-3/22, Obregón, Crónica.
[54] *Ibid.; Col. Doc. Inéd.*, XIV. 480.

be only vaguely determined. From Guatimape he evidently marched up the Río Nazas past Indé to Santa Bárbara and perhaps a short distance beyond. He then turned about and retraced his steps for a short distance to the southwest before crossing the mountains of Tôpia.[55]

When Ibarra first reached the Río Conchos it is impossible to say. On his entrada of the prior year he is supposed to have discovered mines at Indé and San Julian, but the mines at Santa Bárbara were not mentioned as having been discovered at that time. Indeed, evidence is not lacking to show that the mines of Santa Bárbara were not discovered until after the settlement of Indé in 1567 by Rodrigo del Río. There is more basis for the conjecture that the Conchos country was reached by one or the other of Ibarra's first two entradas, or probably by both of them. The settlement of this country was delayed until after the return of the governor and his men from their entrada to Sinaloa, Sonora, and Chiametla.

After he had explored as far north as the Río Conchos, Ibarra decided to alter the direction of his march, and so he turned back for a distance and then began to ascend the mountains to the west in the direction of Tôpia. His route through the mountains was substantially the same as that which had been taken by Martín de Gamon the year before. As has been pointed out, Gamon's entrada may have been the same one which Martín de Rentería commanded and turned back when he thought that his guides were misleading him. That Ibarra was now following Gamon's route was evidenced, says Obregón, by the fact that they discovered the place where Gamon executed the native guides. The tree from which the Indians had been hanged was found to be

[55] A. G. I., 1-1-1/20, Memorial del Lcdo. Juan de Ybarra. On this occasion, says Mota Padilla (*Nueva Galicia*, p. 207), Ibarra also discovered Cuencamé.

dead, although there was no sign of injury by fire or lightning! Obregón piously declares that this was evidence of divine condemnation. Near the same place they also found remains of carts which some unnamed friars had taken there.[56]

As they continued their journey, the difficulties of the Spaniards multiplied; the mountains became higher, more rocky, and so precipitous that at times they had to crawl on their hands and knees. The innumerable crags and ravines necessitated frequent detours and unloading and reloading of pack-animals. No natives were encountered. In fact, so desolate was the land that there was an absence even of birds. On one occasion, while crossing over a high mountain pass, a snow-storm overtook them, and the cold was so intense that about forty horses were frozen to death. One horse was frozen standing upright and fifteen days later was found in that position![57]

After the storm had passed, the governor with the maestro de campo and twenty-six chosen men started on a reconnoitering tour to locate the native settlement of Tôpia. The rest of the men remained under the command of Captain Hernando Ramon.[58] Ibarra and his companions marched ahead, "quite doubtful of the certified statements which had been made by the five discoverers, although they were men of integrity."[59] Finally, from a high mountain, they could see in the distance a great valley. But descent into the valley was attended with great difficulty. Once the maestro de campo tripped and fell and surely would have been killed, says Obregón, had it not been for his helmet.

[56] *Col. Doc. Inéd.,* XIV. 478; Herrera, *Historia General,* I. 35-36; A. G. I., 1-3-20/11, Francisco de Ybarra, Información de méritos; Monumentos de la Dominación Española, MS 2, p. 243, Bancroft Library.

[57] A. G. I., 1-1-3/22, Obregón, Crónica; A. G. I., 1-3-20/11, Francisco de Ybarra, Información de méritos.

[58] *Ibid.; Col. Doc. Inéd.,* XIV. 480.

[59] Referring to Salvador Ponce and his companions.

When they reached the floor of the valley, the governor
drew up his men in battle-array, for he feared that they
were in an inhabited land and liable to be attacked. Marching
in this order, they came to a fair-sized stream, which was
crossed with difficulty, for it was in flood; on the opposite
bank they found some fields of maize and beans. Later they
sighted some native women, clothed from the waist down in
cotton cloth, but they fled on the approach of the Spaniards.
A short distance beyond they found a native settlement composed of several stone and adobe houses and a remarkable
fort made of stone ramparts about a lance length in height,
with a ditch running about it, and an outer defense of cactus
plants. At first sight it appeared to be a settlement of some
importance, and so Ibarra and his companions were filled
with enthusiasm.

Since the Indians adopted a hostile attitude, the governor
determined to storm the fort. He assembled his men on the
brow of a small hill, distant about an arcabus shot away,
where he could dominate the fort. Then he ordered Antonio
de Betanco and some picked men, among them being Rodrigo
del Río, Salvador Ponce, Alvaro de Mata, Juan de San Po,
Amador López, and Pedro de Montoya, to undertake an
assault upon the fort. Betanco was chosen to lead the attack, because he had earnestly requested of the governor that
he be selected for all tasks in which the danger was greatest.
The Spaniards were wont, when attacking natives unaccus-
tomed to fire-arms, to rely mostly on the noise of their guns
to terrify their opponents into submission. But on this occasion the natives shouted so lustily that the reports of the
guns were deadened, and so had no effect. But when
Rodrigo del Río, the sharpshooter of the expedition, sniped
one of the natives, they took heed of the arcabus. Then
the Spaniards, led by the maestro de campo, rushed the fort,

and although the natives fought fiercely with bows and arrows, clubs, spears, darts, and lances, they were unable to withstand the besiegers. Betanco was the first to scale the walls, and he was closely followed by Rodrigo Verdugo and the rest. Verdugo was accidentally shot in the arm at this time by one of the soldiers who was outside the fort on the hilltop with the governor.

After the Spaniards had captured the fort, the Indians deserted their homes and fled to the mountains for safety. Though none of the assailants was killed in the attack, a few were wounded. After the defeat of the natives, the Governor and his men established themselves in the fort. Later, by dint of friendly persuasion and a few presents, they were able to reassure the fugitives, and to induce them to return to their homes.[60] Ibarra and his men remained for some time in Tôpia to rest themselves and their horses and to give their wounded an opportunity to recover. They were rejoined a short time after the battle by the remainder of the expedition, which had been left behind under the command of Ramon.

The arrival of Francisco de Ibarra in Tôpia was not the initial appearance of white men in that province. Obregón, at least, assures us that Tôpia had been discovered by some of the captains of Nuño de Guzmán from San Miguel de Culiacán, which was eighty miles away. Tôpia may well have been visited by some of Guzmán's men when they crossed the mountains to the plains of Guadiana.[61]

The province of Tôpia fell far short of meeting the expectations of the explorers. Instead of being a rich, populous land, it proved to be nothing but a narrow, deep, valley about two miles wide and sparsely settled by some

[60] A. G. I., 1-1-3/22, Obregón, Crónica.
[61] Cf. p. 24.

very inferior natives belonging to the Acaxées nation.[62] Likewise, instead of the settlement being composed of "white, many-storied, terraced-houses," it was made up of a few squatty, adobe hovels. The Acaxées, however, understood the art of cultivation and raised, in so far as their limited cultivatable soil would permit, a quantity of maize, beans, and calabashes. Their raiment was not sumptuous; the men wore in front of their persons a square piece of tanned deer-hide secured to a cord tied around the waist. The women wore long petticoats of chamois, cotton, or agave fibre. What they lacked in dress, they substituted with a great variety of ornaments; and the practice of painting the face and body was common among them. In morality, the standards of the Acaxées were extremely low. Arlégui[63] attributes the vilest practices to them. That these people were cannibals was evidenced by the great number of human bones scattered about the village.[64] They hunted human beings for food as they hunted deer or other game. Concerning the cure of wounds, Obregón says that the Indians of Tôpia used no herbs or medicine; they merely sucked their wounds and went on a diet. Since these natives were idol worshippers, Ibarra, with great Christian zeal, ordered the idols overthrown and had crosses erected in their places. Then the padres preached to the natives, extolled the merits of Christianity, and condemned the evil practice of cannibalism.

[62] "The Acaxées inhabit the valleys of the mountain regions of Tôpia and San Ándres in Durango and Sinaloa" (Bancroft, *Native Races,* I. 614). "The principal nation in which mountains is the Real of Tôpia, is the Acaxées" (Ribas, *Historia de los Triumphos de Nuestra Santa Fee entre gentes las más bárbaras y fieras del Nuevo Orbe,* Madrid, 1645, p. 471).

[63] Arlégui, *Chrónica de Zacatecas,* pp. 154-157.

[64] *Ibid.,* pp. 180-182; Ribas, *Historia de Los Triumphos,* pp. 6-7, 175.

The disillusionment occasioned by the discovery of the real Tôpia had a most depressing effect upon the soldiers. To revive their spirits and overawe the natives, the governor ordered a celebration in the form of military maneuvers, gun-firing, flag-raising, and speeches. He did not attempt to make a Spanish settlement in Tôpia because of the inaccessibility of the place. It was not considered a desirable land, or *tierra cómoda*.[65] The natives, in fact, considered the Christians as witches who must have come from the sky, for they had regarded their settlement as being inaccessible. The lands surrounding Tôpia were also uninviting and sparsely populated. From the high mountains surrounding Tôpia the Spaniards could see to the west level stretches of land dotted with Indian settlements, and, at a great distance, they saw the South Sea.

The governor decided to make the west coast his goal, but, before attempting to lead his whole army out of those rugged mountains, he thought it advisable to discover the easiest and safest descent. For that purpose he selected the same twenty-six men who had captured Tôpia to accompany him and the maestro de campo.[66] After leaving Tôpia, they descended and ascended various mountain ranges until they came to a deep valley, which was sparsely settled like Tôpia. Upon the approach of the Spaniards, the natives deserted their pueblo and left a great supply of maize. Thanks to the able guidance of a cacique of Tôpia named Cayayn, the Spaniards were able to manage a safe descent from the mountains, but not without extreme hardships. They finally came to a river, which they later learned would lead them to Culiacán. This was the Río Culiacán, which Bancroft erroneously says was the "Río Suaqui, or Sinaloa, now the Fuerte."[67]

[65] A. G. I., 59-6-15, Información de Bartolomé de Arriola.
[66] A. G. I., 59-4-3, Antonio Gotelo de Betanco sobre Francisco de Ibarra, México, 5 de junio de 1566, y 9 de diciembre de 1567.
[67] Bancroft, *North Mexican States and Texas,* I. 107.

Some hostile natives, probably Tebacas, met them on the Río Culiacán and attempted to kill Cayayn because he had guided the Spaniards to their country. But, notwithstanding this opposition, they marched in safety as far as the pueblo of Matoen. At that place the cacique Cayayn took leave of them and returned to Tôpia.

CHAPTER V

ON THE COAST OF THE SOUTH SEA

The discovery of the Indian settlement on the upper Río Culiacán greatly encouraged Francisco de Ibarra and his men. The pueblos were so well constructed and their inhabitants so culturally advanced that the Spaniards thought surely they were now about to realize their hopes of discovering another Mexico or Peru. But their enthusiasm was turned to grief and chagrin when they heard that but one day's journey distant was a pueblo belonging to an encomendero of San Miguel de Culiacán. The Indians of Matoen and other pueblos between Culiacán and the Acaxées of Tôpia belonged to the Tebaca nation[1] and were *salteadores,* or savages who refused to live in settled communities under Spanish control. They partook of the life of the pueblos of Culiacán, but paid no tribute, nor were they subject to encomenderos. Their remarkable intelligence was explained by the fact that they had for some time been in contact with Spanish civilization.[2]

When Pedro de Tovar, the alcalde mayor of San Miguel, which was under the jurisdiction of the audiencia of Nueva Galicia, heard of the arrival of Ibarra and his men, he went to welcome them. Tovar treated the Governor of Nueva Vizcaya kindly, gave him and his men food and other necessities, and sympathized deeply because of the evil turn their

[1] Orozco y Berra, *Geografía*, p. 334.

[2] Ribas, *Historia de los Triumphos*, p. 28; A. G. I., 1-1-3/22, Obregón, Crónica; A. G. I., 59-4-3, Betanco sobre Ibarra. "After excessive hardships he came to the coast of the South Sea, in lands fronting California which long ago Cortés attempted to settle" (A. G. I., 1-1-1/20, Memorial del Lcdo. Juan de Ybarra).

fortunes had taken. He then suggested that the provinces of Sinaloa and Chiametla, situated to the north and south of Culiacán, might offer satisfactory alternative goals, where they could repair their fortunes. Because of the great trials his men had endured, Ibarra was reluctant to subject them to additional hardship in recrossing the mountains. He was inclined, therefore, to listen to Tovar's advice, and determined to try his fortune in Sinaloa. But, to avoid any possible conflict with the Spanish residents of Culiacán, he refused to go to San Miguel, for he was particularly distrustful of the possible behavior of his men. Since he wished to retain the good favor of Tovar, he was anxious that the maltreatment of the residents of San Martín and Aviño should not be repeated in San Miguel, and thus he marched in a northerly direction, keeping close to the foot of the mountains and to the east of Culiacán.[3]

Although they were in a "tierra de guerra," the Spaniards were not opposed by the Indians. They were able to secure the natives' good will by kindly treatment and strict adherence to the policy of respecting their property and their persons. Ibarra's humane policy was the secret of his remarkable success and explains how he and his twenty-six soldiers were able to accomplish so much on this expedition into Sinaloa. The Indians of the Río Sebastián de Evora, now the Río Mocorito, welcomed the Spaniards and offered the services of two hundred of their warriors. Their generous offer was accepted willingly, and with his allies Ibarra resumed his march to the north through an uninhabited stretch of territory until he came to the Río Sinaloa, or, as it was then known, the Río Petatlán. This name was first applied to the river and to the natives of that area at the

[3] A. G. I., 1-1-3/22, Obregón, Crónica.

time of Nuño de Guzmán, because their huts were covered with a rush known by the Mexicans as *petates*.[4]

Prior to the arrival of the Governor of Nueva Vizcaya, the situation of the Spanish settlers in Culiacán had been most precarious. Living in the midst of numerous hostile Indians and far beyond the settled frontiers of New Spain, they were in constant dread of the savages. The hostility of the natives dated back to the cruel régime of Nuño de Guzmán, who left for his successors a heritage of hate and a keen desire for revenge on the part of the natives. Many of the encomiendas were deserted, others were in revolt, and the Spaniards were forced to remain constantly on guard. Beyond the confines of San Miguel all evidences of Guzmán's conquest in that region had been obliterated.[5] The advent of Ibarra in Culiacán had, therefore, been most opportune and probably prevented the desertion of that most important outpost. Without resorting to force, he was able to quiet the natives and to influence many of them in the Río Mocorito region to return to their pueblos. These Indian settlements were then repartitioned among the Spaniards. Obregón contends that Ibarra did not interfere with the rights of the inhabitants of Culiacán; but Mota Padilla disagrees and states that the Governor of Nueva Vizcaya, on pretense that there was no religious instruction in those lands and they were consequently subject to confiscation, repartitioned *among his own men* the settlements of San Sebastián de Evora (Mocorito) and Petatlán, which belonged in encomienda to Pedro de Tovar and Cristobál de Tápia.[6]

About a league from the pueblo of Piastla, in Petatlán, the explorers met a native array of about six hundred war-

---

[4] "Todos los pueblos de los indios cobiertas las casas de esteras, a las cuales llaman en lengua de México *petates*, y por esta causa le llamamos Petatlán" (Bancroft, *Native Races*, I. 575, note 243) ; A. G. I., 59-4-3, Betanco sobre Ibarra.

[5] Bancroft, *North Mexican States and Texas*, I. 107.

[6] Mota Padilla, *Nueva Galicia*, p. 208.

riors in full war regalia. This was not a hostile demonstration, for, on the contrary, the visitors were received very kindly, and, like the natives of Mocorito, the Indians offered to ally themselves with the Spaniards. The Governor thanked them and gave them presents of trinkets. Then Fray Azevedo attempted to explain to them the elements of the Christian religion. These natives, who belonged to the Guazaves tribe,[7] were a partially naked lot; the men wore cotton breech-cloths, and the women wore cured deer-hide skirts. They cultivated beans, maize, calabashes, and cotton, and lived in small settlements of adobe and rush huts. Near at hand were mountains where they sought shelter when attacked, and the South Sea was about fifty miles away.

While Ibarra was in Petatlán, his interpreter died, and thus is was necessary to find another one or discontinue the journey. Fortunately he heard that, in the land of the Ocoroni, a tribe living farther to the north, there was a Christian squaw who was acquainted not only with the Aztec language, but also with many other native tongues. He sent a messenger to her requesting that she act as his interpreter. Although she could not read, the messenger took her a written message from the governor to convince her that she was really being summoned by the white men and was not being duped by some other savages. She was willing and returned to Petatlán accompanied by a dozen warriors. This interpreter's name was Luisa, and she was the wife of the cacique of Ocoroni. Although she was held a captive in Ocoroni, she was really the ruler of that tribe, for, because of her great wisdom and ability in governing, she was greatly sought after by various chieftains. It seems that

---

[7] "Los Guazaves . . . distante diez, y doze leguas de la villa" [San Juan de Sinaloa] (Ribas, *Historia de los Triumphos,* p. 153); "Habitadores de San Pedro Guazave y de Tamazula, orillas del río Sinaloa" (Orozco y Berra, *Geografía,* p. 332).

she was a native of Culiacán and had fled to escape paying tribute. She was captured on five different occasions by the Indians north of Culiacán and had acted as many times as the consort of different caciques. So well had she served the Ocoroni that their pueblo was said to be the best managed in the province of Sinaloa. She understood the dialects of the natives from Culiacán to Sonora and Corazones, and, though she was somewhat inexperienced in the use of the Mexican tongue, she soon revived her knowledge of that also. In a short time she became a capable and obedient servant of the Spaniards. When she came to Ibarra, she was only clothed in a cotton skirt from the waist down, so the governor made her presents of dresses and glass beads.

Accompanied by a hundred braves of Petatlán, the Spaniards resumed their march to the north. Their next destination was Ocoroni. When they had approached to within a mile of that pueblo, they were met by messengers sent by its caciques to learn the purpose of the Spaniards' visit. At the same time they protested the presence in their lands of the natives of Petatlán, who were their bitter enemies. They were appeased when Ibarra assured them of his peaceful intentions and guaranteed the good behavior of his allies.

Ocoroni was a good-sized pueblo of about four hundred houses built of reed-matting. The site of the pueblo was on a mountain slope, near a crag, and close to a small stream. This position, naturally, was chosen for protection against their enemies. The Ocoroni were brave fighters, and they had an expert, well-equipped force of about five hundred warriors. The evident prosperity and advancement of the Ocoroni pleased Ibarra greatly. He harangued the natives on matters of religion and peaceful living and succeeded in reconciling them with their erstwhile enemies, the Petatlán Indians. In token of friendship, the two tribes exchanged bows and arrows. After these ceremonies the natives of Petatlán returned to their own lands.[8]

From Ocoroni Ibarra and his men went to the pueblo of Ciguini, which was not a great distance away, although some very difficult mountainous country intervened. Ciguini and Ocoroni were probably located between the Sinaloa and Fuerte rivers. With some Indian guides obtained at Ciguini, the explorers continued their march to the pueblo of Tegueco on the Fuerte. They were now in the heart of the province of the Sinaloas, which was a general name for the tribes living in that district. The original limits of Sinaloa can be but vaguely determined. They were probably the Río Mayo on the north and the Río Sinaloa on the south. The eastern and western boundaries were the Sierra Madre and the shores of the South Sea.[9] This strip of territory was said to be inhabited at that time by about thirty thousand natives. They were slightly more advanced in intelligence than the average native of northern Mexico. They wore cotton clothes, tilled fields of maize and beans, and were skilful hunters and fishermen. Although there were many fertile valleys in Sinaloa, through which flowed innumerable streams, the greater part of that territory was mountainous. In the mountains were to be found a great store of metals, especially lead and silver.

The pueblo of Tegueco, located on the Río Fuerte[10] about fifty miles from the sea and fifteen miles from the foot of the sierras, was one of the most populous native settlements in Sinaloa.[11] In warriors alone, it boasted about

[8] A. G. I., 1-1-3/22, Obregón, Crónica.

[9] "The Province of Sinaloa is the most northerly of Nueva Galicia. It is forty-two leagues from Culiacán and one hundred and fifty leagues from Guadalajara. San Juan de Sinaloa was founded but could not be maintained" (Herrera, *Historia General*, I. 24).

[10] The Fuerte was known in colonial days as the Suaqui.

[11] "Seis leguas al Oeste del ultimo de sus pueblos (the Sinaloas) seguian los teguecos o tehuecos" (Orozco y Berra, *Geografía*, p. 332).

one thousand men, who were feared by all the natives in that region. Surrounding the pueblo were fields of maize and calabashes, which, in addition to abundant game and fish, supplied them with food. The river at that place was wide, and, although the stream was swift, the natives ventured out on it in small boats. Though the warriors of Tegueco were drawn up in battle array on the approach of the Spaniards, they received the newcomers kindly, and, like the other natives, they offered their services. But the Spaniards were suspicious of them and thought it inadvisable to remain there. Therefore, after the padre, through Luisa, the interpreter, had instructed them in the rudiments of Christianity, they turned back to the Río Sinaloa to await reinforcements.[12]

A log fort was constructed on a favorable site on the Río Sinaloa, and there Ibarra and his men remained, while Fray Azevedo returned to Mexico City, and some soldiers went to Tôpia for their companions who had been left there. These soon rejoined their leader at his camp on the Río Sinaloa.[13] In the meantime, the maestro de campo went to Culiacán in pursuit of deserters, among them being Rodrigo Verdugo, the soldier who had been wounded in the attack on Tôpia. Because of the exemplary past services of these men, they were treated very leniently. Ordinarily the punishment for desertion was hanging. When Betanco returned to Sinaloa, he brought with him from Culiacán supplies of all sorts such as foodstuffs, horseshoes, powder, clothing, and shoes.

After the arrival of his reinforcements, Ibarra returned to the Río Fuerte to undertake the founding of a villa. This

According to Ribas (*Historia de los Triumphos*, p. 171) the Teguecos lived on the Fuerte about four leagues above the Zuaques.

[12] A. G. I., 1-1-3/22, Obregón, Crónica.

[13] *Ibid.;* A. G. I., 1-3-20/11, Francisco de Ybarra, Información de méritos.

decision was dictated by various circumstances. In addition to the obvious advantage of a Spanish settlement in that region as an aid in the work of Christianizing the natives and in exploiting their lands, the governor regarded the establishment of a villa and the apportionment of its lands as a satisfactory means of rewarding his soldiers. Many of them had received no pay for their services, and, since the entrada had failed to enrich them, they were very disheartened. So, as a makeshift and salve for their disillusionment, the Governor decided to found a town and apportion encomiendas in its vicinity.

The site selected was on the fertile banks of the Fuerte at a place called Carapoa, only five miles north of Tegueco.[14] Factors which determined the selection of Carapoa were: that it was situated in the midst of fertile meadows; that there were mountains near by which contained rich mineral deposits; and that surrounding it were many native settlements which could be repartitioned among the Spanish settlers. In sum, the town-site was ideal and was said to surpass anything in Culiacán or Chiametla. On the occasion of the founding of San Juan, Obregón says that Ibarra made a speech to his men, telling them that it had always been his greatest desire to lead them to discoveries and riches greater even than those of Mexico and Peru, but this lay in God's keeping. They should not forget, he said, that it was their duty to take advantage of every opportunity to convert the natives and thereby increase both the Heavenly Kingdom and that of his Catholic Majesty. Then a mass was said "to illuminate their understandings," and, after that, the villa was founded. The date of the founding of San Juan de Sinaloa, the name given to the new pueblo, was probably May or June, 1564. Municipal officials were appointed by the Governor, and the lands were distributed among the

---

[14] Ribas, *Historia de los Triumphos*, p. 28.

soldiers in accordance with their rank and services. A church was built, but its dedication was deferred until the return of Pablo de Azevedo, who had gone to Mexico for more religious to assist him in his missionary work. After the founding of San Juan, Ibarra sent Antonio de Betanco to Culiacán for more settlers and live-stock, such as cattle, swine, and sheep. These were given the settlers by the Governor free of charge.[15]

In June, 1564, there arrived in Sinaloa Juan de Zaldívar y Mendoza, a resident of Guadalajara, with news that Pedro Morones was dead. Zaldívar also gave Ibarra a royal cédula ordering him to continue his work of conquest and settlement even though he entered lands which had already been discovered—providing that he found them without churches and religious.[16] The subjugation of Chiametla had been entrusted by royal grant to the oidor of Nueva Galicia,[17] but he was unable on account of insufficient funds to undertake the enterprise. Thus the conquest of Chiametla, postponed time after time during Morones' lifetime, was never undertaken. That large and alluring province, extending from the mountains to the ocean and from Compostela to Culiacán, was, in 1564, a most promising field to exploit. Because of the apparent failure of Ibarra's efforts up to that time and the keen disappointment of his followers, it is not surprising that he should have looked toward Chiametla with longing eyes. When he first arrived in Culiacán from the wilds of Tôpia and was met by Pedro de Tovar, the conquests of Sinaloa and Chiametla were suggested to him. But, as has been narrated above, he first went to Sinaloa, for he probably thought that it was unwise to encroach on the oidor's grant. The receipt of the news of the death of

[15] A. G. I., 1-3-20/11, Francisco de Ybarra, Información de méritos; Col. Doc. Inéd., XIV. 481.

[16] Mota Padilla, Nueva Galicia, p. 208.

[17] Cf. p. 97.

Morones changed the situation entirely, for Ibarra regarded the oidor's commission as having terminated with his death.

Although it was then the rainy season, and most of the streams were in flood, Ibarra decided to start for Chiametla at once. After placing Antonio de Betanco in charge of the new pueblo of San Juan de Sinaloa, the Governor started for Chiametla with twenty picked horsemen.[18] He went by way of Culiacán, where he and his men were well received by Tovar and the inhabitants of San Miguel. There they were supplied with clothing, food, horses, and everything necessary for the undertaking. The alcalde mayor of Culiacán was at all times so generous in assisting Francisco de Ibarra and his men that to him belongs considerable credit for the success of the settlements in Chiametla and in Sinaloa. "Pedro de Tovar," according to Obregón, "was a most virtuous man, the most gentlemanly in the kingdom; in whom was to be found all Christianity, honor, and generosity." He was married to Doña Francisca de Guzmán, daughter of Gonzalo de Guzmán, one-time governor of Cuba. She was a lady "whose piety was equalled only by her great beauty."

Francisco de Ibarra did not decide precipitously on the conquest of Chiametla. From Culiacán he sent word to his uncle Diego telling him about his proposed undertaking, and requested his advice. Diego's reply was prompt and favor-

---

[18] Ibarra's memorial of his services, to be found in *Col. Doc. Inéd.*, XIV. 463-484, reads in his own words, "Fue a la provincia de Chiametla, que es por la banda del norte en la cual poblo la villa de San Sebastian donde se proveyo de cierta cantidad de soldados y de bastimientos, y otras cosas necesarias, para entrar la tierra adentro en demanda de nuevas tierras," etc. This passage, and Herrera's statement that Ibarra went north from Sinaloa, founded San Sebastián, and then continued farther northward into northern Sonora and Chihuahua, has caused Bancroft (*North Mexican States and Texas*, I. 108, note 20) considerable confusion, for he declares that "to go so far south in order to undertake a trip to the far north would be a strange proceeding." This, however, is exactly what took place. A. G. I., 59-4-3, Betanco sobre Ibarra; A. G. I., 1-1-1/20, Memorial del Lcdo. Juan de Ybarra.

able. At the same time, he sent his nephew and his followers
necessities in the form of clothing and munitions. With a
force considerably augmented by recent arrivals from both
Culiacán and Mexico, and all well equipped, Francisco set
out for Chiametla. Obregón says that Ibarra started for
Chiametla from Culiacán in April, 1566, during the rainy
season. The date as given in Ibarra's own información was
1564, and this is supported by the testimony of several witnesses. He entered Chiametla not later than 1565 and was
engaged for eleven months in the conquest. Bad roads,
heavy rains, and swollen rivers made the going extremely
difficult, and it was only after surmounting great hardships
that the Governor and his men finally reached the confines
of the province of Chiametla.[19]

The boundaries of Chiametla cannot be determined other
than that the province centered about the Mazatlán and
Cañas rivers, midway between Compostela and Culiacán,
with the Río Piastla as the northern boundary. Because of
the rich gold and silver deposits in that district, Nuño de Guz-
man had founded a Spanish villa on the Río Chiametla and
had partitioned the natives among his followers. But, because
of the ferocity of the Indians and the forbidding character
of the land, the settlement of Chiametla had a short life.
The intractable Indians rebelled about two years after the
founding of the settlement, killed their encomenderos, destroyed the pueblos, and then fled to the mountains. There
they lived like wild beasts in caves in the most inaccessible
parts of the mountains whither the Spaniards were unable
to follow them. In time these natives forgot all their Christian teaching and relapsed into barbarism. Since Chiametla
lay directly across the main road from Compostela to Culiacán, the savages became a real menace to communication

---

[19] A. G. I., 59-4-3, Betanco sobre Ibarra; A. G. I., 1-3-20/11, Francisco
de Ybarra, Información de méritos; A. G. I., 1-1-3/22, Obregón,
Crónica.

between the two places and actually threatened the existence of Culiacán, then an isolated frontier post. The difficulties Coronado encountered while passing through Chiametla were but one example of numerous like instances. Though the Spaniards had long lost control of Chiametla, the value of the province was not forgotten. Its reconquest was urged as being necessary to the retention of Culiacán. But the real desire of petitioners like Valiente and Morones was to win fortune and fame for themselves in a province whose wealth they greatly overestimated.

After marching for five days, Ibarra came to the pueblo of Caguacán, which was on the southern frontier of Culiacán. The natives of that pueblo belonged to the encomendero, Juan Arias. At that particular time these Indians were in a state of revolt, but, on the appearance of Ibarra and his men, the rebels were cowed immediately, for the reputation of the Governor of Nueva Vizcaya as a conquistador appears to have preceded him. Without the firing of a shot, the natives of Caguacán were returned to the obedience of their encomendero. From Caguacán, Ibarra's band moved on under the guidance of some Caguacán natives to the Río de Piastla, which marked the northern boundary of Chiametla. There they discovered a pueblo named Piastla. Its inhabitants received them kindly, gave them food, and even offered to serve in the expedition.

Since Piastla was the first native settlement which they encountered in Chiametla, Ibarra took possession of it in the name of his Catholic Majesty. The act of possession was written and recorded in due legal form by the Governor's secretary, Sebastián de Quiros. A cross was erected in the center of the pueblo and the building of a church was begun. From Piastla messengers were sent to settlements on the Río Chiametla demanding their submission. The messengers were received peaceably by the natives of Chiametla and returned to the Governor with promises of submission and with numerous gifts. From Piastla, Ibarra continued to the Río Chiametla, receiving submission of the natives as he went. These particular natives were evidently well acquainted with the Spaniards, for they had traded with travelers passing to and from Culiacán and Compostela. A camp was established on the Río Chiametla a few miles from one of the larger Indian pueblos. This they made their headquarters until a town could be founded.

The natives of Chiametla submitted peacefully and promised to be obedient servants of the Spanish king. In particular they offered their services for the subjugation of their warlike neighbors, the Hinas,[20] who lived in the inhospitable mountains to the east of the Río Chiametla. These natives, called "Caribes" by Obregón, were a savage lot, who practiced cannibalism. They made frequent raids into the plains, harassed the fields of the more civilized and peaceful Indians of Chiametla, and carried off captives to be consumed in their cannibalistic orgies.

After the establishment of his camp, Ibarra accepted the proffered assistance of the natives of Chiametla and determined to attempt the pacification of the Hinas, who inhabited a high and rugged *peñol* named Cacalotlán. He marched to their rocky stronghold, but his demands of surrender were answered by taunts and showers of arrows, lances, and stones. A battle of four hours' duration ensued, and so determined was the resistance of the Hinas that the Indian allies of the Spaniards deserted, thinking that the battle was lost. But finally, when one of the caciques of the defenders was shot, their resistance withered, and they deserted their

---

[20] The Hinas, according to Alégre (Francisco Javier Alégre, *Historia de la Compañia de Jésus,* Mexico, 1841, II. 195), lived in very deep canyons in the heart of the mountains near the sources of the Río de Humace, which empties into the Piastla. Orozco y Berra (*Geografía,* p. 316) states also that they lived on the banks of the Río de Piastla.

peñol fort. They withdrew deeper and deeper into the mountains as they were forced to give up one position after another, but to all the entreaties and promises of the Spaniards they turned deaf ears and refused to cease fighting. At last, in desperation, Ibarra was driven to an act which he seldom employed in his wars with the Indians: he discontinued the attack and ordered the houses and fields of the Hinas to be destroyed. A little later he ordered Captain Hernando Ramon, an experienced and able soldier, to attempt once more the pacification of the natives. Unexpected resistance was encountered by Ramon, for the Indians, driven to fury by the destruction of their homes and their crops, fought with even greater bravery than before. Nine Christian natives and four horses had been killed by the time Ibarra came post-haste to the assistance of Ramon. With the arrival of reinforcements, the Indians disclosed a desire to conclude hostilities. But, as a condition of capitulation, they curiously stipulated that some Negroes whom the Spaniards had with them should not come near them, for they regarded them as evil spirits. Ibarra accepted their terms, but stipulated in turn that they should discontinue their attacks on their neighbors and that they should give up their practice of cannibalism.

Three hundred of the Caribes surrendered and were kindly received by the Governor, who gave them trinkets of various sorts.[21] They were instructed in matters of Holy Faith by Padre Azevedo, who also endeavored to dissuade them from their practice of eating human flesh. So devastating had been that revolting custom that in the whole province there were but five thousand natives, whereas in Guzmán's time there had been that many in a single locality.

[21] Juan Rodrigo Parra testified that Ibarra made *entradas* while in Chiametla to Cacalotean, Mateatlan, and other places (A. G. I., 1-3-20/11, Francisco de Ybarra, *Información de méritos*).

In a small pueblo in the mountains, the Spaniards found two thousand human skulls and a great pile of human bones of consumed captives.[22]

In the conquest of Chiametla, Ibarra was singularly fortunate, for in four battles with the natives not a Spaniard was killed, and only a few were wounded, though a few of their Indian auxiliaries and some of their horses had been killed.

After Francisco de Ibarra had subjugated the greater part of Chiametla, the oidores of Nueva Galicia, claiming authority over that province under the grants to Doctor Morones, attempted to oust him. They first wrote ordering him to leave Chiametla and make way for an alcalde mayor appointed by themselves. They argued that, having failed to discover Copalá, Ibarra was repairing his fortunes at the expense of Nueva Galicia in Culiacán and in Chiametla, both provinces which had been conquered by Guzmán and which belonged to their jurisdiction. They claimed that the Governor of Nueva Vizcaya was proceeding contrary to the terms of his commission, which specified that he was *not* to acquire lands which had once been conquered.[23]

The letter of the oidores, which was not couched in the most polite terms and which branded Ibarra, among other things, as being a delinquent and wrong-doer, was answered by him with firmness and courtesy. He admitted frankly that he had set out from San Juan in search of Tôpia, but misfortune had overtaken him, and he found himself on the shores of the South Sea with dissatisfied men on his hands. While he was in that predicament, he learned about the death of Morones, and, knowing the richness of Chiametla he regarded this as a divinely ordained opportunity to serve God and the king as well as to retrieve his own waning fortunes.

[22] A. G. I., 1-1-3/22, Obregón, Crónica.
[23] A. G. I., 67-1-18, Audiencia de Nueva Galicia al Rey, 10 de septiembre de 1567.

The subsequent ease of the conquest convinced him that it had been God's will that he should be the conqueror of Chiametla. As for the legality of his act, Francisco de Ibarra conscientiously believed that he was acting within the terms of his commission. After all, he asked, were not he and the oidores vassals of the same king, whom they served with one purpose? In the conquest of Chiametla he had won for the crown, at no expense to the royal treasury, tribute, royal fifths, and many converts to the Catholic faith. Did not the results justify the act?

"To the logical argument of Ibarra," says Obregón, "the oidores hardened their hearts with envy," and determined to force his submission. The man entrusted with the unenviable task of arresting the Governor of Nueva Vizcaya was Lorenzo de Padilla, "for they gave him difficult commissions since he was severe and rough by nature."[24] Harsh as may have been Padilla's character, he readily recognized the justice of Ibarra's acts and relinquished his commission after he had returned to Nueva Galicia with his mission unaccomplished. Antonio de Ribera was next delegated to go to Chiametla, where he was received with all the respect due a royal official. His report to the oidores contained nothing but words of praise for the Governor of Nueva Vizcaya, and he actually declared that Francisco de Ibarra deserved a reward for his meritorious services!

After their personal efforts had failed, the oidores next turned to the viceroy and even to the king for assistance in their struggle with the Governor of Nueva Vizcaya. Viceroy Falces' opinion regarding the legality of Ibarra's invasion of Chiametla was made clear on May 31, 1567, when he issued a confirmation of Ibarra's commission and sanctioned all of his acts prior to that date. The viceregal confirmation read as follows:

[24] A. G. I., 1-1-3/22, Obregón, Crónica.

We are informed that Francisco de Ibarra has discovered beyond the mines of San Martín and Aviño many lands and settlements of natives as far as the South Sea, and has baptized many natives and brought them to a knowledge of the Christian faith. He has also brought them to our obedience and has settled with Spaniards the town of Durango in the valley of Guadiana, the town of San Sebastián in the province of Chiametla, and the villa of San Juan in the province of Sinaloa. In all this God and ourselves have been served, and the said Francisco de Ibarra, a good captain and our obedient servant, has been forced to undergo great hardships, and has made great expenditures at his own cost, without salary from us or remuneration whatsoever. Because of all this, and the desire to reward him for various reasons brought to our attention by Don Gaston de Peralta, Marques de Falces, Count of San Estevan, our mayor domo of our kingdom of Navarra, and our viceroy, governor, and captain-general of New Spain, and president of our audiencia and royal chancellery at that place, we have decided to confirm and approve, as we now do confirm and approve to the said Francisco de Ibarra the commission awarded him by Don Luís de Velasco, our viceroy, as captain and governor of the lands which he might discover and settle beyond the above mentioned mines. By virtue of the said commission, and once more if necessary, we name him as our captain and governor of all the lands and provinces beyond the said mines which have been discovered and settled by others of our vassals. In all of this he shall retain the same instructions and powers granted him by the Viceroy Don Luís de Velasco, and by the oidores of the said our royal audiencia, to exercise and discharge all the duties concerning and appertaining to a captain and governor. We command all persons residing in the lands and provinces already discovered, both by land and sea, that is to say, those who are already there, and those who might come later, to regard him and obey him as their captain and governor. He shall judge them in all cases criminal and civil that shall arise, giving decisions in the first instance, and allowing appeals to go before the royal audiencia which resides in the City of Mexico, and before no other body. In all of this we grant him complete powers in accordance with the provision which he possesses. Given in the City of Mexico, May 31, 1567. The Marques de Falces. (Rubric)[25]

In reply to an appeal of the audiencia of Nueva Galicia that it be allowed to name a governor and administer justice in Chiametla, "which had been granted to Morones, but had been usurped by Ibarra," Viceroy Falces answered at length on July 7, 1567. He declared that, since the royal cédula

[25] A. G. I., 58-3-8, El traslado de la provisión que el señor marques de falces visorey dió á francisco de Ybarra.

to Morones had not been put into effect and since Francisco
de Ibarra had, with great labor and expense to himself, conquered that region, and since the inhabitants were content
under his government, the royal service could not be justified
without more sufficient cause to take steps which would only
result in disturbing the Spaniards and the natives. Falces
did not deny that the territory occupied by Ibarra rightfully
belonged to Morones, but it did not appear that, on the death
of Morones, the audiencia took steps to appoint someone
for the place, nor did it take measures to oppose Ibarra's
entry on the ground that it was going to appoint a person
conforming to the king's mandate. There was no one in
Nueva Galicia who could have done at his own expense what
Francisco de Ibarra had accomplished, and so they ought not
to pay him badly for his service nor put him in a position to
defend himself. In conclusion, Falces advised the audiencia
of Nueva Galicia to consider how important it was for the
Spaniards to avoid discord among themselves because of
the bad example it set the natives. He suggested that both
sides present their case to the king for his consideration; as
for himself, he would not consent to do more.[26]

In a letter dated August 5, 1567, the Viceroy discussed
the matter of Chiametla with the oidor Contreras. Since
news came to Mexico that Nueva Galicia was contemplating
forcible steps against Ibarra, Falces endeavored to convince
the oidores that Ibarra was acting within his rights as
granted by his commission. Their attention was directed to
the royal instructions enabling the Viceroy to undertake the
work of exploration and settlement. It was in accordance
with these instructions that Velasco had granted Ibarra his
commission and that Falces had confirmed it. Once more
the Viceroy proposed that all parties write to the king and

[26] A. G. I., 58-3-8, Traslado de la carta del señor visorey de la nueva
españa que escrivió á esta real audiencia sobre lo de Francisco de Ybarra,
México, 7 de julio de 1567.

present their claims. In the meantime, Falces did not believe Francisco de Ibarra should be disturbed in his governorship.[27]

On September 10, 1567, the oidores finally accepted the Viceroy's advice and wrote the king. They protested the legality of Ibarra's occupation of Chiametla and contended that it was directly contrary to his commission *not to enter occupied lands*. They declared that not only had Ibarra acted contrary to the letter of his commission, but he had no authority to apportion encomiendas. Later the audiencia of Nueva Galicia prepared for the king an información showing that Governor Ibarra had exceeded his authority in entering Chiametla, and in granting encomiendas to his followers. The king was asked to order a visitation of the province of Nueva Vizcaya, and to take a residencia of Ibarra's governorship.[28]

Because of the grave and persistent accusations of the officials of Nueva Galicia, a residencia of Francisco de Ibarra was actually ordered at a later date. Other charges trumped up by the audiencia, and the eventual investigation will be considered later. But, as regards the administration of Chiametla, a compromise was finally arranged. Ibarra was to remain in control of the province, but it was agreed that appeals from his decisions, originating in Chiametla, should proceed to the audiencia of Nueva Galicia for final adjudication. This arrangement was acceptable to Ibarra since Guadalajara was much nearer Chiametla than was Mexico.[29]

After the pacification of Chiametla, Ibarra decided to make a permanent Spanish settlement and to repartition the

[27] A. G. I., 58-3-8, El traslado de la carta que escrivió el visorey á esta real audiencia con el señor licedo contreras sobre lo de Fran. de Ybarra, México, 5 de agosto de 1567.

[28] A. G. I., 67-1-18, Audiencia de Nueva Galicia al Rey, 10 de septiembre de 1567; A. G. I., 67-1-18, Audiencia de Nueva Galicia al Rey, 4 de marzo de 1569.

[29] A. G. I., 1-1-3/22, Obregón, Crónica.

native inhabitants of the province. The site of the new town was that which the Governor had chosen for his camp on the Río Chiametla. It was on the west slope of a hill, about a stone's throw from the river, a spot unincumbered by undergrowth or trees.[30] The new town, which was named San Sebastián, for it was founded on that saint's day (January 20), was duly organized with a cabildo and municipal officials. It was also provided with a church and priest. The lots were apportioned among the soldiers according to their merits. The founding of San Sebastián was of great importance in protecting the route from Compostela to Culiacán. In and around the villa there settled a number of Spanish farmers who raised maize and vegetables to support the workers of the mines near by. Throughout Chiametla many changes were made in the old encomiendas; pueblos were repartitioned by the Governor to reward his friends, and many new encomiendas were apportioned.[31]

In addition to San Sebastián, other Spanish settlements arose around the various mines in Chiametla. The most noteworthy of these were Pánuco, Copalá, and Nochestan. All were located in the mountains to the north and west of San Sebastián.[32] The mines of Las Charcas, twenty-five miles east of San Sebastián, were settled by an independent

[30] *Ibid.;* A. G. I., 1-1-1/20, Memorial del Lcdo. Juan de Ybarra; the subjugation of the natives was accomplished in six months; it was after that that San Sebastián was founded (A. G. I., 1-3-20/11, Francisco de Ybarra, Información de méritos).

[31] *Col. Doc. Inéd.,* XIV. 481, 484; Bancroft, *North Mexican States and Texas,* I. 110; A. G. I., 1-1-1/20, Memorial del Lcdo. Juan de Ybarra.

[32] Lope de los Rios gives the names of the mining settlements as Pánuco and Pala; but the latter name was probably meant for Copalá. Juan Rodrigo Parra mentions another mine by the name of Guadalupe. His testimony is confusing for he states that before Ibarra could arrive at the mine of Guadalupe, which had already been settled by the Spaniards, the Indians killed all of the settlers, or about twenty-three persons. The governor returned later to settle the mines of Guadalupe, but because they were not sufficiently rich, the project was abandoned (A. G. I., 1-3-20/11, Francisco de Ybarra, Información de méritos).

movement from San Martín, for soon after the pacification
of Chiametla, eight soldier-miners, principally Portuguese,
set out from San Martín prospecting for mines. They
crossed the high mountains to the west and arrived in
Chiametla. There they discovered and began to work the
mines of Las Charcas. These mines, according to Obregón,
were the first to be worked in Chiametla. Some years later,
however, the natives of that locality rebelled, drove out the
miners, and destroyed the settlement. Many other mines
were discovered in Chiametla and produced a large quantity
of silver and quicksilver.[33]

Two years after Ibarra's conquest of Chiametla, Lope
Fernandez and some other miners went from Durango to
San Sebastián searching for mines, but Captain Hernando
Trejo, Ibarra's lieutenant-governor of Chiametla, refused
to grant them permission to prospect for fear they would
arouse the natives. They then went to Sinaloa, where the
Governor was at the time, and received his permission to
prospect. They returned to Chiametla and were quite successful in locating productive silver veins.[34]

But not all of these discoveries and improvements were
accomplished on Ibarra's first visit to Chiametla. The first
entrada, which resulted in the conquest of Chiametla and
the founding of San Sebastián, occupied the conquistador
for eleven months. He then returned to Sinaloa and, after
an extended journey to the far north, returned to Chiametla,
where he resided the greater part of the remainder of his life.
The Indians of Chiametla were kept in order with difficulty,
both because of their warlike nature and because of the

---

[33] Obregón claims that, at an earlier date, when he was returning from
a voyage to the "Isla Cardena de la Carnifería," with Antonio de Luna,
his father-in-law, he discovered some mines in Chiametla. When he
joined Francisco de Ibarra he told him about these mines. They were
rediscovered and proved to be very productive. He does not give the
names of the mines.

[34] Ibid.

extreme ruggedness of the lands which they inhabited. For that reason, Ibarra spent most of his time in Chiametla and seldom went over the mountains to Durango.

Shortly after the founding of San Sebastián, the Governor's forces were somewhat augmented by new arrivals from Mexico and Guadalajara, for it appears that Salvador Ponce had been sent to get recruits in Nueva Galicia and Mexico. He was able to enlist only a few men, but these were thankfully received by Ibarra, and Ponce was rewarded by being appointed alguacil mayor of Chiametla. This, in the opinion of Obregón, was small reward to Ponce, because he had spent over five thousand pesos on the conquest of Nueva Vizcaya. The soldiers brought by Ponce were sent to Sinaloa, from which place the governor planned to undertake an expedition to the far north to the "Plains of the Cows," or the buffalo country. Other arrivals who were later to play leading rôles in the history of Nueva Vizcaya were Hernando de Trejo and Baltasar de Obregón. Since Ibarra was making plans to conduct a great expedition beyond the northern frontier, he was most desirous of leaving his recent conquests in Chiametla in competent hands. He therefore communicated with Hernando de Trejo, "a gentleman of parts, ability, and military experience," and offered to appoint him lieutenant-governor of Chiametla. Trejo accepted, and at Compostela he met Baltasar de Obregón, who was also bound for Chiametla. This marks the initial entry of Obregón into Nueva Vizcaya, and henceforth his *Chronicle* is based on personal observation and is more trustworthy than the preceding chapters, which were founded on documentary evidence and hearsay.

Obregón's mission to Chiametla was to warn Ibarra that a Juan de Avellaneda had procured, "by underhand means," a royal mandate charging the Governor of Nueva Vizcaya and his men with the theft of seven hundred horses at San

Martín. This fact lends considerable basis to the accusations of Diego de Colio.[35] Obregón and Trejo agreed to make the journey together and started alone through the wilderness which separated them from Ibarra. At that time Obregón was in ill-health; so, because of his infirmities and the danger of the Indians, he sought to confess himself before he started on his long journey, but the Franciscan friar in Jalisco, "because of the bad opinion he had of soldiers who killed Indians," refused to confess him! With great uneasiness, the travelers pursued their solitary journey; without mishap they arrived safely in San Sebastián. There they were received by the Governor of Nueva Vizcaya, who was forewarned by Obregón, "so that the coming of Avellaneda was made unnecessary." How Obregón's warning could have assisted Ibarra it is difficult to imagine.

Trejo was appointed Ibarra's lieutenant in Chiametla, but he stipulated first that he and the vecinos should be granted repartimientos and the forced performance of certain personal services on the part of the natives. The Governor agreed to grant them encomiendas, but he flatly refused to subject the natives to personal service, contending that that was contrary to his commission. But he agreed that, in the mines and in the homes of the Spaniards, they could employ natives from their encomiendas if they paid for their services and gave them religious instruction. At this time Ibarra addressed an información to the king asking that he be confirmed in his title of governor and be granted a salary of two thousand ducats. The request was evidently conceded about a year prior to his death.

The advantages and benefits attending the occupation of Chiametla were many. From the spiritual standpoint, thousands of natives were won to the Catholic faith. Many of

[35] Cf. p. 114.

these had been cannibals, and thus an end was put to their revolting practice. Ibarra estimated that from Guzmán's time to his own more than thirty thousand natives had met death at the hands of the cannibals![36] Since the Spaniards were prone to exaggerate the number of natives, Ibarra may also have exaggerated in this instance, but the mute evidence of thousands of human skulls was substantial basis for estimation. After his subjugation of Chiametla, Ibarra declared that there occurred not a single war between the natives, and, with the absence of prisoners of war, their human feasts came to an end.

Another important result which followed the occupation of Chiametla was that it afforded safe travel to and from Culiacán. Prior to Ibarra's subjugation of Chiametla, Culiacán was being rapidly deserted, and the mines in its vicinity were abandoned because of the Indian menace. Now that the route to Culiacán was safe once more, tradesmen and merchants could go there with safety. With the settlement of Chiametla and the increased supply of foodstuffs from that province, Culiacán was rehabilitated and prospered. Since maintenance of Culiacán was indispensable to the Spanish advance into the northern frontier, the work of Ibarra in Chiametla occupies an important place in the history of northern expansion in New Spain.

A result of the conquest of Chiametla which probably won greatest favor in the eyes of the treasure-hunting Spaniards was the opportunity to exploit rich mineral resources. Many silver mines were discovered in Chiametla, and, though their production up to the time of Ibarra's death was small, this was not due to low grade ore, but rather to a scarcity of labor and excessive prices of implements and foodstuffs. The Spanish residents of Chiametla

[36] A. G. I., 1-1-1/20, Memorial del Lcdo. Juan de Ybarra.

maintained themselves with difficulty, for almost everything cost about double the prices prevailing in Mexico City.[37]

In addition to its rich mines, Chiametla possessed other noteworthy advantages. Along the coast were good fisheries, said to be "adequate to supply all New Spain with fish." On the coast, also, were extensive salines, where could be collected with little effort an unlimited supply of salt, which was deposited by the high tides. The salines were of inestimable value in the operation of the silver mines. The fertile valleys of Chiametla were well adapted to the cultivation of maize, beans, fruits, and cotton. The grazing industry had received a good start before Ibarra's arrival in the province, for some of the cattle lost by Coronado when he passed through Chiametla on his journey to Cíbola had multiplied into the thousands. In short, so valuable were the services of Francisco de Ibarra in rewinning Chiametla, that it is not surprising that his indiscretion was overlooked in view of his greater services.

[37] A. G. I., 1-1-1/20, Memorial del Lcdo. Juan de Ybarra; A. G. I., 66-6-22, Los oficiales reales de Durango al rey, Durango, 1 de marzo de 1579.

CHAPTER VI

THE EXPEDITION TO PAQUIMÉ (CASAS GRANDES)

When Francisco de Ibarra left Sinaloa to undertake the conquest of Chiametla, he appointed Antonio de Betanco as his lieutenant-governor of the province of Sinaloa. After the departure of the Governor the natives exhibited a hostile attitude, and Betanco immediately busied himself in fortifying San Juan. A log palisade about four hundred yards square with towers at the four corners was erected about the villa. But an attack did not materialize, for so prudent was Betanco in handling the natives that he was able to maintain peace, and during the eleven months of Ibarra's absence not a single Indian was killed by the Spaniards.[1]

After the safety of San Juan had been assured, Betanco undertook to pacify the remainder of the province and to secure supplies. He first went to Tegueco, located on the Río Fuerte a short distance below San Juan. The inhabitants, who were rebellious at the time, fled on the approach of the Spaniards and refused to return to their pueblo. Betanco decided to use force, and an attack was ordered with as much noise as possible to frighten the natives into submission, and thus to avoid bloodshed. The plan was successful, for, terrified by the noise of the guns, the Indians fled in every direction. The soldiers pursued them and captured a number of their squaws and children and returned with them

[1] A. G. I., 1-1-3/22, Obregón, *Crónica*. According to Ribas (*Historia de los Triumphos*, p. 28) Ibarra left in charge of San Juan, as captain and justicia mayor, Estevan Martín de Vohorques. The curate of the church of San Juan was Hernando de Pedrosa. It must have been some time later when Pedrosa took charge, for Obregón says that there was no one in Sinaloa to say mass during the eleven months when Ibarra was away (A. G. I., 59-4-3, Betanco sobre Francisco de Ibarra).

to their camp. The braves did not dare to attack while their women were prisoners, and so hovered about the camp and indicated that they wished to make peace. Their friendly overtures were accepted, and order was restored in Tegueco.[2]

The maestro de campo continued his march down the river, receiving the friendly submission of the numerous Indian settlements along the way. One of the more important of these was named Urigue or Vrigoe. Here, as in Tegueco, the natives were subdued with little effort, because of their fear of the fire-arms of the Spaniards. Finally, Betanco came to the mouth of the Río Fuerte and inspected it carefully to determine its possibilities as a harbor. The river formed a small inlet as it entered the sea, and, though it was not highly satisfactory, he ascertained that it could at least accommodate seagoing vessels. From the South Sea, Betanco and his companions returned to San Juan by way of the pueblo of Ciguini, which was located a short distance to the southeast of Tegueco. The inhabitants of Ciguini received him kindly, but when he ordered them to furnish him some "burden-bearers," they refused. Their insubordination was soon curbed, after one of their leaders had been severely flogged. Betanco then returned to San Juan without further incident.

The maestro de campo, acting under instructions of the Governor, would not allow his men to work the mines which they had discovered in Sinaloa until the Indians were sufficiently pacified, for it was the well-advised policy of Francisco de Ibarra to subordinate everything to the subjugation and domestication of the savages. This caused great discontent among the soldiers and some of them conspired to desert the province, but at that time there arrived a letter from the Governor telling about the conquest of Chiametla and announcing that he was sending Fray Pablo de Azevedo

[2] A. G. I., 1-1-3/22, Obregón, Crónica.

and some soldiers to Sinaloa to make preparations for an expedition to the far north. He also ordered Betanco to prospect for more mines. A few soldiers were sent out by Betanco, and in a short time they returned with many favorable ore samples. But when some of the dissatisfied soldiers became petulant and threatened to make trouble, Betanco attempted to cow them into submission by threates of arrest and imprisonment. His efforts were unsuccessful, for on the following day the uprising occurred. "Thanks to the Vizcainos," says Obregón, "who on innumerable occasions proved to be the most loyal and valiant of Ibarra's followers," the incipient revolt was checked, and the ring-leader was cast into irons. The rest of the culprits were not punished because of Betanco's desire to maintain concord among his followers.

Another letter from the Governor arrived stating that he was on his way to Sinaloa and that, pending his arrival, the maestro de campo and Fray Pablo should reconnoiter to the north of Sinaloa. In accordance with the Governor's orders, Betanco, Azevedo, and twenty soldiers marched as far north as the Río Mayo. They found the Indians of that region greatly in need of maize, for the Río Mayo had flooded all of their fields. The Fuerte was also in flood up to the fort and hindered the building of houses. At the beginning of the harvest season there was such an abundance of maize that the soldiers and Indians burned it, but now, as a result of the floods, the natives were reduced to dire want and wandered through the mounains hunting roots, herbs, and game. Had it not been for the forethought of Betanco, who had carefully guarded a little patch of maize, famine would have compelled the desertion of Sinaloa. Eleven months elapsed before Ibarra returned to San Juan de Sinaloa. In that time the new settlement prospered greatly under the solicitous care of Betanco.

As Francisco de Ibarra was returning to Sinaloa to undertake his projected trip to the far north, he stopped at Culiacán, where he was well received by Tovar, who once more supplied him and his men with many necessities for the journey.[3] From Culiacán, Ibarra went to Mocorito, where he lent effective assistance to newly-established cattle ranches. Then he visited the native settlements of Petatlán and Ocoroni, and, finding the natives obedient and peaceful, he continued to San Juan de Sinaloa, where he was received most enthusiastically by the Spaniards and the natives. The reception was marked by a formal parade of the soldiers and the Indians, the latter gaily bedecked in plumage and strings of shells. The Indians danced before the Governor and shot their arrows into the air to signify their great joy at his safe arrival.[4]

The Governor was pleased with the development of San Juan and also with the news of the recent discoveries of mines and native settlements. He remained in Sinaloa for twenty days making preparations for his journey;[5] but, since the founding of the new towns of San Juan and San Sebastián had created a drain upon his following, Ibarra was able to assemble not more than sixty soldiers for the expedition.[6] Most of these were arcabuceros. They were well equipped for such a long journey with arms, munitions, supplies, and about three hundred horses. Fray Pablo was the only friar taken on the entrada; another

[3] A. G. I., 1-3-20/11, Francisco de Ybarra, Información de méritos.
[4] A. G. I., 1-1-3/22, Obregón, Crónica.
[5] "Francisco de Ibarra returned to Sinaloa and in *the same year* went north beyond Sinaloa to investigate reports of many Indian settlements" (A. G. I., 1-1-1/20, Memorial del Lcdo. Juan de Ybarra).
[6] Betanco (A. G. I., 59-4-3, Betanco sobre Francisco de Ibarra) states that forty soldiers went on the entrada. Melchior Enríquez (A. G. I., 1-3-20/11, Francisco de Ybarra, Información de méritos) testified that he was one of the thirty soldiers who left Sinaloa with Ibarra. Beaumont (*Crónica de Michoacán*, V. 533) relates that Ibarra was accompanied by fifty soldiers, together with Pedro de Tovar and Fray Azevedo.

Franciscan was left in Sinaloa to look after the spiritual needs of its inhabitants. They had two interpreters: Diego de Soberaños, Ibarra's personal servant, and Luisa, the Indian squaw whom he had obtained from the Ocoroni. It was planned that they should march and live together in groups of fours and fives, each group with its own native servant to cook for it. As the safety of Sinaloa was a matter of concern to the Governor, he proposed to leave his maestro de campo in charge. Betanco did not wish to accept the post of lieutenant-governor, because of his desire to accompany the Governor, and it was only by virtue of much persuasion that he finally acquiesced.[7]

All preparations for the journey having been completed, they took leave of the maestro de campo and the vecinos of San Juan. The latter were somewhat disgruntled because they had not been allowed to 'encomendar' more natives. This gave Betanco some trouble later. The date of Ibarra's departure, as given by Obregón, was May 1, 1567. This date seems to be erroneous, for, according to Obregón himself, Ibarra first went to Chiametla in the spring or summer of 1564 and after a lapse of about eleven months he returned to Sinaloa; and then, in twenty days, he departed for the far north. That would place the entrada about the middle of 1565, which seems to be the more logical date. This is also supported by Ibarra's información, which states that the entrada was made six or seven years prior to July, 1572. Lastly and most conclusively, Betanco wrote a letter in Mexico on June 5, 1566, giving a complete account of the entrada.[8]

The Governor sent ahead the main body of his expedition under the command of Pedro de Uncueta, while he

<hr/>

[7] A. G. I., 59-4-3, Betanco sobre Francisco de Ibarra.

[8] *Ibid.;* A. G. I., 1-3-20/11, Francisco de Ybarra, Información de méritos.

himself, with a few soldiers, went to examine the supposedly rich mines that had been discovered by Antonio de Betanco. In the absence of Ibarra, the expedition passed over the mountains north of San Juan and arrived in the valley of the Río Mayo. There they halted for a time while Ponce, Obregón, and five other soldiers searched for food. A short distance up the river, in the mountains, they found a large native settlement named Temosa or Tenmoca and several other little settlements. The Spaniards were able to appropriate all the foodstuffs they desired, for the Indians cultivated maize, beans, and calabashes in quantity.

The natives of the lower Río Mayo, as well as of the region near the mouth of the Río Yaqui, constituted a group of sedentary Indians who spoke two dialects of the Cahita language—the Mayos and their northern relatives, the Yaqui. Regarding the culture of these Indians, Bandelier says:

The Mayos were independent of the Yaquis, and the relations between the two groups were far from being always friendly. There even existed on the part of the latter a tendency to crowd and overwhelm the former, in that gradual but persistent manner which is characteristic of Indian warfare. Still, there was no difference in degree of culture. Settled each along the bank of a considerable river, which bore the name of its respective tribe, they planted Indian corn, cotton, calabashes, beans, and tobacco, improved the mescal varieties of the American agave, hunted, fished, and fought their neighbors, as well as among themselves. Owing to the almost tropical climate, their dwellings appeared frail, canes and boughs forming the framework, palm-leaves the outer protective shell. Split up into a number of autonomous villages, each one governed after the well-known tribal system, the entire dialectic cluster only coalesced temporarily and at rare intervals, for self-protection, in case insult offered by one of their villages to outsiders led to threatened revenge on a larger scale. No central head existed, either for war or in peace. Still it is not improbable that each group may have constituted a sort of barbaric confederacy, although it is certain that it did not possess the consistence which we admire in the "League of the Iroquois." Gentilism certainly prevailed, and there are traces of similar esoteric clusters to those discovered by Mr. Cushing among the Zuñis, and which, guided by his observations, I have since found in existence among the Queres, Tehuas, and the Tiguas, in New Mexico. Fetichism characterized their religious beliefs, as well as those of all other southwestern Indians, and the absence of the conception of one supreme being is as plain among them as elsewhere.

These two clusters dwelt, for the most part, about the mouths of the two rivers bearing their names; they held but a portion of the course of each stream, and it cannot be said that their sway extended any distance into the Sierra Madre. East of them, Indians speaking what may be dialects of the Tarahumar and Tepehuan idioms occupied the valleys and fastnesses. These tribes are little known, some of them have disappeared by name, and what we know of their condition recalls that of the Yaquis and Mayos, locally varied through environment.[9]

The Governor rejoined his men while they were in the valley of the Mayo. From there they marched for five days up the Río de Los Cedros, one of the northern branches of the Mayo. This stream was called Los Cedros because of the great growth of cedars which lined its banks.

From the headwaters of the Río de Los Cedros, the explorers were forced to work their way over high, rugged mountains which were covered with a thorny underbrush. After losing several horses, they reached the ridge of the sierras. That mountainous country was inhabited by natives known as Umaredas.[10] It was learned that there were more than twenty Umareda settlements and that, farther in the interior, there were larger pueblos with more civilized inhabitants. But as the Spaniards marched northward, they discovered that the natives became more savage. For three days they struggled through the almost impassable mountains, their every step being impeded by the Indians who were a menace, not only at their front and rear, but also overhead on the precipitous crags.

[9] A. F. Bandelier, *Final Report of Investigations Among the Indians of the Southwestern United States,* Papers of the Archaeological Institute of America, American Series, Cambridge, 1890, III. 48-53.

[10] It is impossible to identify these Indians. They may have been the Huvagueres mentioned by Orozco y Berra (*Geografía,* p. 351).

They were now on the southern edge of Sonora. They descended from the mountains and for two days marched down a narrow valley, in which there were natives who cultivated fields of maize and beans. When they arrived within a short distance of a pueblo named Oera, the Governor ordered camp pitched on a carefully chosen site of level ground which could be easily defended, for he had heard a great deal about the warlike natives of that region. Messengers were sent to the pueblo to announce the peaceful purpose of their visit. They were peaceably received by the natives, and were sent back to Ibarra loaded with presents of foodstuffs and promises of a friendly reception.

Oera was located in a small valley bearing the same name. Through it flowed a small affluent of the Yaqui River. Oera had about two thousand inhabitants of whom four hundred were warriors. These natives, who belonged to the Yaqui nation, were much more intelligent than those who lived in the mountains to the south. The men wore cotton mantas, and the women were clothed from the waist down in deer-hide skirts. Though they hunted game for food, they also raised, in irrigated patches, maize, beans, and other vegetables and fruits. The natives of Oera were sun worshippers, a superstition which Fray Azevedo immediately endeavored to correct.

From Oera the explorers continued their march in a northerly direction, crossing almost impassable mountains, and descending into deep, rocky arroyos. On the fourth day they reached the summit of a high mountain from whence could be seen the valley of the Río Yaqui. Their guides told them that in that valley there had once been a Spanish settlement which was later destroyed by the natives. This settlement can probably be identified with Coronado's town of San Gerónimo. Fearing that the natives might still be dangerous because of the knowledge of their past victory over the Spaniards, the Governor decided to exercise the utmost caution while passing through Sonora.[11]

For four days the party went up the Yaqui Valley, passing many settlements and pueblos located about ten and twelve miles apart along the banks of the river. That province, according to Obregón, was inhabited by about twenty thousand natives who were divided into two linguistic groups, "Caytas" and "Pima Aytos." According to Bandelier's classification, the Caytas (Cahitas) were the Mayos and the Yaqui, whereas those natives north of the Yaqui in the southern heart of Sonora were the southern Pimas, or Nebomes, to distinguish them from the Arizona Pimas.[12] The Pima Aytos of Obregón were evidently the Nebomes. Their social organization and their religious system were analogous to those of the Yaqui. Their language, however, was quite different. Ribas describes them as follows:

The Nebomes were settled on the banks of creeks with running water. Their houses were better and more durable than those of other nations, for the walls were made of large adobes, which they manufactured out of clay and covered with flat roofs of earth. Some of these houses they built even much larger, with loop-holes like forts, in order that, if they should be attacked by enemies, the people of the village might retire into them and make use of their arrows.[13]

They were skilful farmers and cultivated maize, beans, chili, melons, and fruits. They were very anxious to obtain iron implements to till their fields, and hovered about the camp of the Spaniards in hopes of securing them. To obtain salt, they often made raids upon their neighbors, the Yaqui, who lived along the coast of the South Sea. The Nebomes were savage warriors.

The Spaniards were now among savages who used poisoned arrows. Obregón states that the poison was ob-

---

[11] Sonora (Señora) was that region lying between the Yaqui and the Sonora rivers. Obregón called the upper Yaqui region Sonora, and it is so considered in the present treatise.

[12] Bandelier, *Final Report,* I. 53.

[13] Ribas, *Historia de los Triumphos,* p. 360.

tained from a tree which grew extensively in those regions to a height of about ten to twelve feet and was said to resemble the olive. To touch it was dangerous, and the superstitious Indians even claimed that it was deadly to sleep in its shade. The juice of the tree was a milk-like liquid and was very poisonous. The Indians would dip their arrow-heads in the sap, and any wound, however small, when touched by the poison, proved fatal within twenty-four hours. Bancroft is of the opinion that the poison was obtained by other means: "Some travelers say that this poison was taken from rattlesnakes and other venomous reptiles, which, by teasing, were incited to strike their fangs into the liver of a . . . deer which was presented to them, after which it was left to putrify, and the arrows being dipped into the poisonous mass, were placed in the sun to dry." Bandelier, however, scoffs at this suggestion.[14] The poisoned arrows of the Sonora Indians caused the Spaniards great anxiety, and they were constantly on the lookout to find a counter-poison. Finally, their efforts were rewarded, for some natives showed them a plant which counteracted the poisonous herb. It was similar to the "moat-weed," and had a yellow flower like the *maxtuerco de Castilla.* The roots of this plant were boiled in water and the solution was applied to the wound. Even this remedy was not always a sure cure, for often the wound never healed. For example, the wound of Pedro de Montoya, who was shot by a poisoned arrow, remained open for twenty years.[15]

The first large native settlement found in the upper Yaqui Valley was Guaralpi. It had about six hundred houses, and near the pueblo were many large fields under

---

[14] Bancroft, *Native Races,* I. 578; Bandelier, *Final Report,* I. 77.

[15] A. G. I., 1-3-20/11, Información rescivida sobre la que dió el gobernador Francisco de Ybarra de los servicios en la SS. á S. M. y de su calidad y mérito pa. suppca. á S. M. q. remuneraje de los q. de haga mrds., México, 12 de enero de 1573.

irrigation. About a five days' journey beyond Guaralpi, they found another large pueblo with about five hundred houses. It was called Cumupa. Ibarra was now in the land of the Ópatas. "The villages of the Ópatas were small, their houses detached, and only for one family. A slight foundation of cobble-stone supported a framework of posts standing in a thin wall of rough stones and mud and a slanting roof of yucca or palm leaves covered the whole."[16]

From Cumupa the expedition moved with great difficulty to the northeast through some rugged mountains, where several horses and much baggage were lost. The next settled district discovered was a valley called Zaguaripa, inhabited by the Jovas, cognates of the Ópatas.[17] There the Spaniards found the natives plotting to destroy them. Desertion of their guides, the abandonment by the Indians of their pueblos, and the lighting of signal fires, warned the Governor to be on his guard, and, when the Indians killed fourteen of the horses with their poisoned arrows, he knew that a general uprising impended. Messengers sent to Zaguaripa returned with the news that the pueblo was on the verge of war. Since the natives of Zaguaripa could not forget their victory over Coronado's lieutenant, Alcarez, at San Gerónimo so many years before, Ibarra determined to deflate their swollen pride. To assist him in punishing the natives, he chose six soldiers, and set out for the pueblo on horseback.[18]

[16] Bandelier, *Final Report,* I. 58.

[17] To the Jovas "pertenecen los pueblos de San José Teopari, Los Dolores, *Sahuaripa,* donde hay tambien opatas, Ponida, Santo Tomás, Arivetzi, San Mateo Malzura" (Orozco y Berra, *Geografía,* p. 345).

[18] Sahuaripa, located on the Río Aras, an affluent of the Yaqui in eastern Sonora, is designated on some seventeenth century maps (in the Bancroft Collection) as Caguaripa and Saguaripa. It is presumed that they are the same Zaguaripa which was discovered by Ibarra. If Cumpas in northern Sonora is identical with Cumpa, which was discovered by Ibarra, our supposition regarding the location of Zaguaripa is destroyed.

When Ibarra arrived at Zaguaripa, he found that the pueblo, "which was built like a fort," had within it about six hundred warriors, and on the roofs of the houses were assembled the women and children armed with clubs and stones. After considering the situation carefully, he was impressed with the difficulty of attacking, and made peace overtures by means of an interpreter. He was answered by shouts and jeers. Then he ordered the attack. When the Indians discovered that their poisoned arrows had little effect on the Spaniards, because of their armour, they soon lost heart and abandoned their pueblo. So precipitously were they driven from their houses that they were not able to take anything with them. In the attack on Zaguaripa seven Spaniards were able to overcome with little difficulty several hundred Indians.

After his victory, Ibarra took possession of the pueblo and assembled all of his followers within it. To protect the horses, he ordered each soldier to care for two of them. Also, no Negro or Indian servant was to leave the camp without permission. To search for food, and also to reconnoiter the surrounding country he despatched Rodrigo del Río and seven soldiers. In the meantime, the Indians surrounded the pueblo in great numbers and waited for their allies, for all of the natives of that region had entered into their plot.[19] Had their confederates arrived, said Obregón, the investing force would have totaled fifteen thousand men. Carefully laid plans were made by the natives for the attack. They planned to discard their bows and arrows and advance in three groups with lances, battle-axes, and stones. For several nights the attack was delayed until a favorable mo-

---

[19] Regarding the custom of the Ópatas to form confederations, Bandelier (*Final Report*, I. 57-8), says, "The Opatas became geographically and politically divided into a number of small tribes, or village communities, autonomous and often hostile towards one another. On the Río Sonora above, confederacies appear to have been formed."

ment when they could take the Spaniards unawares. Finally they were rewarded, for one morning, at about four o'clock, the sentinels were discovered asleep. At a given signal the Indians started the attack. They were so confident of success that they had provided themselves with cords to bind the prisoners, whom they planned to eat.

Fortunately for the Spaniards, just before the attack Fray Azevedo had arisen to recite matins, and one of the sentinels, was preparing to go on guard. These two aroused the camp just in time to allow the soldiers to seize their arms. The Indians were forced to retire, and thus a serious disaster for Francisco de Ibarra was averted.[20] The Governor prepared against further attack by doubling the guards and placing them on horseback. The Indians began to lose hope and deserted by the hundreds. They then decided to change their plan of procedure: they would let the Spaniards march into the mountains, and waylay them in some narrow pass where it would be impossible to use their horses.

Some time after the battle Rodrigo del Río and the soldiers who had gone with him on the reconnoitering expedition returned to the pueblo. Their return was a great relief to Ibarra, who had feared that they had been killed by the Indians. News of the battle was communicated by signal fires to all the natives for miles about; indeed, in two days' time the news reached Sinaloa, but the natives there did not dare to rebel, because Antonio de Betanco had the situation well in hand.

Since the hostility of the natives did not abate, Ibarra decided to leave Zaguaripa before another attack was made. For two days the explorers marched through a mountainous

---

[20] Betanco's account of the battle was as follows: "All of the Indians of Sonora had joined in a plot, and at four o'clock in the morning they attacked the Spaniards. The latter, however, discharged their guns, and a dozen on horseback charged and repelled the natives and caused them to flee" (A. G. I., 59-4-3, Betanco sobre Francisco de Ibarra).

country until they came to a pueblo of about two hundred houses. Since the houses had been constructed for defensive purposes, the pueblo might be called a fortified village. Protection from enemies, who threatened the Ópatas from the Chihuahua side of the mountains, was the cause of the superior and defensive mode of building. The inhabitants, however, had deserted their houses when the Spaniards appeared. After much persuasion, Fray Azevedo was able to induce them to return to their pueblo, but even then the Spaniards did not trust them, and that night a dozen men kept watch on horseback; to insure that the guards kept awake, Ibarra ordered bells put on the horses. These precautions discouraged the Indians, who had been awaiting a favorable opportunity to launch another attack, and they abandoned their plan.

The land inhabited by the sedentary Indians of Sonora and their allies did not extend farther to the east of the last-mentioned pueblo. The explorers now crossed the final range of mountains and descended to the plains inhabited by Indians who were said to be bitter enemies of the Ópatas.[21] These, called Querechos by Obregón, were nomadic, plains Indians, classified by Bandelier as belonging to the Suma nation. He divides them geographically into two branches, one part near the El Paso region; the other in a valley in which the ruins of Casas Grandes are situated. The Sumas, who roamed near the Río Grande, were, he says, very similar to the Apaches; they lived in frail abodes, their dress was very scant, and they lived entirely by the chase. The Sumas of the Casas Grandes, on the other hand, were a more docile and sedate stock, and they had more stable settlements. "How far they had been agricultural

---

[21] "I cannot overlook here the very positive statements of the Ópatas of eastern Sonora that the people living at Casas Grandes were always their bitter enemies" (Bandelier, *Final Report*, I. 91).

already (in the seventeenth century)," Bandelier continues, "it is impossible to determine."[22] According to Obregón, however, the habitations of the Indians of Casas Grandes were either caves or straw huts, and he states specifically that they were not agricultural.

After leaving Zaguaripa, Ibarra probably crossed the sierras to the east and emerged on the plains near the ruined pueblo of Paquimé, or Casas Grandes, in northwestern Chihuahua. Though none of the evidence at hand states directly that he turned to the eastward, a careful examination of the return route tends to verify this conjecture. On the other hand, the explorers may well have followed one of the northern affluents of the Yaqui River and so have reached the deserted pueblos of the Gila Valley. But that would have carried them much farther than they appear to have gone. On the second day after reaching the plains, they were met by a great number of the Querechos, who had heard of their arrival and had come to welcome them. They received the Spaniards with great enthusiasm. They sang and danced about the camp, employing the customary ceremonials when worshipping the sun, for they probably regarded the Christians as supernatural beings. In answer to queries put to them, they said that the settlement of Cíbola was farther to the north. They also said that, many years before, some Spaniards had visited that region and performed wonderful miracles and cures. Without doubt they referred to Cabeza de Vaca and his companions. It is significant that none of the Indians spoke about Coronado, and thus we are to infer that Coronado did not pass through that region and that the pueblos visited by Ibarra were probably not those of the Gila region.

[22] *Ibid.*, p. 90.

Paquimé was located on a river which flowed in a northerly direction. This stream, now known as the Casas Grandes River, empties into an inland basin, the Laguna de Guzmán, thus forming a separate drainage system between the Río Grande in the east and the Yaqui in the west. The pueblo, as described by Obregón, was one of great size and had many terraced houses six and seven stories in height. Most of the houses, however, were in ruins, after the rains, and the wooden supports had rotted away. But traces still remained of painted walls, flagged paving, and beautiful courts. Traces were also found of metals which had been smelted. Below some of the houses were estufas or dugouts, where the Indian kept warm in the winter, for it snowed a great deal in that country and was very cold for several months in the year. Remains could be seen of canals which had conducted the pueblo's water supply from the river. In addition to the pueblo, there were other groups of houses scattered along the river banks for a distance of about eight leagues.[23]

A very excellent description of the ruins of Casas Grandes as they appeared in 1884 is to be found in Bandelier's *Final Report*. Interesting and pertinent extracts are presented here:

Half a mile south of the present village (Casas Grandes) are the famous ruins from which the name Casas Grandes, or Great Houses, derives its origin. They lie on the southern extremity of a terrace which rises above the river bottom, and is traversed by several small gulches running in the main from northwest to southeast. . . . Besides being quite extensive for Southwestern ruins, they are also compact, so that the population, if we take into consideration the fact that the houses were several stories high, may have amounted to three or four thousand souls. In that case it would have been by far the largest Indian pueblo in the Southwest, and twice as large as the most populous village known to have existed farther north. . . . The site is well selected, commanding an

[23] A. G. I., 59-4-3, Betanco sobre Francisco de Ibarra; A. G. I., 1-3-20/11, Francisco de Ybarra, Informacion de méritos; A. G. I., 1-1-3/22, Obregón, Crónica.

extensive view. The ground is gravelly, as the terraces generally are, and ledges of rock protude here and there. The cultivable bottom land commences at the foot of the terrace which is only a few feet above it. A part at least of the pueblo, therefore, was built on ground unfit for cultivation, but adjacent to such as was tillable, and not farther from the river than a quarter of a mile. No enemy could approach Casas Grandes in the daytime without being discovered.

The walls exposed in the ruins are in places two or sometimes three stories high, and their thickness varies between 0.40m. (16 inches) and 1.2m. (4 feet). . . . Most of the rooms are large, with some exceptions, and the door-ways are of quite a good size. The air-holes and apertures for light deserve the name of windows; they are round, rectangular, and elliptical or oval. . . . The lintels of the doors as well as of the windows were of wood, and mostly 0.15m. (6 inches) thick. They seemed, from the impressions which were left, to have consisted of flat, or half-round pieces, but I could not determine the kind of timber used. Of the roofing or ceiling I saw but one specimen. Round beams from 0.13 to 0.17m. in diameter (5 to 7 inches), supported a superstructure of octilla poles and earth. The floors were of earth, and the walls were covered in places with a thin coating of whitewash, and I noticed traces of fire on them.

A wall with two superposed grooves, the upper clearly the groove of the ceiling, seems to indicate a flight of steps; but I could not determine positively whether it was a staircase or not. If it was, the inhabitants in Casas Grandes had made quite an important stride in architectural progress. Of ladders I saw no trace.

The question of the form of these edifices, whether they were like the pueblos of the north, with retreating terraces, or with a central tower, as Casa Grande, or massive blocks with straight walls to the top, is a difficult one to determine. The conical shape of the mounds would lead to the inference that the central parts were higher than the outer ones; on the other hand, there are outer walls still standing which are three stories in height. . . . The ruins of Casas Grandes stand close together, even appearing to be crowded in a small compass. Alleys, rather than streets, separate the various mounds; and although the width of these passages must have been greater when the edifices were intact, there is nowhere, as far as I was able to detect, any square of public yard of considerable extent.[24]

The only inhabitants seen by Ibarra were some wild, nomadic Querechos, who, instead of living in the houses, lived in caves and straw huts. They did not till the soil, but lived solely by hunting. The Spaniards asked them

[24] Bandelier, *Final Report,* II. 544-547.

about the ancient residents of Paquimé. They replied by signs, that, because of wars with their enemies, that people had moved farther north, about a six days' journey down the river. They also said that about four days to the west were other large houses, inhabited by people who wore clothes and practiced agriculture. It was most unfortunate that Ibarra had no interpreters who could intelligently question the Querechos, for he had no reason to know that he was so close to the New Mexican pueblos. Men who later went to New Mexico with Espejo (1582) declared that Ibarra had actually approached within a two days' journey of the first of the pueblos of New Mexico. Francisco de Ibarra, therefore, did not enter the territorial limits of the United States. Rodrigo del Río and Obregón explored down the Casas Grandes River for some distance, but did not find any inhabited settlements. They were inclined to disbelieve the stories of the Querechos and so gave up their attempt and returned to Paquimé.

The soldiers had endured the difficulties and dangers of crossing the mountains of Sonora because of their eagerness to find great settlements and untold riches. But when their high hopes had been dissipated, signs of unrest began to appear, and many would have deserted and returned to Sinaloa but for the dangers of returning by way of Sonora. Because of the unrest and actual plotting among the soldiers, as well as because of the scarcity of food and clothing, Ibarra called a council of war to decide on the best plan of action. A few, among them Rodrigo del Río, Baltasar de Obregón, Salvador Ponce, Bartolomé de Arriola, and Fray Pablo de Azevedo, expressed an earnest desire to continue farther to the north. Rodrigo del Río, Hernando de Tovar, Cristóbal de Osorio, and Baltasar de Obregón volunteered to return to Sinaloa for reënforcements and supplies, if Ibarra and the rest of his men would await them at Paquimé.

But the remainder of the soldiers insisted that they should all return to San Juan, and then establish a villa on the Río Yaqui. Since the latter opinion prevailed by but one vote, the Governor decided much against his will to order the return. "So, because of fear and cowardice," declared Obregón, "they lost the honor and profit of discovering New Mexico which went to others at an expenditure of much less effort."[25]

Because of the poisonous herb of Sonora, Ibarra was persuaded to take a different return route to Sinaloa. It was planned to keep farther to the east on the southward march, but it soon became evident as they progressed that, in endeavoring to avoid danger, they encountered greater hardships. For five days they marched south, keeping to the east of the Sierra Madre. When Ibarra decided that they had marched far enough south, he gave orders to cross the mountains. The advisability of turning west so soon was opposed by Rodrigo del Río and Baltasar de Obregón, and, as later proved to be the case, they were justified in their opposition, for they had not succeeded in avoiding the Indians of Sonora.

The mountains were the most difficult imaginable; they were high and rugged and broken into numerous deep canyons. To increase the difficulty of their predicament, their food supply gave out, and they were finally driven to the extremity of eating roots, wild amaranth, leather-shields, shoes, and horse-flesh. Even the blood of the horses was utilized; it was first dried and then used as food. A certain weed which some of them ate caused temporary insanity. Ibarra himself was a victim of this weed, and one night, after eating some, was restrained with difficulty from throwing himself into the camp-fire. Not only did they lack food,

[25] A. G. I., 1-1-3/22, Obregón, Crónica; *Col. Doc. Inéd.,* XIV. 482-483.

but they had no salt, which was most essential when living practically on meat alone.[26]

After they had marched for about eleven days through the mountains, the expedition came to a large river, probably one of the eastern branches of the Yaqui.[27] Rafts were made to attempt a crossing, but the swift current destroyed them as fast as they were launched. For several days they struggled to manage a crossing, and in the meantime they became weaker and weaker from hunger. Once, when an adventurous soldier tried to swim his horses across, two were drowned in a whirlpool. Many were of the opinion that they would never get out alive and so confessed themselves and prepared for the end. Finally, it was discovered that by attaching ropes to the rafts, a safe crossing could be made. But even after all had crossed the stream, their difficulties did not cease, for, because of the precipitous walls of the canyon, no exit could be discovered, and though they searched for fifty miles up and down the river, they were unsuccessful.

It was finally proposed by Ibarra that they should abandon their horses and excess baggage and follow the stream on foot. But this was opposed on the ground that without their horses they could not protect themselves against the Indians. Then Obregón volunteered to search for a trail. Though he was very weak from hunger, he claims that God gave him strength to climb the mountain and find a way out for his companions. From a high mountain he could recognize far to the south the Sonora Valley. He returned to

[26] A. G. I., 1-1-1/20, Memorial del Lcdo. Juan de Ibarra.

[27] This was not the only river encountered by Ibarra on his return journey, for he says in his información (A. G. I., 1-3-20/11, Información de méritos) that for eight days they marched through the mountains for a distance of about thirty-five leagues, and they crossed *two large rivers*. According to Ibarra's *Relación* (*Col. Doc. Inéd.*, XIV. 482-483), "On their return they had to cross a high, rough mountain range for more than thirty-five leagues, and *some large swollen streams*."

Ibarra with the good news and received as his reward the commendation of the Governor that "he did not expect less from such an able soldier." With the assurance that their hardships were nearly over, the soldiers summoned their reserve strength and followed Obregón. A lone Indian whom they chanced to meet said that Sonora was but a three days' journey away. Next they discovered a little Indian settlement which, fortunately, was well supplied with food. There they remained for a while and rested before continuing to the Río Yaqui and the South Sea.[28]

In passing through Sonora, Ibarra tried to avoid the native settlements, but when the Indians killed some of his horses, he sought an opportunity to avenge his loss. One night he caught the Indians off guard, and punished them severely, but in the fight Pedro de Montoya and Juan Rúiz were wounded by poisoned arrows. As has been noted elsewhere, Montoya's wound never healed. They reached the South Sea probably in the vicinity or slightly to the north of the Bay of Guaymas. That region was known as Huparo or Uparo. It was inhabited by a domestic, peaceful people, who were the enemies of the Yaqui, or, as they were called, Yaquimi.

From Uparo the explorers marched south over more mountains until they came to the pueblos of the Yaquimi located near the mouth of the Yaqui River. They were well received and were given supplies of fish, maize, and calabashes. The Yaquimi, as described by Obregón, were a peaceful, handsome people, who wore their hair down to the waist, but had no clothes, and covered their nakedness with leaves. They were very numerous, their number being estimated at over fifteen thousand.

[28] According to Betanco they were thirteen days in crossing the mountains.

The economic possibilities of the country which he had just explored seemed to impress the Governor of Nueva Vizcaya, for he sounded the bay at the mouth of the Yaqui River to determine its possibilities as a port. The estuary was found to be sufficiently deep to accommodate sea-going vessels and was thought by the Governor to be suitable as a port of entry for all of that northwestern region. But Paquimé, which by way of the Yaqui River was about three hundred miles from the sea, was inaccessible from the west, owing to the mounains and the danger of the poisonous herb of Sonora. The interior route by way of Santa Bárbara was thought to be the most desirable approach to northern Chihuahua.[29]

The possibilities of Yaquimi so impressed Ibarra that he expressed a desire to found a town in that province. Ten soldiers were sent to Sinaloa to request of the maestro de campo sufficient soldiers and supplies for the new settlement. Betanco replied that he could not spare the men and begged the Governor to return immediately, for he feared that trouble was brewing among the Spanish settlers of San Juan because of Ibarra's refusal to grant repartimientos. He therefore decided to return to Sinaloa, but promised the Indians of Yaquimi, who were most reluctant to see him leave, that he would return very soon. A great number of the natives accompanied him as far as the Río Mayo, where they killed and robbed the Mayos. It was impossible for Ibarra to reconcile the Yaqui and the Mayos, for they had been enemies from time immemorial. Three days after leaving the Río Mayo, the explorers arrived in Sinaloa.

[29] In Obregón's *Chronicle* is to be found the following table of distances:

Río de Sinaloa—60 leagues from Guayabas, port of San Miguel de Culiacán.
Río de Yaqui—40 leagues from Sinaloa.
Valles de Señora—30 leagues from Yaquimi and 40 leagues from the sea.
Paquimé—30 to 40 leagues from Valles de Señora.

A great celebration was held by the Spanish settlers and the natives of San Juan in honor of the safe return of their Governor. Their joy was intensified because they had heard that the expedition had been lost in the battle of Zaguaripa. Quite to the contrary, not a single Spaniard was lost on the journey. On their expedition to Paquimé they had been absent about seven months.[30] As has been noted elsewhere, a determination of the route of the entrada, and the northernmost point reached, must be left largely to conjecture. Evidence seems to support the theory that Paquimé was really the Casas Grandes of northwestern Chihuahua, and that supposition is accepted by the present writer. Several sources state that the explorers went two hundred leagues north of Sinaloa and about three hundred leagues north of Chiametla, but those distances, quite obviously, would have carried them far into the New Mexican pueblo region, whereas it is certain that *Ibarra did not see any of the Pueblo Indians*.[31] Great discrepancies in estimating distances were quite possible because of the difficult nature of the territory traversed.

Soon after his return to Sinaloa, the Governor rewarded his men for their faithful services by granting them encomiendas. As a preliminary step, he ordered Antonio de Betanco to make a thorough investigation of the province and to take a census of the inhabitants. The first encomienda was granted to Betanco. The remainder of the men were granted pueblos according to their merits and services. More settlers arrived from Culiacán, and those soldiers who did not care to remain in Sinaloa were allowed to depart.

[30] A. G. I., 1-3-20/11, Francisco de Ybarra, Información de méritos.
[31] *Ibid.;* A. G. I., 59-4-3, Betanco sobre Francisco de Ibarra; A. G. I., 1-1-1/20, Memorial de Lcdo. Juan de Ybarra; *Col. Doc. Inéd.,* XIV. 481-482. In the last two of the preceding sources it is stated that Ibarra discovered, about three hundred leagues to the north of Chiametla, great settlements with inhabitants who wore clothes of cotton cloth, and who irrigated their fields. Francisco de Ibarra saw remains of such habitations, but he *did not see* the inhabitants.

The wide vision of Francisco de Ibarra, as well as his ambitious zeal to extend to the utmost the frontiers of Nueva Vizcaya, was evidenced by the fact that he actually contemplated exploration by sea. He hoped "with the aid of God and His Majesty, and his health permitting, to explore the Gulf of California, and settle the peninsula[32] which he hoped possessed great riches. Also, up the coast from Chiametla and in the islands of Las Marías fronting Chiametla, was a great supply of pearls which he intended to fish."[33] Antonio de Betanco, in writing to the king, said that Ibarra hoped to discover the "English Strait," which was thought to be located at about the forty-fifth degree of latitude, for it was the belief of many Spaniards that the English had knowledge of this strait which connected the two oceans.[34] Ibarra undertook the construction of two ships at Sinaloa, but progress was slow, owing to his illness and lack of funds. The ships, still uncompleted, were destroyed when the natives of Sinaloa revolted in 1569.[35]

Betanco realized the utter impossibility of the enterprise ever being undertaken by Francisco de Ibarra, and petitioned the king asking that he be granted a commission to embark on the expedition. His request was refused, probably because he asked for assistance from the royal treasury. In his petition to the Royal Council, Betanco gave a complete account of Ibarra's trip to Paquimé. The petition was signed in Mexico, on June 5, 1566, for he had been allowed to return to Mexico immediately after the Governor's return from Paquimé in order to bring his family to San Juan.[36]

[32] It is to be noted that at this time California was thought to be a peninsula.

[33] A. G. I., 1-1-1/20, Memorial del Lcdo. Juan de Ybarra.

[34] A. G. I., 59-4-3, Betanco sobre Francisco de Ibarra.

[35] Ibid.; A. G. I., 1-1-1/20, Memorial del Lcdo. Juan de Ybarra.

[36] Betanco had married a daughter of Gutierrez de Badajoz, one of the captains in the conquest of Mexico (A. G. I., 59-4-3, Betanco sobre Francisco de Ibarra).

The date of the petition is significant, because it is indubitable evidence that Francisco de Ibarra returned from Paquimé *prior* to June, 1566. Since he spent seven months on the expedition, it shows that he left Sinaloa for the far north in the fall of 1565.[37]

Some time after Ibarra's return to Sinaloa, news came to him of the Cortés-Ávila conspiracy. He immediately sent two soldiers to the audiencias of Nueva Galicia and Mexico, offering to render any assistance they might require. While waiting for an answer, he assembled all of his available men and marched to Chiametla. At that place news was received from Nueva Galicia that the rebellion had been put down and the culprits jailed and that all was quiet in Mexico.[38]

After the final departure of its Governor, the prosperity of San Juan de Sinaloa was short-lived. The accumulated grievances of five years of Spanish oppression finally culminated in the determination of the natives to expel their oppressors from their lands.[39] At first they did not dare to do more than kill horses and cattle and burn houses that were somewhat removed from the villa. As the spirit of the Indians became more unruly, and their destructive practices increased, many of the Spaniards who had no encomiendas, mines, or other interests to hold them in Sinaloa deserted the province and went to Culiacán and Chiametla. In a short time so few remained in San Juan that they were unable to protect themselves against the natives when the revolt finally

[37] Bolton and Marshall (*Colonization of North America,* p. 56) have accepted Obregón's erroneous date, June, 1567, as the time when Ibarra started for Paquimé.

[38] A. G. I., 1-1-3/22, Obregón, Crónica; A. G. I., 1-1-1/20, Memorial del Lcdo. Juan de Ybarra. The revolt was checked by the execution of the Ávila brothers, August 3, 1566.

[39] The date of the rebellion is not positive, though there is much reason to believe that it occurred about 1569. According to Obregón it broke out five years after the founding of San Juan. Mota Padilla says that the Indians of Sinaloa revolted when Ibarra went to Nombre de Diós in 1569 to safeguard his interests in that place.

occurred. The two friars, Azevedo and Herrera, and several Spaniards were killed.[40] A few of the settlers managed to escape and retired southward to the Río Petatlán, where a new settlement was founded called San Felipe y Santiago.

Francisco de Ibarra was unable to go to the assistance of Sinaloa, for at that time, 1569, he had gone with about two hundred men to defend his jurisdiction over Nombre de Diós.[41] A certain Diego de Guzmán was ordered by Ibarra to go to Sinaloa to punish the natives. He recruited about fifty soldiers in Chiametla and Culiacán and went to Sinaloa, where he found the native settlements deserted; and, since the Indians refused to come out of their hiding places, he could do nothing with them.[42] The bodies of the friars were recovered and were taken to Culiacán for burial. The religious historians piously chronicle that Azevedo's body was miraculously preserved, shrunken to the size of a child of three years—a proof of his innocence. Ribas' version of the revolt differs in some particulars from the above. He relates that a company of vecinos of Sinaloa went to the Suaqui nation for maize and were kindly received. Then, without warning, the Indians attacked and killed all but one. When the inhabitants of San Juan received the news, they withdrew into their fort and sent word to Culiacán. The cabildo of Culiacán immediately sent twenty-four men under Gaspar Osorio to aid Sinaloa. Osorio and his followers marched with all haste to the Río Petatlán. A little beyond the river they met the survivors of Carapoa (San Juan)

[40] Obregón mentions but one Spaniard as being killed; nothing is said about the murder of the padres.

[41] Mota Padilla, *Nueva Galicia,* p. 208. According to Juan de Ibarra (A. G. I., 1-1-1/20, Memorial del Lcdo. Juan de Ybarra) Francisco de Ibarra was unable to render assistance because of his infirmities, and because of the expense which would be entailed in outfitting an expedition.

[42] Guzmán learned that the revolt of the natives had been caused by the harsh tactics of a mulatto who collected tribute from the natives (Riva Palacio, *México á través de los siglos,* II. 365).

bound for Culiacán. Osorio finally persuaded them not to abandon the province, but to settle a villa on the Petatlán where the natives were more peaceful and where they would be nearer Culiacán.[43]

The vicissitudes of Sinaloa to the end of the century can be noted briefly. For many years after the revolt, the region north of the Sinaloa River was abandoned to the savages. It was not until 1583, under the governorship of Diego de Ibarra,[44] that the Spaniards again undertook the conquest of Sinaloa. At that time Pedro de Montoya was given authority to make a new entrada. He marched north from Culiacán with about thirty-five men. At first the Suaqui were peaceful and did not interfere with the settlement of San Felipe y Santiago, which was relocated a half league above the old settlement of San Juan. But later, after some of the settlers had returned to Culiacán, they found an opportunity to massacre Montoya and his men.[45]

The survivors of Montoya's expedition were intent on deserting Sinaloa, when they were met at the Río Petatlán by Juan López de Quijada bearing a commission from the new governor of Nueva Vizcaya, Hernando de Bazan, as the lieutenant-governor of Sinaloa. Accordingly, San Felipe was reëstablished on the Sinaloa. In April, 1585, Bazan and one hundred Spaniards arrived in Sinaloa. Shortly thereafter he sent Captain Gonzalo Martín and eighteen men into the mountains to locate the natives. The Indians were found in a well protected *peñol,* and, in the fight which ensued they killed all but two of the Spaniards.[46]

When Bazan heard of the death of his lieutenant and his men, he tried by every means possible to bring on a general

---

[43] Ribas, *Historia de los Triumphos,* pp. 28-29.
[44] Not Trejo, as stated by Bancroft (*North Mexican States and Texas,* I. 113).
[45] A. G. I., 67-1-17, Carta de Diego de Ibarra al Rey, México, 15 de octubre de 1583.
[46] Ribas, *Historia de los Triumphos,* p. 30.

battle with the savages, but without success. He then went as far north as the Río Mayo, where the natives were friendly and hospitable, but he returned the kindness of the Mayos with treachery, for on the pretext that they were accomplices of the Suaqui, he seized several and put them in chains. The captives were sent to Mexico, but Viceroy Villamanrique intervened on their behalf and ordered their release. Bazan's entrada came to naught; he left Sinaloa and appointed Melchior Tellez as comandante at San Felipe. Pedro Tovar succeeded Tellez, but soon he and other settlers deserted the villa, and finally only five remained. One of these, Bartolomé Mondragon, was appointed comandante of Sinaloa in 1589. Though they were weak in numbers, the five vecinos of San Felipe were not lacking in zeal, and they are said to have made many trips into the northern interior in search of mines. Had it not been for them, all of the advantages gained by Francisco de Ibarra in Sinaloa would have been lost.

Their single-handed efforts in withstanding the natives were finally rewarded, for, in 1595, Alonso Díaz and twenty-five men were sent from Durango by the Governor to build a fort at San Felipe. From that time on the inhabitants of San Felipe enjoyed the protection of a presidio. It appears also that many settlers came to San Felipe at about this time. According to the statements of the Jesuit annalists, Ribas and Alégre, eight permanent churches and sixty temporary churches were erected by their order in Sinaloa in the last decade of the sixteenth century. The Jesuit fathers are also credited with six thousand converts in the years 1591 to 1597.

CHAPTER VII

In the mountains to the east of Chiametla was located the native province of Guazamota. The inhabitants of that province, a very warlike and degenerate lot, were accustomed to raid the settlements of northern Zacatecas and then flee to their mountain retreats, where it was almost impossible to pursue them. Since Francisco de Ibarra had a large force of well-equipped men under his command in Chiametla, which he had organized to take to Mexico to help put down the Cortés-Ávila revolt, he decided to employ it in the subjugation of Guazamota. The principal object of the expedition, however, was the lure of reported rich mines in that province.

From Chiametla he marched into the mountains of Guazamota east of the Río San Pedro in southern Durango. The Indians were hunted down and pacified without much difficulty. Then the Spaniards turned their attention to prospecting for the anticipated rich mineral deposits, but, although they discovered a few mines, the ore was too low-grade to be worked with profit. And, since Guazamota was mountainous and unsuitable for cultivation or for grazing, Ibarra was forced, after spending six months in the province, to abandon it.[1]

From Guazamota the Governor returned to Durango after an absence of three years. One of his first acts after his return was to undertake the settlement of the lands north of Guadiana, which he explored in 1563-1564. Because of failing health Francisco was not able to undertake this task

[1] A. G. I., 1-1-1/20, Memorial del Lcdo. Juan de Ybarra; A. G. I. 1-3-20/11, Francisco de Ybarra, Información de méritos.

personally, and he commissioned Rodrigo del Río to act for him. After he had been equipped by the Governor with everything necessary for the undertaking, Rodrigo left Durango in 1567 and first went to Indé.[2] There he made a settlement and began to work the mines, which proved to be extremely productive. The silver mines of Indé contributed materially to the royal revenues from Nueva Vizcaya; in fact, the oidores of Nueva Galicia complained that it was not until after the mines of Indé were exploited that the crown received any return whatsoever from Nueva Vizcaya.[3] The production of the mines, however, was greatly hampered by the constant warfare which was waged against the savage Tepehuanes who infested that region. These campaigns proved to be a drain, not only on the resources, but also on the man-power of the settlement, so that by 1573 it was reduced to but ten inhabitants. The Governor attempted to save the mines from desertion, but without avail, for in

[2] This date is substantially correct, for Ibarra himself (A .G. I., 1-3-20/11, Francisco de Ybarra, Información de méritos) says that Rodrigo del Río was sent to Indé three years after the entrada of 1563. The interrogatorio in the same información states that by May, 1570, the mines of Indé had been settled three years; that is, since 1567. Pedro Vituno testified (ibid.), "About three years after what was related above (i.e., the entrada of 1563) the governor commanded Rodrigo del Río, this witness, and other soldiers to settle the mines of Indé which had been discovered on the first entrada. The mines of Indé have now been settled more than two and a half years." Gonzolo Rodríquez, another soldier who accompanied del Río to Indé, testified that the date of the settlement was three years prior to the date of the información. Since these witnesses actually accompanied Rodrigo del Río, their evidence should be more trustworthy. Ibarra's Relación (Col. Doc. Inéd., XIV. 477) is alone in assigning the date of the settlement of Indé as 1563, "a few days after his return (i.e., May, 1563) Ibarra sent Rodrigo del Rió and some soldiers to the mines of Indé to settle them." This evidence has been accepted by Bancroft, and by Bolton and Marshall (Colonization of North America, p. 56). In a letter to the king, dated December 9, 1567, Antonio Betanco announced his intention to inform the king about recent events which had taken place since he last wrote on June 5, 1566. He then mentioned the discovery and settlement of the rich mines of Indé. It is clear, therefore, that those mines were first worked, and a settlement established, between June, 1566, and December, 1567.

[3] A. G. I., 67-1-18, Diego de Colio al Consejo, 15 de febrero de 1570.

1575 Doctor Orozco reported that the mines of Indé, after having been worked for six years had been abandoned on account of the Indian menace and because of the inefficient administration of those who had been placed in charge of the settlement by Ibarra.[4]

After the founding of a Spanish settlement in Indé and the subjugation of the Indians in the immediate vicinity, Rodrigo del Río, who had been appointed alcalde mayor of Indé, was ordered by the Governor to make settlements farther north in the Conchos Valley. Rodrigo, with men and supplies furnished at the personal expense of the Governor, effected, in the latter part of 1567, the settlement of Santa Bárbara in the San Bartolomé Valley, located seventy-five miles north of Indé on the Río Florido, an affluent of the Conchos. The mines of the Santa Bárbara district proved to be rich in silver, and it was said that the production was limited only by the scarcity of native labor. The Indians who lived immediately to the north of Santa Bárbara belonged to the Conchos tribe, a branch of the Tarahumares, who inhabited a large part of the great plateau north of Durango.[5] The Conchos were in a very low state of development and could not compare with the Jumanos and Passaguates, who lived to the north of them. They did not wear clothes of any sort, nor did they have permanent habitations. They knew nothing about cultivation, but lived on ground mesquite, prickly-pears, calabashes, roots of various sorts,

[4] *Col. Doc. Inéd.,* XIV. 477; XVI. 564-565; A. G. I., 1-1-1/20, Memorial del Lcdo. Juan de Ybarra; A. G. I., 67-1-18, El Obispo de Nueva Galicia al Rey, 23 de diciembre de 1573.

[5] The Conchos "se estiende hasta las orillas del río grande del Norte. Por la parte del septentrional confina con los languneros y al Mediodía tiene algunos pueblos de los tepehuanes y valle de Santa Bárbara" (Alégre, *Historia de Compañia de Jésus,* II. 58). Concerning the Tarahumares, Orozco y Berra (*Geografía,* pp. 318-25) says, "Al Oriente tienen el río de los Conchos y al Poniente la Sinaloa, Sonora y las regiones del Nuevo Mexico, al Norte y al Austro la Nacion de los Tepehuanes." Cf. Bandelier, *Final Report,* I. 94-100, on the Tarahumares and the Tepehuanes.

and wild game. They have been described as a lazy, filthy, quarrelsome, and physically repellent people.[6] During the lifetime of Francisco de Ibarra, Santa Bárbara was the Spanish outpost on the northern frontier.[7]

It has been thought by some that Francisco de Ibarra was the discoverer of the mines of Mazapil and that they were under the jurisdiction of Nueva Vizcaya.[8] But he himself at no time claimed to be the discoverer of Mazapil, and, indeed, it appears that he never explored east of the Río de Nieves. The eastern boundary of Nueva Vizcaya was never defined in Ibarra's lifetime; certainly the frontiers of Spanish settlement did not extend farther to the east than the present boundaries of the state of Durango. The territory to the east of Zacatecas was much less inviting than that to the north and west, and therefore it was to the latter region that Ibarra devoted his attention. The mines of Mazapil were probably discovered in 1568, or a short time before, by some miners from Zacatecas. The audiencia of Nueva Galicia took possession of Mazapil and organized it into an alcaldía mayor.[9]

In November, 1568, Francisco Cano, a lieutenant of the alcalde mayor of Mazapil, explored to the north of Mazapil

[6] J. L. Mecham, "The Second Spanish Expedition to New Mexico," in the *New Mexico Historical Review*, I. 269; also "Antonio de Espejo and His Journey to New Mexico," in the *Southwestern Historical Quarterly*, XXX. 122-123.

[7] *Col. Doc. Inéd.*, XVI. 564-565; Herrera, *Historia General*, I. 35-36; Monumentos de la Dominación Española, MS 2, p. 243, Bancroft Library; A. G. I., 1-3-20/11, Francisco de Ybarra, Información de méritos.

[8] Amador (*Zacatecas*, p. 215) says, "There is some foundation to the belief that Ibarra discovered the mines of Mazapil, for Padre Tello states, 'Cuando Francisco de Ibarra se metió en la Galicia, como es el Matzapil, Saltillo, Guadiana, Tzinaloa, Chiametla y San Sebastián, y todo lo demas'." "Francisco de Ibarra discovered the mines of Conction, Masapíl, Charcos, San Ándres and others," says Obregón.

[9] Amador (*Zacatecas*, p. 21) states that Mazapil was part of the alcaldía mayor of Zacatecas, together with Fresnillo, Sombrerete, Nieves, and Piños.

as far as the Laguna de Parras, called the Laguna de Nuevo
Mexico. He wrote most encouragingly regarding the fertility of the new lands, and, above all, he advocated the occupation of that region because of its proximity to Pánuco on
the Gulf Coast, which would make communication with the
interior much easier and shorter than by way of Mexico.
He reported that three large rivers flowed into the lake,
and two flowed out towards the "North Sea."[10]

Much of the territory which Cano explored had been
visited the year before by Father Pedro de Espinareda, who
went from San Martín to Pánuco preaching to the natives.
Although he learned from the natives that far to the north
there was a great lake and that about the lake were numerous
people who had gold in abundance, with commendable moder-
ation Espinareda opined that the metal must be copper.
It seems, however, that he attempted to reach the lake, but
lost his way and returned to San Martín. From Nombre
de Diós, on January 20, 1567, he wrote an account of his
journey to the oidor Orozco. Like Cano, he recommended
the pacification and occupation of the region between Pánuco
and Zacatecas, for that would open direct communication
from Spain to Nueva Galicia.[11]

The fame of the mines of Mazapil spread so rapidly
that by 1569 over one hundred and fifty Spaniards had
flocked there to seek their fortunes. The Indians of that
region were extremely savage and gave the miners considerable trouble. It was probably because of the Indian menace

[10] *Col. Doc. Inéd.,* XIX. 538; A. G. I., 67-1-18, Audiencia de Nueva
Galicia al Rey, 4 de marzo de 1569; A. G. I., 67-1-18, El Obispo de
Nueva Galicia al Rey, 31 de marzo de 1569; A. G. I., 67-1-18, El
Obispo de Nueva Galicia sobre Francisco Cano y las Minas de Masapil,
17 de diciembre de 1568.

[11] A. G. I., 67-1-18, Lcdo. Orozco al Rey, Guadalajara, 4 de marzo
de 1567.

that the Spanish population of Mazapil decreased to thirty in 1573.[12]

After his expedition to Guazamota, Francisco de Ibarra devoted the remainder of his life, insofar as his health would permit, to the administration of his province, and in particular to the exploitation of the mines he had helped to discover. Availing himself of his right to bring into his government all settlements that were not provided with a church and a missionary, he despoiled many encomenderos and seized their holdings.[13] On his expeditions, he invariably followed the subjugation of a province or a district by granting encomiendas to his followers. Since Indian labor was so essential to the working of the mines and the cultivation of the fields, the control of encomiendas was jealously guarded. Ibarra's interference in Culiacán, Sinaloa, and Chiametla resulted in the confiscation and repartitioning of encomiendas, and it is not a matter of surprise that the officials of Nueva Galicia protested vigorously. The despoiling of encomenderos, quite as much as the diverting of royal revenues, turned them against the Governor of Nueva Vizcaya. Though it is perfectly true that Francisco de Ibarra repartitioned lands and natives in Culiacán, Sinaloa, and Chiametla where encomiendas had already been granted, his acts were not illegal. In Culiacán, according to Obregón, although Mota Padilla holds an opposite view, Ibarra merely assisted Pedro de Tovar in reconquering his rebellious natives who were then partitioned *among the inhabitants of Culiacán*. In Sinaloa, and in Chiametla, encomiendas had been granted as far back as the time of Nuño de Guzmán, but most of these had been deserted; the natives had relapsed into barbarism, and the land had fallen into disuse. To

[12] A. G. I., 67-1-18, Audiencia de Nueva Galicia al Rey, 4 de marzo de 1569; A. G. I., 67-1-18, El Obispo de Nueva Galicia al Rey, 23 de diciembre de 1573.

[13] Bancroft, *Mexico*, II. 598.

Francisco de Ibarra, who reconquered these lands, belonged the spoils of the victor. The oidor Alarcón accused Ibarra, when partitioning lands, of neglecting to set aside any for the royal service. Also, he contended that, when the conquistador invaded Chiametla, he partitioned lands which in prior times had been set aside as royal domain.[14] These were errors into which the Governor might easily have fallen; also, he might as easily have rectified them by reassigning royal lands. But concerning this point no evidence is at hand. Alarcón also accused Ibarra of having interfered with the encomiendas of San Martín.

The audiencia of Nueva Galicia never looked with favor upon the new government of Nueva Vizcaya, but seized every opportunity to challenge Francisco de Ibarra's jurisdiction, for it believed that it had been defrauded of territories rightfully belonging to it by virtue of original discovery.[15] This clash of interests occurred even prior to the granting of Ibarra's commission. When Doctor Morones heard that Viceroy Velasco had been given royal permission to undertake the conquest of Copalá, he protested against the annexation of Copalá to Mexico. His argument was that Copalá was much nearer Compostela and that it would be more convenient to administer that province from Nueva Galicia than it would be from Mexico.[16] But his protests were futile, for, according to the terms of the commission granted Francisco de Ibarra in 1562, he was created governor and captain-general of *uninhabited* lands extending be-

[14] A. G. I., 67-1-18, Doctor Alarcón á su Magestad, 10 de abril de 1571.

[15] In 1570 the authority of the audiencia of Nueva Galicia extended over Compostela, La Purificación, and Culiacán on the South Sea; and, in the interior, over Guadalajara, Jérez de la Frontera, Santa María de los Lagos, Zacatecas, San Martín, Sombrerete, La Nieves, Los Ranchos, Chalchihuites, Aviño, Santiago, Fresnillo, Mazapil, Jocotlán, Guaxacatlan, Añalco, Guachinango, and Espiritu Santo.

[16] A. G. I., 67-1-18, Morones al Rey, Compostela, 8 de octubre de 1559.

yond Aviño and San Martín, and in matters of superior control he was subjected to the audiencia of Mexico. This im-
plied, of course, that judicial appeals from Nueva Vizcaya
were to go to Mexico for final decision. Royal tribute, also,
was to be taken direct to Mexico. The oidores of Nueva
Galicia took immediate affront to this provision and cited
certain laws enacted by Charles V, made for the good government of the Indies, which provided that appeals from
governors should go to the nearest audiencia. There was no
question but that Ibarra's government was nearer Guadalajara than it was to Mexico; in fact, communication between
Nueva Vizcaya and Mexico was maintained by way of
Guadalajara. The audiencia of Nueva Galicia sent notice
to Ibarra reminding him of the law on appeals, but he
declared that he did not intend to submit to Guadalajara.
Nor was the audiencia of Mexico willing to acknowledge the
rights of the audiencia of Nueva Galicia. The latter audiencia was later constrained to petition the king to issue a
cédula stating that his law on this matter was to be obeyed.[17]
This, they said, was particularly desirable, because the great
distance to Mexico prevented litigants from presenting their
cases, and thus they had to forego justice. Also, Nueva
Vizcaya was declared to be a menace to good government in
Nueva Galicia because the major portion of the population
of Nueva Vizcaya was declared to be made up of criminals
and fugitives from justice. Among these they enumerated
debtors, married men who had escaped to avoid being sent
back to Spain to their wives, and foreigners who were trying
to avoid being deported.[18]

[17] The audiencia wrote two letters concerning this matter, one dated
January 31, 1563, and the other, April 18, 1563. Both letters were written
in Guadalajara and were signed by Oseguera, Morones, and Alarcón
(A. G. I., 67-1-18, Audiencia de Nueva Galicia al Rey, 18 de abril de
1563).

[18] Colio (A. G. I., 67-1-18, Diego de Colio al Consejo) mentions
Martín López de Ibarra, royal treasurer of Nueva Vizcaya, and Bar-

Ibarra and his officials were even accused of defrauding the royal treasury. He was charged with maintaining three royal treasury officials at exorbitant salaries; and it was not until after the settlement of Indé and Santa Bárbara that he began to pay the royal tribute of one-twentieth. But even then salaries of the royal officials for the prior four years were deducted from the king's tribute, and nothing remained for the treasury. The fact that the mines of Nueva Vizcaya paid a tribute of but one-twentieth, whereas those of Nueva Galicia paid one-tenth, was protested by the oidores of Nueva Galicia as being unfair. They cited as an example of great injustice in this connection the fact that Culiacán, a great distance beyond Chiametla, paid one-tenth, whereas Chiametla paid but one-twentieth. Because of the discrimination in favor of Nueva Vizcaya in the matter of tribute, it was a common practice for the settlements which properly belonged to Nueva Galicia to transfer their allegiance to Nueva Vizcaya and pay their tributes through the latter government. For example, the mines of San Lucas and San Buena Ventura near Durango, which originally belonged to Nueva Galicia, were occupied by Francisco de Ibarra, and their silver returns were thus cut from one-tenth to one-twentieth, greatly to the prejudice of the royal treasury. The mines of Aviño, which belonged to the jurisdiction of Nueva Galicia, arbitrarily transferred their allegiance to Ibarra's government. Such "evil tendencies," claimed the officials of Nueva Galicia, were prevalent all along the frontier and should be curbed.

tolomé de Arriola, royal accountant, as men who had wives in Spain. The oidor Contreras (A. G. I., 66-5-14, Averiguaciones de Contreras, 1570) mentions by name three murderers whom Ibarra harbored without punishment. Cf. A. G. I., 67-1-18, Alarcón á S. M., 10 de abril de 1571; A. G. I., 67-1-18, Audiencia de Nueva Galicia al Rey, 4 de marzo de 1569; A. G. I., 66-5-14, Averiguaciones hechas por el Ldo. Contreras y Quebara sobre lo tocante de la visita del real consejo de Indias, 1569.

They then suggested certain remedial measures which should be adopted if order was to be restored.

In the first place, since the population of Nueva Vizcaya was so small, they suggested that that province be placed under the jurisdiction of Nueva Galicia. Ibarra and his officials should be dismissed and their places taken by alcaldes mayores appointed by Nueva Galicia. In the event that the above suggestions were not adopted, they pleaded that at least all appeals from Nueva Vizcaya should go to their audiencia instead of to Mexico. They asked also that royal tributes be paid through the treasury officials at Zacatecas, which would do away with "the customary fraudulent practices in Durango," and dispense with the high salaried officials.[19]

The officials of Nueva Galicia received a gentle rebuff from Viceroy Falces, when, on May 31, 1567, he confirmed Ibarra's commission as governor of Nueva Vizcaya and re-asserted the authority of the audiencia of Mexico over Nueva Vizcaya in the matter of appeals. It is to be noted in particular that the conquest of Chiametla by Francisco de Ibarra was recognized by the viceroy as a real service to God and to the king. In view of the fact that Ibarra had performed signal service for the crown at his own expense, even though in doing so he may have trespassed his territorial jurisdiction, and, since he was really working for the advancement of the royal interests, the viceroy felt that his acts should be condoned.[20]

[19] A. G. I., 67-1-18, Alarcón á S. M., 10 de abril de 1571; A. G. I., 67-1-18, Diego de Colio al Consejo; A. G. I., 66-5-14, Averiguaciones de Contreras, 1570.

[20] A. G. I., 58-3-8, El traslado de la provisión que el señor marques de falces visorey dió á francisco de Ybarra en que parece confirmió la que le avia dado don Luys de Velasco, México, 31 de mayo de 1567; A. G. I., 67-1-18, Audiencia de Nueva Galicia al Rey, 10 de septiembre de 1567.

Falces' successor, Martín Enríquez, had a different opinion regarding appeals from Nueva Vizcaya. In reply to an order from Madrid, August 10, 1572, that the viceroy make a report regarding the matter of appeals from Nueva Vizcaya, with complete information regarding distances, advantages on either side, and the viceroy's own opinion regarding the best course to be adopted, he replied on March 19, 1573, that, since Nueva Galicia was nearer, and since the cost would be less, it was his opinion that the king should order appeals sent to Nueva Galicia instead of to the audiencia of Mexico.[21] The Royal Council of the Indies acted immediately upon the viceroy's suggestion, and a cédula was issued on May 26, 1573, which declared that all appeals from Nueva Vizcaya should be made to and through the audiencia of Nueva Galicia. The audiencia of Mexico was ordered not to receive appeals from Nueva Vizcaya. This cédula was supplemented by another, dated February 18, 1574, which ordered appeals sanctioned by the governor and other justices of Colima and Zacatula to go to the audiencia of Nueva Galicia and to no other place for final adjudication. The viceroy and oidores of Mexico protested this decision and presented reasons why it should be rescinded. They contended that the trade carried through Colima and Zacatula, which were ports on the South Sea, was destined ultimately for Mexico, the commercial center. Mexico should therefore decide matters relative to the commerce of those places. Regarding appeals from Nueva Vizcaya, the viceroy made the interesting remark that it might be convenient some time in the future to move the audiencia of Guadalajara to Nueva Vizcaya, or to erect a new audiencia.[22]

[21] A. G. I., 58-5-9, Enríquez al Rey, 19 de marzo de 1573.
[22] A. G. I., 58-5-9, El Virrey y Audiencia de Mexico, 31 de octubre de 1576; A. G. I., 87-6-3, El Rey al Virrey Enríquez, 27 de octubre de 1571.

Measures to prevent further defrauding of the royal treasury were also adopted by the Royal Council. On October 27, 1571, it declared that no salaries of provincial officials should be paid from the royal treasury, but only from tributes, and if there were no tributes, there could be no salaries. Henceforth the officials of Nueva Vizcaya were ordered not to draw their salaries from the royal chest.[23]

Nombre de Diós constituted a bone of jealous contention between Nueva Galicia and Nueva Vizcaya. Ibarra's attempt to assert his claims over that villa at the time of its official establishment in 1563 was apparently futile, for the audiencia of Nueva Galicia, basing its claim on Colio's act of possession in its name, organized a government for the villa, partitioned lands among its citizens, and declared that appeals from the decisions of the local justices were to be heard in Guadalajara. It is not stated that the officials who had been appointed by Ibarra were displaced. There is reason to believe that Colio merely performed an act of possession and took no part in the naming of officials, since Alonso García, alcalde ordinario appointed by Colio, was also the alcalde ordinario named by Ibarra. The provision regarding appeals had been ordered by Viceroy Velasco, so he must have understood clearly that Nombre de Diós was not included within Ibarra's jurisdiction. Thus for several years appeals from Nombre de Diós went to Nueva Galicia, the elections of local officials were confirmed by the audiencia, and Nombre de Diós was inspected by the alcaldes mayores of San Martín as well as by the oidores of Nueva Galacia. In short, the jurisdiction of the audiencia of Nueva Galicia over Nombre de Diós was complete and absolute. Such was the situation in the middle of 1569, when Francisco de Ibarra entered Nombre de Diós and forcibly assumed con-

[23] A. G. I., 58-5-9, El Virrey y Audiencia de México, 31 de octubre de 1576.

trol of the city. The circumstances which led to his interference have been described by the oidor Alarcón:[24] In
Nombre de Diós there were two officials by the name of
Sosa;[25] one was an alcalde and the other a regidor. One of
them murdered a man who had taken refuge in the Franciscan monastery at that place, and, in hopes of escaping punishment, they connived at transferring the allegiance of their
villa to Nueva Vizcaya so that Francisco de Ibarra might
judge the case. When the audiencia of Nueva Galicia heard
of the defection of Nombre de Diós, it ordered Diego de
Colio, alcalde of San Martín, to regain possession of the
city. Colio went to Nombre de Diós, but, on June 18,
1569, while he was executing the order of the audiencia,
Francisco de Ibarra entered the place with about forty armed
men and forcibly expelled Colio,—so violently, he said, that
one of his fingers was broken! All the officers of the cabildo
were forced to resign and were replaced by officers named
by Ibarra. The audiencia of Nueva Galicia would not
consent weakly to be despoiled. The oidor Juan Bautista de
Orozco went in person to Nombre de Diós and arrested
some of the ring-leaders in the defection of the town. He
learned that most of the residents of Nombre de Diós
were loyal to the audiencia and that the Sosas were the only
ones who wanted to separate. Having reappointed the local
officials, Orozco returned to Guadalajara.[26]

Francisco de Ibarra, on the other hand, was unwilling to
let the matter drop. No sooner had Orozco departed than

[24] A. G. I., 67-1-18, Alarcón á S. M., 10 de abril de 1571.
[25] Riva Palacio (*México á través de los siglos*, II. 365) calls one
Francisco Soto.
[26] Mota Padilla (*Nueva Galicia*, pp. 208-209) has a different version.
He says that Diego de Colio, the alcalde mayor of San Martín, because
of his debts to Francisco de Soto (Sosa), and to other residents of
Nombre de Diós, proposed to transfer the jurisdiction of Nombre de
Diós from San Martín to Nueva Vizcaya. The audiencia of Nueva
Galicia thereupon ordered Juan Bautista de Orozco, oidor and visitador,
who was at that time in Zacatecas, to defend the jurisdiction of the
audiencia.

the Governor reappeared in Nombre de Diós at the head of about one hundred men and reassumed control of the town.[27] The alguacil mayor of Guadalajara, Lope Sánchez de Urrechiga, who attempted to restrain Ibarra, was arrested with several of his soldiers, and all were taken to Durango and imprisoned. After an incarceration of several days, Urrechiga managed to escape. Orozco was now aroused to fury and assembled about one hundred men in San Martín. A conflict seemed imminent and was prevented only by the intervention of Diego de Ibarra, at that time alcalde mayor of Zacatecas, who referred the matter to the viceroy.[28] In the meantime, Viceroy Enríquez and the audiencia of Mexico took possession of Nombre de Diós, "in trust," until it should be decided what was to be its permanent status. An alcalde mayor was appointed by the Viceroy to govern the villa in the interim. As was so customary in colonial administration, official red-tape was unwound very slowly; for years no final decision was reached regarding the disposition of Nombre de Diós. In 1593 the case was brought to the attention of Viceroy Velasco II. He decided that appeals or disputes between the alcalde mayor of Nombre de Diós and his lieutenants and other officials should go to the governor of Nueva Vizcaya for decision. This provision, however, was disregarded, so the villa presented an información to the king asking that the viceroy's provision be enforced. The royal reply, May, 1596, was a request that "the king be informed completely regarding this matter so that he might decide."[29] In 1608 the villa presented an información advocating annexation to Nueva Vizcaya. It claimed that Nom-

[27] Francisco de Ibarra went to Nombre de Diós with two hundred men, says Riva Palacio (*México á través de los siglos,* II. p. 365).

[28] Mota Padilla, *Nueva Galicia,* pp. 308-309; A. G. I., 66-5-14, Averiguaciones de Contreras, 1569.

[29] A. G. I., 139-1-2, El Rey al Virrey Enríquez, 31 de mayo de 1576; A. G. I., 67-1-18, Alarcón á S. M., 10 de abril de 1571; A. G. I., 67-1-3, Información de Nombre de Diós, 1608.

bre de Diós rightfully belonged to Nueva Vizcaya, because it had been discovered by Francisco de Ibarra, and that he had appointed justices for it in accordance with authority vested in him by royal cédulas. Informaciones, petitions, and protests from Nueva Galicia and Nueva Vizcaya, as well as from Nombre de Diós, remained unanswered. Thus the viceroy ruled the disputed place until 1611, when, by royal order, it was restored to Nueva Vizcaya.[30]

The culmination of the bitter criticism to which Francisco de Ibarra was subjected by the oidores of Nueva Galicia was the institution of a residencia or searching inquiry into his official conduct as governor of Nueva Vizcaya. In response to innumerable charges brought against him, a royal cédula was sent to the viceroy on August 10, 1570, commanding him to send some one to Nueva Vizcaya to take the Governor's residencia. Particular charges which the king wanted investigated were: that Ibarra harbored criminals and men of bad character who had fled from justice in Nueva Galicia and elsewhere; that Ibarra exceeded the terms of his commission in entering Chiametla, which had been granted to Doctor Morones; and that he founded towns and organized encomiendas outside his authorized territory. These matters were to be investigated carefully, and if Ibarra and his officials were proved guilty, they were to be permanently deprived of their offices; if proved innocent, they were to be reinstated.[31] Because of the difficulty of selecting a competent person to take the residencia, the viceroy delayed action. On July 1, 1571, another royal cédula was received ordering the viceroy to cause Francisco de Ibarra to appear before the alcaldes del crimen in Mexico so that they might investigate certain "excesses" he had committed against the audiencia of Nueva Galicia in connec-

---

[30] A. G. I., 103-3-1, Registros, 1554-1671.
[31] *Ibid.*

tion with Nombre de Diós. On May 18, 1572, a third royal
cédula was issued demanding that the governor of Nueva
Vizcaya be summoned before the justices of Mexico.[32]

In compliance with the royal wishes, the viceroy ordered
Francisco de Ibarra to appear before the alcaldes del crimen
within fifty days to answer charges preferred by the oidores
of Guadalajara. But once more action was delayed on ac-
court of Francisco's serious illness. The viceroy granted him
four months' grace within which to appear. In the meantime, he ordered an investigation made in Nueva Vizcaya
to determine if Ibarra had really been disobedient to the
audiencia of Nueva Galicia. Constantino Bravo de Lagunas,
a resident of Mexico, and Simon de Coca were sent to
Nueva Vizcaya in December, 1572, to conduct the investigation.[33] When the report of the investigation was received
by the viceroy, he decided that Ibarra was innocent of all the
accusations, and, on the contrary, had actually endeavored
to avoid disagreement with the authorities of Nueva Galacia.
For example, when the oidor Orozco went to Nombre de
Diós to remove the justices appointed by Ibarra, the latter
voluntarily withdrew to avoid trouble. It was the opinion
of Enríquez that the charges should be dropped, and he and
the audiencia of Mexico voted that all accusations should be
dismissed.[34]

Francisco de Ibarra's guilt demands a cautious scrutiny
of the charges made by the oidores of Nueva Galicia,
for they were extremely prejudiced and prone to invent
or magnify grievances real and imaginary. The low

[32] A. G. I., 66-5-14, Audiencia de Guadalajara al Rey, 24 de diciembre
de 1572.

[33] A. G. I., 58-5-9, Oficiales de Nueva España al Rey, 10 de diciembre
de 1572.

[34] A. G. I., 58-3-8, Enríquez al Rey, México: (a) February 5, 1572;
(b) April 28, 1572; (c) May 30, 1572; (d) October 10, 1572; (e) December 6, 1572. A. G. I., 58-5-9, Enríquez y oidores al Rey, México:
(a) December 16, 1572; (b) March 19, 1573.

character of Ibarra's following, certain criminal actions charged against him, and aspersions on his character must be regarded as gross exaggerations. It must be admitted, on the other hand, that on more than one occasion he overstepped the bounds of his jurisdiction, and, although these very acts redounded to the service of his Catholic Majesty, they constituted a bold usurpation of authority and justified the protests of the audiencia of Nueva Galicia.

CHAPTER VIII

ECONOMIC ORGANIZATION OF NUEVA VIZCAYA

The principal occupations of the Spanish settlers of Nueva Vizcaya, as in other parts of Spanish America, were farming, grazing, and mining. Although the last attracted a larger percentage of people and has monopolized a disproportionate share of attention in the telling of the historical development of Nueva Vizcaya, yet a large portion of the population lived by farming and grazing. The dependence of the miners for their sustenance upon the farmer and the cattle-raiser of the immediate vicinity of the mines is obvious, when one considers the difficulties of transporting bulky foodstuffs over long stretches of desert and mountain trails. Although agriculture was stimulated by mineral wealth, which gave new impulse to population, yet in most cases the hold once gained by the farmer was not relinquished, even after the mines were abandoned.

Farming was from the beginning recognized as a basic occupation, and the Governor of Nueva Vizcaya was untiring in his encouragement of agriculture. He induced settlers to come to his province and often assisted them with loans of seeds, agricultural implements, and stock.[1] In most cases, however, the land was settled in accordance with detailed instructions laid down in royal ordinances, for the Spanish crown was deeply interested in encouraging agriculture.[2] It provided that the land should be distributed by the viceroy or by a governor, but in all cases the rights of the Indians were to be respected. The settlers were required to build houses, to plant the ground within a certain time, and to

[1] A. G. I., 1-3-20/11, *Información de Francisco de Ibarra.*
[2] *Recopilación de leyes,* II. 40-1.

possess a certain quantity of stock. The final title of possession was not acquired till after a residence of four years.

Nueva Vizcaya, being largely mountainous and semi-desert, was not particularly favorable to agriculture. But, where there was any soil at all, it was very fertile and could be made to produce abundantly as soon as it was moistened. Agriculture, therefore, was principally by irrigation, but it was not practiced on a large scale, on account of the meagerness of the soil and the primitive methods in use.

Maize, which was the most important food-plant of the natives of Nueva Vizcaya prior to the Spanish conquest, continued to be the principal article of food. A favorite food prepared from the maize was the corn tortilla, which continues to the present time to be the staff of life of the Mexican peon. The corn was prepared by placing it in water to which a little lime was added. It was then allowed to soak long enough to enable the husk to be separated easily from the corn, which was then mashed or ground on a metate. From this paste the tortilla was formed by patting it between the hands into a very thin cake, which was cooked on an earthen pan placed over the fire. Contact with the Spaniards did not seem to modify, among most of the Indians, the primitive method of raising maize. They planted the corn by making a hole in the ground with a sharp-pointed stick, dropping in the seed, and covering it up. As a matter of fact, this is practiced today by some Indians in New Mexico. To loosen the soil about the growing stalk, the Indians used wooden spades and hoes. A contribution of the Spaniards to native agriculture was the introduction of the ox-drawn, iron-shod wooden plow, and of iron agricultural implements.

Of the indigenous plants next in importance to corn was the maguey, or American agave. Although the maguey was not cultivated as extensively within the territorial limits of

Nueva Vizcaya as elsewhere, nevertheless, we have information that it was cultivated at an early date in Sinaloa and southern Durango.[3] The remarkable utility of this plant is noted by Bancroft: "To the Indian it not only gave food, but its leaves covered his hut, and cloth was woven from its fibres; its medicinal qualities were highly valued, and its juice was his favorite beverage, being known to the Aztecs by the name *actli*; but under the rule of the Spaniards the name was replaced by that of *pulque,* which to this day forms the favorite drink of the lower classes."[4] A third indigenous plant, which was widespread in its cultivation, was cotton. Natives who wore cotton clothes were discovered by Francisco de Ibarra in several sections of Nueva Vizcaya.

European grains and plants were first introduced into New Spain by Cortés. The foreign plants proved to be well adapted to the new environment, propagated rapidly, and, when Nueva Vizcaya was founded, there was an adequate supply to be transplanted to the new province. Of European cereals, only wheat was raised to any extent, and, because of want of moisture, it had to be irrigated. We have noted the rapid development of wheat farms in the environs of Durango and Nombre de Diós.[5]

Although many Spanish residents in Nueva Vizcaya were classified as farmers, as a rule they did not personally work the soil. Because of their repugnance to the humble sphere of the farmer, they preferred to be encomenderos. After the conquest of Nueva Vizcaya, therefore, agriculture was carried on only where the work could be performed by Indians, who were virtually in a state of bondage. The system of encomiendas, which was made general for the

[3] A. G. I., 87-5-1, Registros, 1579-1607; A. G. I., 103-3-7, Antonio de Alcega, 12 de mayo de 1596.
[4] Bancroft, *Mexico,* III. 607-608.
[5] Cf. pp. 122-123.

Indies in 1536, was reminiscent of European feudalism. The Indians were the vassals, while their Spanish superiors were the feudal lords. To the encomenderos the king entrusted his wards, the Indians, and they promised to teach, to indoctrinate, and to protect them. There was one main difference, however, between this and the European feudal system, the Indians were not expected to repay their overlords by military service; on the contrary, the Spaniards took possession of the Indians' territory and forced them to work.

The Spanish sovereigns were paternal and humane in their Indian policy, but in practice their laws were ignored. For example, although they ordered that the Indians should not be made to bear burdens, that they should not be taken from their villages and made to serve in the homes of the encomenderos, that their labor should not be exacted except for pay, and that they should not be taken away from their own districts, these laws were violated almost from the beginning. The New Laws of 1542, ordinances resulting from the protests of Bartolomé de Las Casas against the abuses of the encomiendas, sought to correct the evils and eventually to abolish the system. The New Laws, however, were ineffective in operation, and their most vital clauses were repealed in 1545.[6]

Francisco de Ibarra, as we have noted, was empowered by his commission to create encomiendas in Nueva Vizcaya, and he took advantage of this privilege as a means of rewarding his followers. The dependence which the Spanish settlers of Nueva Vizcaya placed on Indian labor can be appreciated, when we read their complaints that they were starving because there were no Indians to work for them.[7]

[6] On the encomienda system, cf. Sir Arthur Helps, *The Spanish Conquest in America and its Relation to the History of Slavery and to Government of Colonies*, Oppenheim ed., New York, 1900-1904, vol. II.

[7] A. G. I., 145-2-21, Pedro Gonzales de Mendoza al Rey, primero de octubre de 1584.

Agriculture in Nueva Vizcaya was based upon native labor, and that native labor was exploited by means of the encomienda system.

The climate and soil of Nueva Vizcaya were remarkably favorable for grazing. On the great plateau in Chihuahua and Durango, at an altitude of five thousand feet and more, the wild pasturage was short, tender, and reproduced rapidly. It was exceptionally nutritious, but disappeared altogether in the dry season because of its short roots. At altitudes lower than five thousand feet the grasses were more vigorous. The stock-raiser could pasture his herd on the uplands during the rainy season and on the lower pastures during the remainder of the year. The relative absence of beasts of prey in that region was also advantageous for grazing.

The Spaniards found no indigenous domestic animals in New Spain, and, therefore, they introduced their own horses, cattle, sheep, and swine. The first importation of cattle was made by Cortés from the West Indies soon after the Conquest, and the first sheep were introduced by Viceroy Mendoza.[8] Thereafter the rapid multiplication of live-stock in New Spain was almost unbelievable. In a short time herds were to be numbered by the thousands, and many cattle roamed in a wild state over the great central plateau.

Not only were climate and geography favorable for the establishment of the grazing industry in Nueva Vizcaya, but the Spanish government was very paternal and fostered grazing by legislation. In 1533 a law was passed making all pasture-ground free to both Spaniards and Indians. In 1538, during the viceroyalty of Mendoza, the first alcaldes de mesta were appointed by the cabildo of Mexico.[9]

[8] "It is probable that the first sheep introduced were not Merinos; particularly they were not of the Léon, Segovian, or Sorian breed" (Alexander de Humboldt, *Political Essay on the Kingdom of New Spain*, London, 1811, III. 50-51).

[9] *Actas de Cabildo del Ayuntamiento de México,* Segundo Libro de Actas, Mexico, 1889, II. 113; *Recopilación de leyes*, II. 135-138.

MESTA (N)

The *mesta,* established after that of Spain, was a league of stock-raisers for the promotion of their interests, and held ordinary jurisdiction for the punishment of petty offenses, as thefts of cattle, encroachments, damage to property and the like. Every year the city council appointed two as alcaldes de la mesta from among the owners of cattle. These, together with five other members of the league, met in session twice a year, on January 16th and August 31st. On these occasions all disputes about the right of property and other questions were decided. Regulations might then also be issued for the guidance of the stock-raisers, but required the viceroy's or governor's approval to become valid. Owners of three hundred head of small cattle and twenty mares or cows were ipso facto *hermanos de la mesta,* that is, members of the league.[10]

It is to be presumed that the jurisdiction of the alcaldes de la mesta extended over Nueva Vizcaya while it was under Francisco de Ibarra's governorship, although no reference to the institution of the mesta in this early period is at hand.

Cattle multiplied most surprisingly on the plains and in the valleys of Nueva Vizcaya. By 1586 Diego de Ibarra had thirty-three thousand head of cattle, and Rodrigo del Río had forty-two thousand head.[11] It appears that the cattle became so numerous that they were slaughtered only for their hides and hoofs; the carcases were left to rot on the plains. Thomas Gage's description of grazing in Guatemala (c. 1625) might apply also to Nueva Vizcaya. He met one farmer who owned forty thousand head of cattle, and heard of a man who bought six thousand head at two dollars and a quarter per head.[12] Since grazing was undisturbed by the government, the stock-raisers of New Spain were able to compete successfully with the Old Country. "In the sixteenth century before the interior consumption had been augmented by the number and the luxury of the whites, New Spain supplied Europe with more hides than

[10] Bancroft, *Mexico,* III. 615, note 47. For the mesta in Spain, cf. Julius Klein, *The Mesta,* Cambridge, 1920.

[11] Bolton and Marshall, *Colonization of North America,* p. 58.

[12] E. G. Bourne, *Spain in America,* New York, 1904, pp. 299-300.

at the present day. Father Acosta relates that a fleet which
entered Seville in 1587, carried 64,340 Mexican hides."[13]
Sheep raising did not become an important industry in
Nueva Vizcaya until the eighteenth century. The raising
of horses and mules, however, was a flourishing industry,
especially in the valleys of Guadiana and Poaña. Since the
horse was one of the Spaniards' most effective instruments
when waging war upon the Indians, safety demanded that
they should restrict its use to themselves. Such was the
nature of an order of Charles V to the first audiencia of
Mexico. It was faithfully observed until the time of the
Mixton War, when Mendoza allowed certain Aztec chieftains to ride at the head of their warriors. But, as the
stock-ranches increased, and wild horses became numerous
along the northern frontiers, the Spanish prohibitions were
of no avail, and before the end of the century Tepehuane
chiefs were able to command numerous troops of mounted
warriors.[14] This situation developed with the expansion of
the frontiers until, by the middle of the eighteenth century,
the Indians of central Canada were found mounted on Spanish ponies by Hudson's Bay Company traders.

Mining was the paramount industry. The discovery of
deposits of precious metals was the object of practically all
the entradas of the sixteenth century. The main object of
search was silver. The great mineral wealth of Nueva Vizcaya, when made available for exploitation by Francisco de
Ibarra, caused a "rush" into the new "El Dorado." The
discovery of the mines, the settlement of numerous mining
towns, and the administrative organization of the district
have been outlined in the preceding chapters. A clearer
understanding of the industry, however, can be obtained by

[13] Humboldt, *Political Essay*, III. 49.
[14] García, *Los Mineros Mexicanos*, p. 179.

a brief examination of the mining laws then in operation and the methods employed in working the mines.

At the time of the Columbian discovery all mines were regarded as belonging to the crown. In 1504, however, the privilege of seeking and operating mines was extended to all Spaniards, provided their claims were first officially registered and they engaged to take the precious metals to the casa de fundición (royal smeltery) to be assayed, taxed, and stamped. In 1526 a royal ordinance so extended private rights as to make the mines practically common property.[15] They were open to all free inhabitants, Spaniards and Indians, and only certain officials and friars were prohibited from holding claims. In 1584 the pretense of royal ownership was definitely abandoned, for a decree of that year declared that in the future the mines were to belong outright to those who discovered them, rather than as a concession of the crown.[16]

The quinto, or king's portion of the mineral production, was based, therefore, on the old custom of requiring large royalties from the miners for the privilege of developing the mines. At the time of the Discovery, the proportion was two-thirds, but, to facilitate the development of the mines, it was successively reduced to one-half, one-third, one-fifth, and in some districts, to one-tenth and even to one-twentieth. In Nueva Vizcaya under Ibarra's régime the mines paid a royalty of one-twentieth. Because of its attachment to the mercantile doctrine, the Spanish government fostered the development of mines in every way possible. For example, acts were passed exempting mining implements, supplies, and slaves of the mining operators

[15] The law, dated November 9, 1526, is given in full in Puga, *Cedulario*, pp. 12-21. It was repeated and reformed in 1551, 1563, 1568, and 1575.

[16] C. H. Haring, *Trade and Navigation between Spain and the Indies in the Time of the Hapsburgs*, Cambridge, 1918; Bancroft, *Mexico*, III. 580-581.

from attachment for debt, and miners were not to be imprisoned for debt.[17]

In addition to the royal mining laws, ordinances were published by Viceroy Mendoza which not only supplemented the king's laws, but seemed actually to supplant them. The first ordinance was published on August 30, 1539; the second, on January 14, 1550. Since Ibarra worked under the last-mentioned ordinance, its general tenor alone needs to be mentioned. The mining ordinance of 1550 provided: (1) that all mine owners were to file titles of possession before a justice, subject to penalty of forfeiture; (2) that a copy of the mine register was to be sent to the viceroy every year so that he might know the location of the mines and the names of their owners; (3) that anyone discovering a vein located at a greater distance than one thousand yards from another mine could file claim on it. The claim was to be eighty yards parallel to the vein and forty yards wide. Within fifteen days after the discovery, the mine had to be registered before the royal officials, with an exact description of its location. If the discoverer failed to register within fifteen days, he could claim but fifty by thirty yards. And, (4) if two men discovered the same vein, the first to register it before a royal official was to be counted the first discoverer. The ordinance also made definite provision for "jumping claims," and established the legal minimum amount of work necessary to hold a claim. These provisions exhibit a marked similarity to our own mining laws on "staking claims."[18] The royal ordinance of 1563, which has been called "The Old Code of Mines," need not be discussed, since it appears that the ordinances of Mendoza were the ones

---

[17] Bancroft, *Mexico*, III. 580-581.

[18] Ordenanzas hechas por el Sr. Visorey don Antonio de Mendoza sobre las minas de la Nueva España, Año de 1550 (Ayer Collection).

actually in force.[19]   These laws protected the discoverers in their tenure of mines and gave them great economic advantages.

Preliminary to a discussion of mining methods and processes of metallic extraction in vogue in Nueva Vizcaya in the sixteenth century, it is necessary to describe the geologic features of that region.   Such an exposition, both brief and readily intelligible to the layman, is found in the following account taken from Bancroft's *History of Mexico:*

On the eastern slope of the Sierre Madre, in Durango, the porphyries sometimes overlay extensive beds of very fine gritstone, and exhibit greater softness than those south of the capital, with large admixture of mica. Quartz is the most common of gangues, and its outcrops in the plateau serve frequently as a guide to prospectors.

The general direction of metallic veins is from the northwest to the southeast, and this being especially the case with the richer kind, it is always taken into consideration on filing a claim. The average breadth of the vein is six feet, except on the Veta Grande of Zacatecas, where it is from thirty to thirty-five feet, the maximum being even seventy-five feet. In some districts, as in Sonora and Chihuahua, the ore lies near the surface, but generally this is not the case, a circumstance which in colonial times, with the prevailing backwardness in drainage and other operations, impeded the search for deeperlying zones in the veins.

There are essentially two forms under which argentiferous ores occur. Near the surface, where exposed to external influence, the metallic substances are generally in the form of oxides, or combined with iron, chlorine, or bromine, and receive from their reddish color the name *colorados*. Those at greater depth have usually retained the condition of all primitive sulphuric bases, and are found in connection with pyrites, galena, or blende. The latter two predominate, and a dark color results, which has given rise to their designation as black ores, or *negros*. They give the greatest part of all the silver produced in the country. The average richness of the ores has been frequently overrated, and the occurrence of enormous blocks of native silver is considered as frequent, while in reality they are very rare, and never larger than those found in European

---

[19] Mendoza's mining ordinances are known to have been in force in 1577 (A. G. I., 58-5-9, Audiencia de México, 10 de diciembre de 1577). For an anlysis of this code, cf. A. S. Aiton, "The First American Mining Code," in the *Michigan Law Review*, III, No. 2, 107. For a summary of the development of Spanish-American mining laws, cf. Santiago Ramirez, *La Propiedad de las Minas*, Mexico, 1883, pp. 86-104.

mines. The average yield is from three to four ounces of silver to the quintal of ore, and the enormous returns of New Spain are due rather to the great abundance of the ore. Gold is obtained chiefly from places in Sonora and the northern regions. In Oajaca it also occurs in rocks, but the exploitation has not proved very profitable. Elsewhere it is rarely found except in connection with argentiferous ores, in some instances in the proportion of about two ounces to the quintal.[20]

The methods applied by the Spaniards in digging out the mineral ore were primitive in the extreme. In following the veins, they dug pits and galleries, but their construction revealed startling defects. For example, they seldom made connecting galleries, and thus ventilation was impossible. Also, the absence of communicating tunnels multiplied the difficulties of carrying out the ore. As Humboldt said, the mines were similar to rooms in a house without connecting doors, so that to move from one room to another it was necessary to go around the house.[21]

Since the art of blasting with gunpowder was not introduced in mining until 1613, the rock had to be broken with iron drills and heavy mallets. All the ore which was taken from the vein was carried out by Indian tenateros—the beasts of burden of the mines. Instead of ladders, the shafts were equipped with a series of beams about five yards in length, placed in pairs in an inclined position of about forty-five degrees and provided with wedge-shaped notches to serve for steps. Up this rude contrivance, the tenateros, working on long shifts, would climb laden with heavy bags of ore.[22] To draw the water from the mines, they used large hide bags attached to ropes which were wound on the drum of a windlass that was turned by a mule. Sometimes the same bags were used to draw up the minerals.

[20] Bancroft, *Mexico,* III. 585-586.
[21] Humboldt, *Political Essay,* III. 235.
[22] *Ibid.;* III. 238-239; Bancroft, *Mexico,* III. 597.

The knowledge which the Spaniards brought to the New World regarding mineral extracting processes was not very extensive. Although they knew about a primitive salt treatment for argentiferous ores, smelting was the process most generally employed prior to the discovery of the silver amalgamation method. Even the natives knew how to smelt real silver ores, but they were unacquainted with the bellows; this was a contribution of the Europeans.[23] Because the Spaniards' methods were ineffective with the more complex ores, they were inclined to avoid them. When la Marcha made his visita of Nueva Galicia in 1550, he reported that there were in the different mining districts a great number of reduction-works, smelters, and refineries.[24] This evidences the almost universal use of smelting in the extraction of silver.

The separation of gold was an easier process. The Aztecs were well versed in placer mining. They would dig a ditch alongside a stream, into which they threw the gold-bearing earth. Then by turning in the water, the dirt was carried away and the gold remained. The prevalence of gold among the treasures of the Aztecs and the Incas did not indicate a greater abundance of that metal; rather, gold was more common than silver because it was easier of extraction. "Till 1545, when the Cerro de Potosí (Peru) began to be worked, Europe appears to have received much more gold than silver from the New Continent. Five-sixths of the booty which Cortéz acquired at Tenochtitlán, and the treasures of Caxamarca and Cuzco consisted of gold; and the silver mines of Porco in Peru, and Tasco and Tlapujahua in Mexico, were very feebly wrought in the times of Cortéz and Pizarro. It is only since 1545 that Spain has been

[23] To increase the intensity of the heat, ten or twelve persons blew upon the fire at once through tubes of copper about two yards in length.
[24] Cf. pp. 52-54.

inundated with the silver of Peru."[25] The amalgamating properties of mercury in combining with gold were well known to the Spaniards, and indeed quicksilver had been used in gold mining from antiquity.

The real explanation of the remarkable increase in the silver returns after the middle sixteenth century was not to be found solely in the discovery of the rich mines of Potosí, Guanajuato, Zacatecas, and Durango, but also in the introduction into New Spain in 1556 of the patio, or American heap-amalgamation process. Although the credit for the invention of this process has been given to a miner of Pachuca, in Mexico, by the name of Bartolomé de Medina, a native of Seville, it appears that Medina did not discover the method, but learned of it from an unknown German companion in Europe.[26]

Medina's process was based on the property of quicksilver to extract the silver from the finely pulverized ore and collect it in the form of an amalgam. The method is defined as cold amalgamation or *por crudo y de patio*. Since the metals destined for amalgamation had first to be reduced to a very fine powder to present the greatest possible contact with the mercury, the metalliferous gangue was first pounded into small pieces by the Indians with heavy hammers and then introduced to the crushing-mill, called an arastre. The arastre was made of four blocks of granite grinding-stones attached to cross-bars of wood made to revolve in a circle about forty feet in circumference. The sides and bottom of the mill were also made of granite. Where water-power could not be obtained, the arastres were kept in motion by mules walking constantly at a slow pace. Generally several

[25] Humboldt, *Political Essay*, III. 401-2. The treasure of Peru has been estimated at over a million castellanos of gold, and fifty thousand marks of silver. The treasure of the Montezumas was in the same proportion of gold and silver.

[26] C. H. Haring, *Trade and Navigation between Spain and the Indies*, p. 158; Humboldt, *Political Essay*, III. 253-254.

arastres were arranged in rows under one shed. If the ore was exceptionally fine, amalgamation took place in the arastre.[27]

When the ore had been reduced to a fine metallic flour, it was thoroughly mixed with water. The moistened paste was then carried to the court of amalgamation, or patio (hence the name of the process), which was usually paved with flags. Here the complex silver minerals were made amenable to quicksilver by being converted into chlorides. This was accomplished by the raw- or cold-amalgamation process, which was the particular contribution of Medina.[28] To facilitate the decomposition of the silver mineral, salt[29] and magistral (sulphates of iron and copper) were worked into the pulp, or torta, which was spread out on the floor of the patio. The contact of these different substances resulted in the amalgamation of the silver. The process proceeded very slowly, extending over a month or more, for the sole extraneous heat was furnished by the sun, and it took some time for the quicksilver to unite with all the silver contained in the paste. When the azoguero, or man in charge of the operation, decided that the amalgamating had ceased, the paste was thrown into vats of water, and the earth was washed away, leaving the amalgam on the bottom. The mercury was then separated from the silver and recovered by distillation.

The particular advantages of the patio process were: (1) it was simple and did not demand great technical knowledge;

[27] For pictures of arastres, as well as a detailed description of the patio process, cf. H. G. Ward, *Mexico in 1827*, London, 1827, II. 434-439.

[28] Medina was only acquainted with the use of salt, and sulphates of iron and copper. In 1590 Alonso Barba invented the hot process, or beneficio de cazo y cocimiento.

[29] Since salt was an essential in the patio process, the explorers were always on the lookout for rock salt mines. The mines in Durango derived most of their salt from the famous Laguna del Piñon Blanco. The mines west of the Sierra Madre got their salt principally from the deposits left by the tides of the South Sea.

(2) it required no construction of buildings, although sheds were often built over the arastres; (3) no combustibles were required; (4) the grinding-machines were easily and inexpensively constructed and could be operated by mule-power; and (5) it was suited to a region where the climate was warm and dry, and where mule-power, labor, and quicksilver were cheaper than fuel and water. Although the loss of quicksilver was large, owing to the formation of calomel which was not recovered, the bullion produced was of a high grade, since refractory silver minerals were hardly attacked.

The new method of extracting silver was found to be such a distinct improvement over the old processes that its adoption in New Spain was almost immediate and universal.[30] In 1562, five years after the discovery, there were thirty-five amalgamation works in Zacatecas. It is impossible to determine exactly the influence of the new process on increased production, for immediately prior to its discovery numerous mines had been discovered. The average yield in New Spain in 1540-1544 was over three times that of the preceding decade, and, in the years 1544-1548, the yield was double that of the prior four years.[31] Since the most prolific mines had already been discovered, it is undoubtedly true that production after 1560 would have declined in proportion to the number of men engaged in mining had it not been for the introduction of the patio process.

[30] The amalgamation process was not introduced into Peru until 1571 by Viceroy Francisco de Toledo. Up to that time the silver was smelted.

[31] C. H. Haring ("American Gold and Silver Production," in *The Quarterly Journal of Economics,* XXIX. 447) gives the following table of average annual silver production in New Spain (reckoned in maravedís) :

August, 1524-November, 1531	2,335,000
November, 1531-July, 1539	47,950,000
August, 1539-May, 1544	152,050,000
June, 1544-December, 1549	269,140,000
January, 1550-March, 1553	405,100,000
March, 1553-August, 1555	507,800,000
August, 1555-January 1560	467,475,000

The widespread adoption of the amalgamation process made the sale of mercury a lucrative source of income. The Spanish crown, in 1559, partly for revenue and partly to keep tab on the mining returns, declared the sale of quicksilver a government monopoly. The principal European sources of supply were the Spanish mines of Almadén, leased to the Fuggers (a German banking house), and the mines of Idria in the Austrian Alps. To refute any claim that the crown did not seek a profit from its quicksilver monopoly, it may be noted that, in 1569, it sold in Mexico quicksilver bought from the Fuggers at an advance of two hundred and fifty per cent. The costs of transportation certainly were not responsible for this increase. All the mercury which was sent to America passed through the Casa de Contratación at Seville. In Mexico City there was established a Tribunal de Azogues composed of several royal officials who had charge of the distribution of the quicksilver. When the quicksilver mines of Huancavelica, in Peru, were discovered in 1564, it was no longer necessary to depend on the Austrian mines, for the deposits of Huancavelica were so productive that they supplied both Peru and a large part of New Spain. It is worthy of comment, however, that the Spanish government exhibited a surprising inefficiency in its administration of the azogue supply. Complaints from the miners of insufficient mercury were unending, and they claimed that the royal returns from the mines were not greater because of an inadequate supply of quicksilver.[32]

Another customary excuse offered to explain why returns were not commensurate with the richness of the ore was the scarcity of labor. The Spaniards often complained that they were starving because the Indians would not work; they also complained that the mines had to be abandoned, or that returns were small, because of the scarcity of Indians. This

---

[32] A. G. I., 67-1-18, Nueva Galicia al Rey, Zacatecas, febrero de 1567.

situation was more pronounced in northern Nueva Vizcaya, for there the Indians of the plains were nomadic and untractable and refused to live in settled communities under the encomienda system. To meet this situation, the Spaniards resorted to Negro slaves and more docile sedentary Indians, who were transplanted from the south. In the later sixteenth century numerous colonies of Tlascalans and Tarascans were settled along the northern frontier. When la Marcha and other visitadores made their tours of investigation in Nueva Galicia, they reported that numerous Negroes were employed in the mines. In his will Francisco de Ibarra mentioned a number of Negroes in the enumeration of his mining properties.

The real labor in the mines, however, was performed by the Indians who were held in encomienda. They were divided into groups and required to work specified times. Compulsory labor in the mines without compensation was first abolished in 1551. This law, as was true of other benevolent acts of the government, was generally disregarded; it was necessary in 1589 to regulate Indian labor more explicitly.[33]

The following is a picture of mining in South America, but it is applicable to the mines of New Spain as well:

It was in the mines, even when the work was not continued beyond eight months in the year, that the Indians suffered their greatest hardships. They were crowded together in great numbers, and worked from week to week and from month to month standing knee-deep in water throughout the coldest season of the year. "Encomendero Rodrigo de Quiroga," to quote an old chronicle, "had six hundred Indians in his repartimiento in the mines, half of them men and the other half women, all from fifteen to twenty-five years of age, and all employed in washing for gold during eight months of the year, on account of having no water in the four other summer months." In 1553, Francisco de Victoria, writing to the Council of the Indies, affirms that at the mines, "there is neither Christianity nor charity, and the abominations cry to heaven. Each encomen-

[33] *Recopilación de leyes*, II, Lib. VI, Tit. XV, Ley 19.

dero puts into the mines his Indians, men and women, old and young, without giving them any rest or more food, during the eight months of the year in which they work, than a pint of maize a day; and the person who does not produce the quantity of gold which is required of him receives blows with a club, or lashes, and if any one hides a grain of gold he is punished by cutting off his nose and ears and exposing them nailed to a pole."[34]

[34] Bernard Moses, *The Spanish Dependencies in South America*, New York, 1914, II. 48.

CHAPTER IX

CONCLUSION

Francisco de Ibarra was conspicuously inactive after his extensive explorations of 1562-1566. The unsuccessful outcome of his various attempts to find Copalá, Tôpia, and other attractive goals must have disappointed and disillusioned him. But it is probable that there remained a sufficient lure in the Northern Mystery to induce the organization of additional expeditions had his health and finances permitted. The journeys of exploration, however, were very expensive undertakings, and, although they resulted in the opening up of vast undiscovered regions, they yielded but a fraction of what they had cost. In financing his numerous expeditions, Francisco expended all of his own fortune, and his uncle Diego was near the end of his own resources. Equally important in explaining his inactivity was his physical incapacity to endure more of the hardships entailed by frontier exploration. Ever since he was sixteen years of age, Francisco had been engaged almost continuously in this most strenuous activity, and the terrible hardships he underwent finally undermined his health, and he contracted tuberculosis. He was subjected to a lingering illness, for, as far back as the time when he went to Paquimé, mention was made of "the Governor's infirmity." It has also been noted that, in 1572, he was so ill that he could not appear before the alcaldes del crimen in Mexico to answer charges brought against him and his administration.[1] There is no indication that he ever left the province of Chiametla during the three remaining years of his life. Finally, in the little mining settlement of Pánuco, in Chiametla, the first

[1] Cf. p. 202.

governor of Nueva Vizcaya succumbed to his infirmities on August 17, 1575.[2]

Francisco de Ibarra's last will and testament had been drawn up in Pánuco on June 3, 1575. This document, which reveals the fact that the conquistador had been ill in Pánuco for a protracted period, reflects interesting side-lights on the character of the man, in addition to giving a complete statement concerning the extent of his estate at the time of his death.[3] It reads in part as follows:

> In the name of God all powerful, and of the glorious and everlasting Virgin, Holy Mary, His Blessed Mother, Our Lady. Know ye who read this that I, Francisco de Ibarra, legitimate son of Pedro Sánchez de Ibarra and of Doña María de Arandía, his true wife, residents of the villa of Durango, in the state of Vizcaya, in the kingdom of Castile, resident in the mines of the province of Chiametla, in the government of Nueva Vizcaya, where I am governor for His Majesty, being ill in body but sane in understanding, and in complete memory, I confess my faith and Catholicism; I believe in the mystery of the divine unity of Father, Son, and Holy Ghost, three persons and but one essence; I confess in Holy Mother the Roman Church, and in that faith and belief I have lived, and in it I protest to live and die. With this divine invocation I order my last will and testament as follows.

The more important sections of the will are presented below in summary:

1. Ibarra requested that, should he die in Chiametla he be buried in the church of San Sebastián; if in Durango he desired to be interred in the church of that place near the high altar. In a later addendum to his will he ordered that his body be placed temporarily in the church of Pánuco. From there his executors were to remove it to Mexico to be placed in the Monastery of Santo Domingo in the chapel built by Diego

---

[2] A. G. I., 1-1-1/20, Memorial del Lcdo. Juan de Ybarra; A. G. I., 67-1-12, Testimonio de Francisco de Ibarra, Pánuco, 18 de agosto de 1575; A. G. I., 66-5-14, Audiencia de Guadalajara al Rey, 16 de septiembre de 1575. "About 1572 Francisco de Ibarra died and was succeeded as governor by his uncle, Diego de Ibarra" (C. W. Hackett, ed., *Historical Documents Relating to New Mexico, Nuevo Vizcaya, and Approaches thereto, to 1773*, collected by Adolph F. A. Bandelier and Fanny R. Bandelier, Washington, 1923, p. 16). The exact date of Ibarra's death has been noted; likewise, his immediate successor was his brother Juan.

[3] A. G. I., 67-1-12, Testimonio de Francisco de Ibarra.

de Ibarra. There a perpetual daily mass was to be said for the repose of his soul.[4]

2. Details for the funeral procession from his house to the church were also arranged. The body was to be accompanied by cofradías, or religious brotherhoods, and alms were to be given to the poor.

3. Arrangements were made for the funeral mass, and a novenario of nine requiem masses were to be said during the three days following the funeral.

4. Innumerable masses were ordered to be said at various churches, chapels, and shrines for the repose of his soul, for the souls of his relatives, and for the souls of those to whom he was obligated. Fees for these masses were to be defrayed from his estate.

5. To the following churches were each given fifty pesos de oro: Durango, Pánuco, Guadiana, and San Sebastián.

6. Many creditors to whom he owed various sums of money were enumerated, and these accounts were ordered to be paid. Typical of such entries are: "Should the heirs of Julian de Soto, who died in Zacatecas, and was a servant of Bolaños many years ago, be found, they should be paid ten pesos; otherwise masses should be said for his soul"; or, "Martín Pérez, the merchant of San Martín, should be paid thirty pesos for iron goods"; or, "Seven hundred pesos are due Cristóbal de Oñate; they are to be paid his heirs if they so desire."

7. Regarding his obligations to Diego de Ibarra, Francisco stated that his uncle had advanced him great sums of money, and that he had spent much of his uncle's estate. The repayment of these was conditioned by Diego's wishes. But Francisco "wished to call attention to the fact, that, at his uncle's solicitation he came to New Spain, and was received into his household. In light of these circumstances this matter should be decided in a manner deemed best." This implies that Francisco de Ibarra regarded himself as the foster-son of Diego, and the assistance he received from Diego as gifts and not loans.

8. His possessions, very vaguely enumerated, were as follows: three water-mills, Negroes (no number given), mules, tools, and other materials appertaining to the mines; "mines which belonged to him through deeds, or donations (the names of the mines not given)"; a reduction-work in the mines of Aviño; a sheep-ranch near Durango; and many other farms (no names).

9. Francisco's inheritance from his parents in Hibar, in Spain, was bequeathed to Diego de Ibarra, in trust, to pay his obligations.

[4] According to Beaumont (*Crón. Mich.*, V. 560-564) Ibarra's remains were transferred to Durango from Chiametla.

10. All royal grants recently made the Governor of Nueva Vizcaya were to be included in his possessions as grants already made.

11. "To the Indians of Chiametla for their good services are to be given two ornaments to cost each one hundred pesos."

12. To a sister in Vizcaya he willed one thousand ducats.

13. He named as executors of the will Diego de Ibarra, Martín López de Ibarra, Hernando de Trejo, and Pedro de Uncueta Ibarra. To these was given complete authority to sell his goods and meet his obligations.

14. After the fulfilment and payment of what was stipulated in the will, the residuum of the estate was bequeathed to his two brothers, Martín Ybañes de Ibarra, and Juan de Ibarra, with the proviso that Martín Ybañes was to inherit the mills, houses, and mines in America, and the estate in the villa of Hibar. Juan de Ibarra inherited all the grants made Francisco de Ibarra by the king, such as the governorship, and the office of alguacil mayor.

15. Martín Ybañes was charged to build a chapel in the City of Mexico to which Francisco's remains were to be transferred, and there a perpetual mass was to be said for the repose of his soul.

16. Finally, he requested his heirs to adopt as their patron saint St. Anthony of Padua, from whom Francisco had received numerous great favors; and he ordered gifts sent to the tomb of the saint in the city of Padua.

The signing of the will was witnessed by eight residents of Pánuco. Between June 3 and August 17, no less than three addenda were attached to the will, for, as new obligations originated, or as Ibarra recalled items that he had overlooked, these were attached to the original document. The third addendum was made only a few minutes before his death. It was signed by the same witnesses, but the Governor, quite naturally, "was unable to sign."

Francisco de Ibarra was but thirty-six years of age when death cut short a career marked by noteworthy achievements. Since the last six or seven years of his life were inactive because of reasons mentioned above, the remarkable deeds of the man are accentuated, in view of the fact that his greatest work was completed before he was thirty years of age. The work of his early years gave promise of even greater services in later life, so it was truly a misfortune for Spanish colonization of the New World that this promising career should have been interrupted and halted by disease and death. But this is not to deny that his actual contributions were great and merit for the "conquistador of Nueva Vizcaya" a prominent place among the foremost Spanish explorers.

With the exception of his quarrels with the oidores of Nueva Galicia, his reorganization of the repartimientos, and incidental references regarding his interest in the exploitation of the mines and in encouraging settlement, we know little about Francisco de Ibarra as a civil administrator. The major portion of his life was occupied in exploration and in fighting the Indians; therefore, we must estimate him primarily as an explorer and as a military leader. His ability to lead men was manifested on numerous occasions. While on the march over the desert or in the high and rugged sierras the safety and comfort of his men was his chief concern. In acting the part of a true leader he never ordered his men to go where he himself was afraid to venture, and he was always foremost in the most perilous situations. Perhaps his most notable achievement was the long march over the mountains to Paquimé and then back across the mountains to Sinaloa, for on this entrada he did not suffer the loss of a single man, and it must be remembered he traversed the full length of the country inhabited by the Indians with the poisoned arrows. The severe sentence he imposed upon Martín de Gamon cannot be taken to imply that he was heartless. Gamon was unquestionably guilty of treason, and, since Ibarra's success depended upon absolute obedience to himself, and since it was known to all that desertion or disobedience called for the death penalty, any other sentence is hardly conceivable. In fact, according to Obregón, the Governor was quite as grieved as anyone over the unfortunate affair. That he could be magnanimous in a similar circumstance was demonstrated upon the occasion of the desertion of Rodrigo Verdugo in Sinaloa. When the hardships of the march depressed the spirits of his men, "like a true captain he animated his soldiers and assisted them as best he could."[5] When booty was being distributed, he never took more than the lowliest soldier. He was so affable, kind, and prodigal in his generosity that he attracted everyone to him, especially his soldiers, who loved him almost to idolatry. His popularity with his men drew from Baltasar de Obregón this eulogy: "The commission granted Francisco de Ibarra was deserved; he proved himself a gentleman, capable, and prudent; his deeds, his life, and his habits proved the truth of all this." Viceroy Velasco referred to Ibarra as "un hombre virtuoso y bastante." It is a noteworthy fact that not a single writer has ever stained the brilliance of his memory. Because of his speedy pacification of the province of Nueva Vizcaya, Francisco de Ibarra has been called "the phoenix of the conquistadores."

A critical estimate of Francisco de Ibarra must concede certain less estimable elements in his character. His ambition to aggrandize his possessions could hardly justify an indictment against him had he not coupled it with a remarkable disregard for the legal rights of others. This was patently exhibited when he invaded the jurisdiction of the audiencia of Nueva Galicia in Nombre de Diós, Peñol Blanco, and Aviño. His interference in Chiametla was more excusable, for there all vestiges of Spanish authority had been destroyed, and that province really constituted virgin territory. It was natural to infer that the grant to Doctor Morones had lapsed with his death. There was some basis of truth in the repeated accusations of various officials of Nueva Galicia that Ibarra did not attempt to restrain his

---

[5] A. G. I., 1-3-20/11, Francisco de Ybarra, Información de méritos.

men, but allowed them to violate the inhabitants of Nueva Galicia with impunity. Whether this was due to lack of control over his men or to contempt for the jurisdiction of Nueva Galicia, it is difficult to determine. The available evidence, however, inclines us to the latter conclusion.

Ibarra's letter of June 6, 1562, telling about the remarkable land of Copalá reveals a degree of exaggeration which was certainly not justified by what he had seen. Here is an instance of falsification quite as serious as that of Friar Marcos himself. The purpose of this wilful exaggeration is quite obvious, for Ibarra concluded his letter with an urgent request that he be allowed to undertake the conquest of those attractive lands. In other words, he made the prospect exceedingly bright to increase the probability of his being allowed to undertake the enterprise.

The oidor Alarcón wrote the king a most venomous criticism of Francisco de Ibarra's Indian policy. He said that the governor of Nueva Vizcaya and his men created great havoc among the peaceful natives and that the friars who accompanied him on his entradas "regarded him as a most unchristian man, and accused him of numerous enormities." As a rule, the Governor's Indian policy was attended by the greatest success. He endeavored to be honest and humane with the natives and always strove to avoid a resort to force. Numerous instances could be mentioned to substantiate this statement. But, on the other hand, certain exceptions to the rule can be noted, perhaps the most marked instance being the violation of his word given to the Indians of Guatimape, when he robbed them of their store of maize.[6]

Since Francisco de Ibarra had been granted a virgin territory out of which he was to carve a province for himself, the measure of his success as an explorer, a colonizer, and an administrator can be determined by making a survey of

[6] Cf. p. 126.

Nueva Vizcaya at the end of his governorship. Such an examination is facilitated by the fact that about that time two lists of settlements were drawn up to show the progress of Spanish colonization in Nueva Galicia and in Nueva Vizcaya. One, compiled by the bishop of Nueva Galicia in December, 1573, enumerated the benefices in his diocese, the annual value of each one, their size, and what ecclesiastical persons resided in them.[7] Unfortunately, the survey is not complete, the benefices south of Zacatecas are omitted, and many important particulars are missing. The character of the second survey is explained by its title: "Relation made by Juan de Miranda, cleric, to Doctor Orozco, president of the audiencia of Guadalajara, concerning the land and settlements from the mines of San Martín to those of Santa Bárbara. Guadalajara, February 26, 1575."[8] In addition to the above, in 1571-1574, López de Velasco, coronista mayor of the Council of the Indies, prepared a dictionary of geographical information for all the Indies.[9] These three sources furnish a fairly complete and accurate picture of Nueva Vizcaya and the northern frontier of Nueva Galicia immediately prior to the death of Francisco de Ibarra.

Durango, situated in the Guadiana Valley thirty miles west of Nombre de Diós, on a site claimed by Ibarra to be the most ideal of any city in New Spain, was the capital of Nueva Vizcaya. In it was located the caja real, and there resided the three officials of the royal treasury. But the Governor did not reside in Durango, for the last years of his life were spent in Chiametla. Martín López de Ibarra, royal treasurer, stayed in Durango and acted there as lieu-

---

[7] A. G. I., 7-1-18, Obispo de Nueva Galicia, 23 de diciembre de 1573.

[8] Relación sobre la tierra y población que hay desde las minas de San Martín hasta las de Santa Bárbara, 1575, por Juan de Miranda (*Col. Doc. Inéd.*, XVI. 563-570).

[9] López de Velasco, *Geografía y descripción universal de las Indias,* Madrid, 1894.

tenant-governor.[10]   Although Durango had but twenty to
thirty families, or a total population not exceeding three
hundred, the surrounding country was populous and productive.   There were about thirty farms in its environs
which produced annually about fifty thousand fanegas of
wheat and maize; and good grazing lands made cattle and
sheep raising profitable.   In addition to the Spanish haciendas, there were many Indian settlements in the vicinity of
Durango.[11]

The mines of Coneto, located to the northwest of Aviño,
were new settlements in 1573, having been founded only
about a year.   In 1574 there were about fifty Spaniards in
Coneto.   Surrounding these mines were also several Indian
settlements.

To the north of Coneto, midway between Durango and
Santa Bárbara, was Indé.   In 1573 there were ten Spanish
families in Indé; but by 1575, the mines, which had been
worked since 1568, were deserted.   Continuous warfare with
the Tepehuanes, who infested that region, and bad government on the part of Ibarra's officials, who were in charge of
the settlement, were the causes of their abandonment.   Because of the same Indian menace and the scarcity of miners,
some very rich mining prospects near Indé known as San
Juan and Todos los Santos remained unexploited.[12]

The most northerly Spanish settlement was Santa Bárbara, seventy-five miles beyond Indé.   In that settlement
were about thirty Spanish families and a small number of

[10] A. G. I., 59-6-20, Información de Martín López de Ibarra, México,
21 de octubre de 1577.

[11] Bancroft, *North Mexican States and Texas,* I. 111; *Col. Doc.
Inéd.,* XIV. 473; XVI. 568; A. G. I., 67-1-18, Obispo de Nueva Galicia,
23 de diciembre de 1573; A. G. I., 1-3-20/11, Francisco de Ybarra,
Información de méritos.

[12] *Col. Doc. Inéd.,* XVI. 568-569; A. G. I., 67-1-18, Obispo de Nueva
Galicia, 23 de diciembre de 1573.   Regarding Santiago and Súchil, no
other information is given than that they were three leagues from San
Martín.

natives. Since the population was small, the production of
the mines was much less than it should have been, for
the average ore produced from four to six ounces per hun-
dredweight. To increase the labor supply, and thereby the
output of the mines, the royal officials of Durango petitioned
the king in 1579 to allow them to import about a thousand
Tlascaltec and other civilized Indians. This policy was later
adopted, and many Tlascaltec colonies were founded along
the northern frontier.[13] Santa Bárbara, situated on the San
Gregorio River, a branch of the Conchos, was surrounded
by many rich farms, where wheat and corn were raised in
abundance.

From San Martín two roads led to the Nazas and thence
to Santa Bárbara; one by way of Aviño and San Juan, the
other by way of Nombre de Diós, Durango, and Coneto.
Along these routes were numerous Indian settlements. In
the valley of San Juan there was an Indian pueblo inhabited
by about three thousand Christianized natives. Beyond San
Juan, in the valley of the Nazas, were several Spanish
ranches and a great number of pueblos inhabited by peaceful
Tepehuanes who cultivated maize along the river banks. On
the Durango road, twenty-five miles from that villa, was
the Indian pueblo of Cacari, which had about two hundred
Christianized natives.[14] A short distance beyond Cacari was
another native town, La Sauceda, with about one thousand
inhabitants. Both of these settlements were surrounded by
tilled fields of wheat and maize. To the northeast of
Sauceda were the sparsely settled mines of San Lucas.[15]
Such was the extent of settlement in Durango and southern
Chihuahua at the close of Ibarra's life.

[13] A. G. I., 66-6-22, Los oficiales reales de Durango al Rey, Durango,
primero de marzo de 1579.

[14] This settlement has been identified with one of the same name on a
seventeenth century Jesuit map in the Bolton Collection.

[15] Col. Doc. Inéd., XVI. 568-569.

Regarding the progress of settlement across the mountains in Sinaloa, Sonora, and Chiametla our evidence is much more unsatisfactory. There were two centers of colonization along the coast of the South Sea: Chiametla and Sinaloa. San Sebastián was the first Spanish town founded in Chiametla, and, in 1575, was quite an important settlement. Near San Sebastián was the mining settlement known as Chiametla. These two places had a combined population of but forty Spanish families and two thousand natives. The last days of Francisco de Ibarra were spent in Pánuco, a mining village located to the north of San Sebastían. Copalá was another mining settlement in Chiametla. The Indians were extremely warlike, and for that reason Ibarra chose to remain in Chiametla to protect the settlers. Evidence of rich silver veins in Chiametla was everywhere apparent, but, owing to the poverty of the Spanish settlers, the treasure output was greatly impaired. Official recognition of the handicaps under which the miners of Chiametla worked was evidenced by royal authorization at a little later date to reduce the king's tribute from one-tenth to one-twentieth.[16]

The extensive conquests of Francisco de Ibarra in Sinaloa and Sonora were practically wiped out by the Indian revolt of 1569. San Juan on the Suaqui (Fuerte), numerous encomiendas, and mines were deserted, and not a Spaniard was to be found north of the Río Sinaloa. On that river there remained a lone outpost, the villa of San Felipe y Santiago inhabited by a few refugees from San Juan. In 1584 Baltasar de Obregón strongly advocated the necessity of repairing the damage done by the natives of Sinaloa before it was too late. Because of the strategic position of the province, its resettlement was prerequisite to further explor-

---

[16] A. G. I., 1-3-20/11, Francisco de Ybarra, Información de méritos; A. G. I., 67-1-18, Obispo de Nueva Galicia, 23 de diciembre de 1573.

ation and settlement of the northwest. Furthermore, the rich mines and fertile valleys of Sinaloa promised ample remuneration. But, as has been noted elsewhere, several years elapsed before an attempt was made to reconquer Sinaloa, and by that time the natives had entirely relapsed into barbarism.

Not only within the territorial limits of Nueva Vizcaya had Francisco de Ibarra been active, for his early fame as an explorer was based on his discovery and settlement of places that were later incorporated into Nueva Galicia. A correct evaluation of his work must necessarily include not only a list of settlements within Nueva Vizcaya but also places in Nueva Galicia which he discovered, settled, and fostered. In 1570 he submitted a list of mines and settlements discovered by himself, but which were not included within the jurisdiction of Nueva Vizcaya. These were: Nombre de Diós, Fresnillo, Nieves, Sombrerete, San Martín, Ranchos, Chalchihuites, and Aviño. From these mines, for a period of about twenty years, silver and gold were extracted totalling in royal fifths over one million pesos de oro. Even though the production was great, it was in no way commensurate with the richness of the veins, for production was limited because of scarcity of labor and quicksilver.[17]

The mines of Fresnillo had been discovered by Ibarra on his first entrada. Since they were on the direct route leading north from Zacatecas, it is not unlikely that they were discovered by an earlier explorer, but the mines were not worked until years later, and no settlement was established until 1567. Fresnillo then assumed some prominence and became the seat of an alcalde mayor. It appears, however, that the mines were not very productive, for in 1575 there was not sufficient income to pay the salary of the local

[17] *Col. Doc. Inéd.*, XIV. 464; A. G. I., 1-3-20/11, Francisco de Ybarra, Información de méritos; A. G. I., 1-1-1/20, Memorial del Lcdo. Juan de Ybarra.

priests.[18]   Nieves, thirty miles northeast of San Martín,
had about twenty Spanish families and a few Indians. No
more Indians could be settled on account of their warlike
nature.   Ranchos, ten miles west of San Martín, had
thirty vecinos. Aviño, situated to the northeast of Durango,
would seem from its location to belong unmistakably to
Nueva Vizcaya. But such was not the case. As has been
noted above, Francisco de Ibarra claimed the dual rôle of
discoverer and founder of Aviño. The weight of evidence
supports his claim. But he himself listed Aviño as one of
his discoveries which was incorporated into Nueva Galicia.
Moreover, his commission granted him jurisdiction over the
lands *beyond* Aviño and San Martín. About 1575 the town
of Aviño had about twenty Spanish families. Surrounding the pueblo were several native settlements.[19]   San
Martín and Sombrerete were two of the largest and most
important settlements in Nueva Galicia which are supposed
to have been discovered by Ibarra. No information regarding their status in 1575 is available.

The anomalous position of Nombre de Diós has been
explained. After 1569 it belonged neither to Nueva Vizcaya
nor to Nueva Galicia, but was controlled directly by the
viceroy of New Spain. In 1569 the population of Nombre
de Diós was about three hundred. The number of inhabitants in 1575 is not given. In addition to the Spaniards there
were many Aztec and Tarascan Indians settled in the villa.
Surrounding it were fifteen or sixteen farms, which produced annually more than twenty thousand fanegas of corn
and thirty thousand fanegas of wheat.

The numerous Spanish settlements in Nueva Vizcaya
and Nueva Galicia that have been enumerated above owed
their origin and most of their prosperity to one man; they

---

[18] A. G. I., 67-1-18, Obispo de Nueva Galicia, 23 de diciembre de 1573.
[19] *Ibid.; Col. Doc. Inéd.,* XVI. 563.

were material monuments to the energy and ability of Francisco de Ibarra. When one questions his contribution to the development of New Spain, the entire northwestern frontier as he left it in 1575 bears mute testimony to the extent of his achievements.

To the Franciscan friars all credit is due for the spiritual conquest of Nueva Vizcaya. Practically all entradas were accompanied by one or more of the missionaries, and soon after the settlement of the mines and pueblos a curate was sent by the bishop of Nueva Galicia to look after the spiritual welfare of the inhabitants. In 1566 the Custodia of Zacatecas was established with five convents: Nombre de Diós, San Juan Bautista in Durango, San Pedro y San Pablo in Tôpia, one in the San Bartolomé Valley, and San Buenaventura in Peñol Blanco. The first custodian was Father Pedro de Espinareda. By 1590 five more convents had been added to the Custodia of Zacatecas; they were: Mapimí, San Juan del Mesquital, San Francisco del Mesquital, Cuencamé, and Saltillo. By 1596 there were fourteen monasteries in the custodia. In 1578 the Custodia of Zacatecas was put under the control of the friars of the Holy Evangel. This was the beginning of the famous province of Nuestra Señora de Guadalupe de Zacatecas, for Zacatecas became the head of the province, which prior to this time had been Nombre de Diós.[20]

It does not appear that any regular convents were founded in Sinaloa. After the murders of Azevedo and Herrera, Sinaloa was left without religious guidance for several years. In 1573 the bishop of Nueva Galicia wrote of two Franciscans, who had recently entered that region,

---

[20] Amador, *Zacatecas*, pp. 198, 211; Bancroft, *North Mexican States and Texas*, I. 116; Bancroft, *Mexico*, II. 719. According to Arlégui (*Chrónica de Zacatecas*, pp. 40-43) recruits to the convent at Nombre de Diós came from the Provincia del Santo Evangelio in Mexico; recruits to Zacatecas came from the Custodia de Michoacán.

"We are not certain that they will remain, though they have built a house among the natives."[21]

The Chiametla region was visited occasionally by friars from Jalisco. Viceroy Enríquez in a letter to the king in April, 1572, set forth the necessity of sending friars to Chiametla. He said, "In the province of Chiametla there is urgent need of friars, for without them, and in the absence of Christian instruction, we cannot hope to retain our hold on that province, since the religious are absolutely essential to the pacification and subjugation of the natives."[22]

Though the achievements of the zealous missionaries were far in excess of their meager numbers, they were all too few to care for the numerous Christians and carry the message of Christ to the thousands of savages demanding their attention. Urgent appeals for more friars were heard from every section of the frontier. The first Jesuits entered Nueva Vizcaya in 1589.

The ecclesiastical jurisdiction of Nueva Vizcaya was not coördinate with its political bounds. It belonged to the diocese of Nueva Galicia, but the great size of the bishopric was regarded as an impediment to efficient administration, and in 1569 the bishop of Nueva Galicia recommended that a new diocese be erected in Nueva Vizcaya. He also suggested that, if the king appointed a new bishop, he hoped he would be a Franciscan, "for they are better equipped to handle the Indians."[23] The diocese of Guadiana, however, was not established until 1620.

The occupation and settlement of Nueva Vizcaya facilitated in many ways the continued development of the neighboring province of Nueva Galicia. By pacifying the natives

[21] A. G. I., 67-1-18, Obispo de Nueva Galicia, 23 de diciembre de 1573.

[22] A. G. I., 58-3-8, Enríquez al Rey, abril de 1572.

[23] A. G. I., 67-1-18, El Obispo de Nueva Galicia al Rey, 31 de marzo de 1569.

who continually harried and menaced the miners of Zacatecas, San Martín, and other places in Nueva Galicia, Ibarra helped in no small measure to increase the production of the mines. Also, the settlement of numerous farmers and cattle and sheep raisers in the environs of Durango and Nombre de Diós resulted in an increased production of foodstuffs which were supplied the miners of Nueva Galicia in greater abundance and at greatly reduced prices.[24] Another contribution of Francisco de Ibarra was the successful accomplishment of a task without which the eventual occupation of New Mexico and California would have been well-nigh impossible. The inadvisability of overstepping a vast expanse of territory menaced by hostile savages who endangered communications was recognized after the failure of Coronado's expedition. Under the leadership of Francisco de Ibarra the settled frontier was advanced from Zacatecas to Santa Bárbara, and from Culiacán to San Juan de Sinaloa. Although he did not subdue and settle all of the present-day states of Chihuahua and Sonora, he nevertheless moved the frontiers far to the north and made possible the next advance of the Spanish flag into New Mexico, Arizona, and California.

"All of the above could not have been accomplished by Francisco de Ibarra and his soldiers alone," says Obregón. "Nothing could have been done, and His Majesty would have lost a great deal had it not been for the assistance rendered by Diego de Ibarra, who financed his nephew without cost to real hacienda." In reviewing the achievements of Francisco de Ibarra, it should never be forgotten that Diego de Ibarra was always in the background, advising and encouraging, and rendering every assistance possible in the form of men, money, and supplies. He is said to have spent more than two hundred thousand pesos on the conquest and devel-

[24] A. G. I., 1-1-3/22, Obregón, Crónica.

opment of Nueva Vizcaya. His returns, though great, never compensated him for his huge expenditures. Diego de Ibarra, a knight of the Order of Santiago and a relative of viceroys, was compelled to spend his last days in reduced circumstances petitioning an ungrateful sovereign for recognition of his great services.

It has been generally believed that Francisco de Ibarra's services were never rewarded, that his estate dwindled away, and that he did not leave enough to pay the large debts which he contracted to fit out his expeditions.[25] A careful examination of his will banishes the impression that he was verging on poverty. His numerous bequests certainly would never have been made had he not had the money to pay them; and furthermore, his final testament failed to mention encumbrances approximating the ninety thousand pesos which his brother Juan de Ibarra claimed he had incurred.[26] Nor were the services of Francisco de Ibarra entirely disregarded by the crown, for on June 1, 1574, the king confirmed his title as governor and captain-general of Nueva Vizcaya for life and granted him an annual salary from the royal treasury of two thousand ducats. After his death, the title and salary were to pass to an heir whom he should designate. Until 1574 the Governor of Nueva Vizcaya had not enjoyed any salary whatsoever. By virtue of the privilege granted him, Francisco named as his successor his brother Juan de Ibarra, then resident in Spain.

After the death of Francisco de Ibarra, Hernando de Trejo assumed the reins of government in Nueva Vizcaya until Juan de Ibarra could arrive from Spain. Since Trejo served without pay, he petitioned the Council of the

---

[25] Bancroft, *Mexico*, II. 598-599.

[26] "Francisco de Ibarra left a debt of more than 90,000 pesos; he expended from his estate, and from other sources, more than 20,000 pesos in those provinces" (A. G. I., 1-1-1/20, Memorial del Lcdo. Juan de Ybarra).

Indies to allow him Ibarra's salary for the time that he acted as governor. After considerable delay the Council finally acted and ordered Trejo to be paid at the rate of one-half of Ibarra's salary.[27] For unknown reasons, the appointment of Juan de Ibarra as governor of Nueva Vizcaya was delayed until February 20, 1576. Then followed additional delays, occasioned in large part by the efforts of the new governor to have his salary increased to six thousand ducats and the title of adelantado bestowed upon him. Also, since Francisco de Ibarra had enjoyed his new privileges and salary for but one year, Juan asked that the governorship descend to one more heir. Only the final request was granted. Before he could embark at Cádiz for New Spain, the governor-elect died, and once more the governorship of Nueva Vizcaya was vacant. The final choice fell upon Diego de Ibarra, and, on November 18, 1576, he was commissioned "governor of the provinces of Copalá, Nueva Vizcaya, and Chiametla for his life and that of an heir, or of another person whom he should designate."[28]

The fortunes of Nueva Vizcaya in the later years of the sixteenth century lie outside the scope of this treatise and are not to be narrated here. It was not a period of remarkable extension of frontiers, but rather one of gradual, methodical, undramatic consolidation of the territories outlined by Francisco de Ibarra. To the "phoenix of the explorers" belongs most of the credit for pioneering the vast northwest of New Spain. But he was more than an explorer; he was a founder of settlements, an exploiter of mines, a patron of agriculture, and a protector of the preachers of the Gospel.

[27] A. G. I., 139-1-2, Registros.
[28] Ibid.; A. G. I., 1-1/20, Memorial del Lcdo. Juan de Ybarra.

BIBLIOGRAPHY

Primary Materials

Manuscript

I. *The Archive of the Indies*

Patronato Real.

1-1-1/20:[1] Descubrimientos, descripciones y poblaciones de este reino de Nueva España. Años 1520 á 1627.

Memorial con documentos del Lcdo. Juan de Ybarra gobernador de la Nueva Vizcaya, junio de 1575.

1-1-3/22: Descubrimientos, descripciones y poblaciones de Nuevo México. Años 1568 á 1602.

Crónica, comentario y narativo por Baltasar de Obregón.

1-3-20/11: Informaciones de méritos y servicios de los descubridores, conquistadores y pacificadores de Nueva España. Años 1573 á 1574.

Información rescivida sobre la que dió el governador Francisco de Ybarra de los servicios en la SS. á S.M. y de su calidad y mérito pa. suppca. á S.M. q. remuneraja de los q. de haga mrds., México, 12 de enero de 1573.

Francisco de Ybarra, Información de méritos, 1574.

1-3-22/13: Informaciones de méritos. Años 1577 á 1579.

Cristóbal de Oñate.

1-3-25/16: Nueva España, Informaciones de méritos. Años 1584 á 1585.

Probanza de los méritos y servicios de Cristóbal de Oñate, México, 23 de enero de 1584.

1-3-27/18: Informaciones de Nueva España. Años 1589 á 1594.

Información de Juan Cortés Tolosa de Montezuma, Guadalajara, 12 de mayo de 1574.

Información de Juannes de Tolosa, Guadalajara, 2 de mayo de 1594.

Cristóbal de Zaldívar.

1-3-30/21: Informaciones de méritos y servicos de descubridores, conquistadores y pobladores de Nueva España. Años 1601 á 1604.

Parecer de la Real Audiencia de México sobre las partes y servicios del testador Juan de Ybarra.

---

[1] Cf. *supra*, p. 6, note 2.

Audiencia de México.

58-2-18: Consultas originales corespondientes al distrito de dicha Audiencia. Años 1586 á 1610.

Diego de Ybarra, Servicios, México, 2 de abril de 1593.

Diego de Ybarra al Rey, México, 25 de febrero de 1596.

El Rey á Diego de Ybarra, Madrid, 20 de agosto de 1600.

Doña Mariana de Ibarra Velasco, 16 de septiembre de 1614.

58-3-8: Cartas y expedientes del Virrey vistos en el Consejo. Años 1536 á 1576.

Velasco al Rey, México, 30 de septiembre de 1558.

Copia de la que me escrivió Franco. de Ybarra de las minas de abiño en 6 de junio 1562 sobre lo de Copalá.

El traslado de la comisión que dió don Luís de Velasco á Franco. de Ybarra para su governador é capitán general, México, 24 de julio de 1562.

Et traslado de la provisión que el señor marques de falces visorey dió á francisco de Ybarra en que parea confirmo la que le avia dado don Luís de Velasco, México, 31 de mayo de 1567.

Traslado de la carta del señor visorey de la Nueva España que escrivió á esta real audiencia sobre lo de Franco. de Ybarra, México, 7 de julio de 1567.

El traslado de la carta que escrivió el señor visorey á esta real audiencia con el señor Ldo. Contreras sobre lo de Fco. de Ybarra, México, 5 de agosto de 1567.

Enríquez al Rey, México, 20 de abril de 1571.

El virrey Enríquez al Rey, México, 4 de mayo de 1571.

Enríquez al Rey, México, 5 de febrero de 1572.

Enríquez al Rey, México, abril de 1572.

Enríquez al Rey, México, 28 de abril de 1572.

Enríquez al Rey, México, 6 de diciembre de 1572.

Enríquez al Rey, México, 28 de septiembre de 1573.

Enríquez al Rey, México, 28 de septiembre de 1573.

58-5-9: Cartas y espedientes del presidente y oidores de México vistos en el consejo. Años 1571 á 1577.

Oficiales de Nueva España al Rey, México, 10 de diciembre de 1572.

Enríquez y oidores al Rey, México, 16 de diciembre de 1572.

Enríquez y oidores al Rey, México, 19 de marzo de 1573.

El virrey y Aud. de Méx. al Rey, México, 31 de octubre de 1576.

58-5-12: Cartas y espedientes del presidente y oidores de México vistos en el consejo. Años 1597 á 1608.

Audiencia de México al Rey, México, 10 de marzo de 1600.

59-4-3: Un libro de cartas escritas á S.M. por sugetòs particulares de N.E. Años 1550 á 1570.

Capitulación de Alonso Valiente par con S.M. en lo de Chiametla.

Manuel Valiente á S. M., Los Ángeles, 18 de mayo de 1556.

Toribio de Bolaños al Rey, México, 29 de abril de 1557.

Antonio Gotelo de Betanco sobre Francisco de Ybarra, México, 5 de junio de 1566.

Una Carta al Rey por Antonio Gotelo de Betanzos, México, 9 de diciembre de 1567.

59-6-15: Informaciones de oficio y parte del distrito de dicha audiencia. Años 1566 á 1567.

Información de Bartolomé de Arriola, Indehe, 11 de marzo de 1570.

59-6-20: Información de oficio y parte del distrito de dicha audiencia. Años 1577 á 1578.

Información de Martín López de Ybarra, México, 2 de octubre de 1577.

59-6-23: Información de oficio y parte del distrito de dicha audiencia. Años 1583 á 1584.

Información de Baltasar de Obregón.

60-1-3: Informaciones de oficio y parte del distrito de dha. audiencia. Años 1591 á 1592.

Información de oficio sobre que dió el Bachiller Ant. de Ybarra, México, 8 de agosto de 1591.

60-1-14: Informaciones de oficio y parte del distrito de dha. audiencia. Años 1612 á 1613.

Información de Martín de Ybarra, 24 de mayo de 1610.

Audiencia de Guadalajara.

66-5-14: Cartas y espedientes del presidente y oidores de la audiencia. Años 1534 á 1576.

Relación sacada en suma de visita general hecha por el señor Ldo. Hernán Martínez de la Marcha, Cacatecas, 19 de abril de 1550.

Averiguaciones hechas por el Ldo. Contreras y Quebara sobre lo tocante de la visita del real consejo de Yndias, 1569.

Visita de Guadalajara, 27 de octubre de 1569.

Averiguaciones hechas por el Ldo. Contreras y Quebara sobre lo tocante de la visita del real consejo de Yndias, 1570.

Visita de Guadalajara, 22 de febrero de 1570.

Audiencia de Guadalajara al Rey, 24 de diciembre de 1572.

Audiencia de Guadalajara al Rey, 16 de septiembre de 1575.
66-6-17: Cartas y espedientes del Governador de Durango. Años 1591 á 1648.
Información de Diego de Ibarra, 9 de agosto de 1582.
66-6-19: Cartas y espedientes de los cabildos seculares de Guadalajara, Zacatecas y Durango. Años 1533 á 1689.
Escudo de armas de la ciudad de Zacatecas, 1599.
66-6-22: Cartas y espedientes de los oficiales de Durango y Zacatecas. Años 1555 á 1698.
Los oficiales reales de Durango al Rey, Durango, primero de marzo de 1579.
67-1-12: Cartas y espedientes de personas seculares del distrito de esta audiencia. Años 1585 á 1599.
Testimonio de F. Ybarra, Pánuco, 18 de agosto de 1575.
Información de Baltasar de Bañuelos, Cacatecas, 5 de octubre de 1587.
67-1-13: Cartas y espedientes de personas seculares del distrito de esta audiencia. Años 1600 á 1611.
Información de Nombre de Diós, 1608.
67-1-14: Información de oficio y parte del distrito. Años 1574 á 1587.
Información de Cristóbal de Oñate.
67-1-16: Informaciones de oficio y parte del distrito. Años 1600 á 1619.
Información de Doña Mariana de Ybarra Viuda, 1610.
67-1-17: Informaciones de oficio y parte del distrito. Años 1620 á 1695.
Carta de Diego de Ibarra al Rey, México, 15 de octubre de 1583.
67-1-18: Libro enpergaminado, contiene varias cartas escritas al Rey por la Audiencia, Obispo y otras personas de la Nueva Galicia. Años 1549 á 1571.
Oidores de N. Galicia al Rey, Compostela, primero de noviembre de 1549.
Carta sobre la visita del Ldo. la Marcha á S.M., Compostela, 18 de febrero de 1551.
Morones al Rey, Compostela, 15 de agosto de 1557.
Ldo. Morones al Consejo, Compostela, 17 de agosto de 1557.
Morones al Rey, Compostela, 18 de septiembre de 1557.
Ldo. Lebrón de Quiñones, 10 de septiembre de 1559.
Morones al Rey, Guadalajara, 2 de enero de 1561.
Oidores de N. Galicia al Rey, 4 de enero de 1561.

Ldo. Seguro al Rey, Guadalajara, 6 de enero de 1561.

El Obispo de Nueva Galicia, 27 de enero de 1561.

Oidores de Nueva Galicia al Rey, 30 de enero de 1561.

Audiencia de Nueva Galicia al Rey, 18 de abril de 1563.

Morones al Rey, Guadalajara, 15 de mayo de 1563.

Audiencia de Nueva Galicia al Rey, 10 de septiembre de 1567.

Obispo de N. Gal. sobre F. Cano y las Minas de Mazapil, 17 de diciembre de 1568.

Audiencia de Nueva Galicia al Rey, 4 de marzo de 1569.

El alcalde mayor de Nueva Galicia Diego de Colio al Consejo de Indias, Minas de San Martín, 15 de febrero de de 1570.

Doctor Alarcón á su Magestad, 10 de abril de 1571.

Obispo de Nueva Galicia, 23 de diciembre de 1573.

Quenta de Fray Juan de Tápia de la jornado q. hizo al Valle de Guadiana y los pueblo q. ajuntado.

87-5-1: Registros de oficio: Reales ordenes dirigidas á las autoridades de Nueva España. Años 1579 á 1607.

Un libro que tiene 1341 Informes de conquistadores de México y otras partes de N. España.

87-6-3: Registros de oficio y partes: Reales ordenes dirigidas á las autoridades y particulares de Nueva España. Años 1560 á 1576.

El Rey al Virrey Enríquez, Madrid, 27 de octubre de 1571.

88-6-2: Cartas y espedientes del Virrey. Años 1539 á 1635.

Hordenancas hechas por el Yll. Dn. Antº. de Mendoza-Minas —1539 (August 30, 1539).

103-3-1: Registros de oficio: Reales ordenes dirigidas á las autoridades del distrito. Años 1554 á 1671.

Registros, 1554 á 1671.

Indiferente General.

139-1-2: Registros: De asientos y capitulaciones para descubrimientos. Años 1530 á 1605.

Annals of Nueva Vizcaya from Francisco de Ibarra to Francisco de Urdiñola. (No title.)

El Rey al Virrey Enríquez, 31 de marzo de 1576.

II. *The Ayer Collection, Newberry Library, Chicago*

Ordenancas hechas por el Sr. Visorrey don Antonio de Mendoza sobre las minas de Nueva España. Año de 1550 (January 14, 1550).

III. *The Bancroft Library*

Durango, Documentos Historicos, 1554-1831.   ↺
Expedición de la Nueva Vizcaya, 1563.
Monumentos de la Dominación Española. No. 2.

PRINTED SOURCES

Actas de Cabildo del Ayuntamiento de México (Segundo Libro de Actas). Mexico, 1889.
BANDELIER, FANNY, editor. *The Journey of Álvar Nuñez Cabeza de Vaca.* New York, 1905.
BOLTON, HERBERT E., editor. *Spanish Exploration in the Southwest, 1542-1706.* New York, 1916.
Cartas de Indias. Madrid, 1877.
Colección de documentos inéditos relativos al descubrimiento, conquista y colonización de las posesiones españolas en América y Oceanía. Madrid, 1864-1884. 42 vols.
Documentos para la Historia de México. Mexico, 1853-1857. 20 vols.
HACKETT, CHARLES WILSON, editor. *Historical Documents relating to New Mexico, Nueva Vizcaya and Approaches Thereto, to 1773* (Collected by Adolph F. A. Bandelier). Washington, 1923.
HALLECK, H. W., editor. *A Collection of Mining Laws of Spain and Mexico.* San Francisco, 1859.
IBARRA, FRANCISCO DE. (Letter to Diego de Ibarra, May 3, 1563), in *Col. Doc. Inéd.,* XIV. 559.
Relación de los Descubrimientos, Conquistas y Poblaciones hechas por el Gobernador Francisco de Ybarra en las Provincias de Copalá, Nueva Vizcaya y Chiametla, in *Col. Doc. Inéd.,* XIV. 463.
ICAZBALCETA, JOAQUÍN GARCÍA, editor. *Colección de Documentos para la Historia de México.* Mexico, 1838-1866. 2 vols.
Nueva Colección de Documentos para la Historia de México. Mexico, 1886-1892. 5 vols.
Información sobre los Acontecimientos de la Guerra, in *Col. Doc. Inéd.,* XVI. 363.
Informe del Cabildo al Rey, 1569, in Icazbalceta *Col. Doc.,* II. 484.
MACNUTT, F. A., editor. *The Letters of Cortés.* New York, 1908. 2 vols.

MIRANDA, J. *Relación sobre la tierra y población que hay desde las minas de San Martín hasta las de Sta. Bárbara, 1575,* in *Col. Doc. Inéd.,* XVI. 563.

Nueva Vizcaya, Documentos para la Historia, in *Doc. Hist. Méx.,* III.

PUGA, VASCO DE, editor. *Provisiones, cédulas, instrucciones de su magestad de esta Nueva España* (1525-1563). Mexico, 1878-1879. 2 vols.

Recopilación de leyes de los reinos de las Indias. Madrid, 1841. 2 vols.

Relación que los Franciscanos de Guadalajara Dieron de los Conventos que tenia su orden, y de otros negocios generales de aquel Reino (Guadalajara, November 8, 1569), in Icazbalceta, *Nueva Colección,* II. 166-176.

Relaciones anonimas de la jornado que hizo á la Nueva Galicia, in Icazbalceta, *Col. Doc.,* II. 248.

TELLO, ANTONIO. *Fragmentos de una historia de la Nueva Galicia,* in Icazbalceta, *Col. Doc.,* II. 343

VALENCIA, FRAY ANGEL. *Carta al Emp.,* in *Cartas de Indias,* p. 110.

VELÁSQUEZ, PRIMO FELICIANO, editor. *Colección de documentos para la historia de San Luís Potosí.* San Luís Potosí, 1897. 4 vols.

VELASCO, LUÍS DE. *Relación de lo que descubrió Diego de Ibarra en la provincia de Copalá llamada Topiá,* in *Col. Doc. Inéd.,* XIV. 553.

SECONDARY REFERENCES

AITON, ARTHUR S. "The Later Career of Coronado," in *The American Historical Review,* XXX (1915), 298-304.

"The First American Mining Code," in the *Michigan Law Review,* III, No. 2, 108-113.

AITON, ARTHUR S. and MECHAM, J. LLOYD. "The Archivo General de Indias," in *The Hispanic American Historical Review,* IV (1921), 553-568.

ALÉGRE, FRANCISCO JAVIER. *Historia de la Compañía de Jésus.* Mexico, 1841. 3 vols.

ALTAMIRA Y CREVEA, RAPHAEL. *Historia de España y de la civilización española.* Barcelona, 1913-1914. 4 vols.

ÁLVAREZ, IGNACIO. *Estudios sobre La Historia General de México.* Zacatecas, 1875-1877. 6 vols.

AMADOR, ELIAS. *Bosquejo histórico de Zacatecas.* Zacatecas, 1892.

ARLÉGUI, JOSÉ. *Chrónica de la Provincia de S. Francisco de Zacatecas.* Mexico, 1737.

BANCROFT, HUBERT HOWE. *History of Mexico.* San Francisco, 1883-1888. 6 vols.

History of the North Mexican States and Texas. San Francisco, 1884-1889. 2 vols.

History of Arizona and New Mexico, 1530-1888. San Francisco, 1884-1889.

The Native Races. San Francisco, 1883-1886. 5 vols.

BANDELIER, ADOLPHE F. *Historical Introduction to studies among the sedentary Indians of New Mexico.* Boston, 1881. (Papers of the Archaeological Institute of America. American Series I.)

Final Report of Investigations Among the Indians of the Southwestern United States Carried on mainly in the years from 1880 to 1885. Cambridge, 1890-1892. (Papers of the Archaeological Institute of America. American Series III-IV.)

Contributions to the History of the Southwestern Portion of the United States (Hemenway Southwestern Archaeological Expedition). Cambridge, 1890. (Papers of the Archaeological Institute of America. American Series V.)

BEAUMONT, PABLO DE LA PURÍSIMA CONCEPCIÓN. *Crónica de la Provincia de S. Pedro y S. Pablo de Michoacán.* Mexico, 1873-1874. 5 vols.

BOLTON, HERBERT E. *The Spanish Borderlands.* New Haven, 1921.

BOLTON, HERBERT E., and MARSHALL, THOMAS MAITLAND. *The Colonization of North America, 1492-1783.* New York, 1920.

BOURNE, EDWARD G. *Spain in America, 1450-1580.* New York, 1906.

CALLE, JUAN DÍAZ DE LA. *Memorial y Noticias Sacras y Reales del Imperio de las Indias Occidentales.* n. pl., 1646.

CHAPMAN, CHARLES E. *The Founding of Spanish California.* New York, 1916.

CORNISH, BEATRICE QUIJADA. *The Ancestry and Family of Juan de Oñate.* New York, 1917. *(The Pacific Ocean in History,* pp. 452-467.)

CUNNINGHAM, CHARLES HENRY. *The Audiencia in the Spanish Colonies*. Berkeley, 1919. (University of California, *Publications in History*, IX.)

✓ DAHLGREN, CHARLES B. *Historic Mines of Mexico*. New York, 1883.

Diccionario Universal de Historia y de Geografía. Mexico, 1853-1856. 10 vols.

FARRAND, LIVINGSTON. *The Basis of American History*. New York, 1904.

FREJES, FRANCISCO. *Historia Breve de la Conquista de los Estados Independientes del Imperio Méjicano*. Mexico, 1839.

HARING, CLARENCE HENRY. *Trade and Navigation Between Spain and the Indies in the Time of the Hapsburgs*. Cambridge, 1918. (*Harvard Economic Studies*, XIX.)
"American Gold and Silver Production in the First Half of the Sixteenth Century," in *The Quarterly Journal of Economics*, XXIX (1914-1915), 433-479.

HELPS, SIR ARTHUR. *The Spanish Conquest in America*. New York, 1900-1904. 4 vols.

HERRERA, ANTONIO DE. *Historia General de los Hechos de los Castellanos en las Islas y Tierra Firme del Mar Océano*. Madrid, 1730. 4 vols.

HILL, ROSCOE R. "The Office of Adelantado," in *The Political Science Quarterly*, XXVIII (1913), 646-668.

HODGE, FREDERICK WEBB, editor. *Handbook of American Indians*. Washington, 1910. (Bureau of American Ethnology, *Bulletin* 30, 2 parts.)

HUMBOLDT, ALEXANDER DE. *Political Essay on the Kingdom of New Spain*. (Translation by John Black.) London, 1811. 4 vols.

HUNTINGTON, ELLSWORTH. *The Red Man's Continent*. New Haven, 1919.

LOWERY, WOODBURY. *The Spanish Settlements within the Present Limits of the United States*. New York, 1911. 2 vols.

MACNUTT, F. A. *Fernando Cortés and the Conquest of Mexico*. New York, 1909.

McGEE, W J. *The Seri Indians*, in Bureau of American Ethnology, *Seventeenth Annual Report*, Part I, pp. 9-296. Washington, 1898.

MECHAM, J. LLOYD. "The Second Spanish Expedition to New Mexico," in *The New Mexico Historical Review*, I. 265-291.

"Antonio de Espejo and His Journey to New Mexico," in the *Southwestern Historical Quarterly*, XXX. 114-138.

MENDIETA, GERÓNIMO DE. *Historia eclesiastica Indiana*. Mexico, 1870.

MOSES, BERNARD. *The Spanish Dependencies in South America*. New York, 1914. 2 vols.

MOTO PADILLA, MATÍAS DE LA. *Historia de la conquista de la Provincia de la Nueva Galicia*. Mexico, 1870.

OROZCO Y BERRA, MANUEL. *Geografía de las Lenguas y Carta Ethnográfica de México*. Mexico, 1864.

PRESCOTT, W. H. *The Conquest of Mexico*. New York, 1843.

PRIESTLEY, HERBERT INGRAM. *The Mexican Nation, A History*. New York, 1923.

RAMIREZ, SANTIAGO. *La Propiedad de las Minas*. Mexico, 1883.

RIBAS, ANDRÉS PÉREZ DE. *Historia de los Triumphos de Nuestra Santa Fee entre gentes las más bárbaras y fieras del Nuevo Orbe*. Madrid, 1645.

RIVA PALACIO, D. VICENTE, editor. *México á través de los siglos*. Mexico, Barcelona, 1888-1889. 5 vols.

SAHAGUN, BERNARDINO DE. *Historia General de las Cosas de Nueva España*. Mexico, 1829. 3 vols.

SOLÓRZANO Y PEREYRA, JUAN DE. *Política Indiana*. Madrid, 1776. 2 vols.

STEPHENS, H. MORSE, and BOLTON, HERBERT E., editors. *The Pacific Ocean in History*. New York, 1917.

TARAYRE, M. E. G. *Exploration Minéralogique des Régions Mexicaines suivie de notes archéologiques et ethnographiques*. Paris, 1859.

TORQUEMADA, JUAN DE. *Monarquía Indiana*. Madrid, 1723. 3 vols.

VELASCO, LÓPEZ DE. *Geographía y descripción universal de las Indias*. Madrid, 1894.

VETANCURT, AUGUSTÍN DE. *Chrónica de la Provincia del Santo Evangelio de México*. Mexico, 1871.

Menologio Francescano de los Varones más Señalados. Mexico, 1871.

WARD, H. G. *Mexico in 1827*. London, 1828. 2 vols.

WINSHIP, GEORGE PARKER. "The Coronado Expedition, 1540-1542," in Bureau of Ethnology, *Fourteenth Annual Report*, Part I, pp. 339-615. Washington, 1896.

WINSOR, JUSTIN, editor. *Narrative and Critical History of America*. Boston, 1889. 8 vols.

WISSLER, CLARK. *The American Indian*. New York, 1922.

ZAMACOIS, D. NICETO DE. *Historia de Méjico*. Barcelona, 1878. 18 vols.

INDEX

Acaponeta River, 23.

Acaponita, pueblo in Nueva Galicia, 84.

Acapulco, Alarcón sails from, 30.

Acatic, 32, 43.

Acaxées Indians, 15, 18; visited by Father Tápia, 85; description of, 131.

Acosta, Father, 210.

Adelantado, nature of office, 3; title requested by Diego de Ibarra, 49; 105.

Agriculture, in Nueva Vizcaya, 204-206; Ibarra encourages, 237.

Aguanaval River, 9.

Ahumada, Pedro de, juez de comisión, 91.

Alarcón, Doctor, oidor, accuses Ibarra, 193; tells of Ibarra's interference in Nombre de Diós, 199; criticises Ibarra's Indian policy, 228.

Alarcón, Hernando de, navigator, 30.

Álava, Basque province, 3; annexed to Castile, 4.

Albarrada, mine near Zacatecas, 46.

Alcaldes mayores, 38; of San Martín, 89; of Zacatecas, 89; 92, 105 f.

Alcaldes ordinarios, 34; of San Martín, 86.

Alcaldía mayor, Nueva Galicia reduced to an, 37; 38; Zacatecas created an, 46; Mazapil organized into an, 190.

Alcarez, Coronado's lieutenant, 169.

Alégre, Francisco Javier, Jesuit annalist, 186.

Alguacil mayor, takes census, 52.

Almadén (Spain), 219.

Alvarado, Pedro de, in Mixton War, 32 f.

Amador, Elias, quoted, 89.

Amazons, islands of the, 19, 21.

Angulos, José de, expedition to Guadiana, 24.

Animals, see Fauna.

Apache Indians, classification of, 14; 172.

Arandía, María de, mother of Francisco de Ibarra, 5, 223.

Araña, Martín de, captain, 116; Gamon envious of, 119.

Archivo General de Indias, 110.

Arellano, see Luna y Arellano, Tristán de.

Arenalo, Hernando de, killed by Indians, 82.

Arias, Juan, encomendero, 145.

Arizona, natives of, 14; 237.

Arizpe, 30.

Arlégui, José, remarks on Seri Indians, 18; authority of, 74, 85.

Arriola, Bartolomé de, treasury officer, 116; lieutenant-governor, 125; advices in council, 176.

Asturias, kingdom of, 4.

Audiencia of Guadalajara, 202; see Audiencia of Nueva Galicia.

Audiencia of Mexico, 35; Nueva Galicia subject to, 37; Oseguera promoted to, 95; Velasco discusses Ibarra with, 102; Ibarra offers assistance to, 183; opposes Audiencia of Nueva Galicia, superior jurisdiction of, over Nueva Vizcaya, 194; authority of, reasserted over Nueva Vizcaya, 196; assumes control over Nombre de Diós, 200; 210.

Audiencia of Nueva Galicia, establishment of, in Compostela, 37; jurisdiction of, officials appointed by, 38; oidores of, petition to move, 39, 51; Mercado commissioned by, 55; claims of, on San Martín, 73; takes steps to suppress rebellion in San Martín, 91; appoints alcalde mayor, 92; political developments in, 93; petition to move to Guadalajara, 98; 134; controversy with Ibarra, 148-152; prepares información on Ibarra, 152; Ibarra offers assistance to, 183; takes possession of Mazapil, 190; opposes Ibarra, 193-203; contests possession of

Nombre de Diós, 198-201; Ibarra invades jurisdiction of, 227; Doctor Orozco, president of, 229.

Ávalos, province, 20, 35.

Avellaneda, Juan de, 155.

Avilés, Menéndez de, adelantado, 3.

Aviño, mines of, 66; discovered by Ibarra, 67, 70; 79; Ibarra writes from, 80; settlement of, 87; development of, 87-88; Ibarra marches to, bad treatment of inhabitants, 115; 227; 233; status of, in 1575, 234.

Ayala, pueblo in Guadiana, 118.

Ayala, Pedro de, bishop of Nueva Galicia, 99.

Azatlán, on the Río Acaponeta, 23.

Azevedo, Pablo de, Franciscan friar, with Ibarra, 113; in Guatimape, 125; in Petatlán, 137; goes to Mexico City, 140, 142; instructs the Caribes, 147; 160; goes to Río Mayo, 161; preaches to natives of Oera, 116; 171; persuades Indians to return to pueblo, 172; advises in council, 176; death of, 184; 235.

Aztec Indians, 15; in Mixton War, 33; with Ibarra, 113; drums of, 119; mining methods of, 215; in Nombre de Diós, 234.

Baimena Indians, 15.

Bancroft, H. H., historian, classification of Indians, 13; quoted, 23; 64; opinion of, on Colio, 93; on the poison herb of Sonora, 168; remarks of, on utility of the agave, 206; geologic description of Nueva Vizcaya by, 213 f.

Bandelier, A. F., comments of, on the Yaqui and Mayos, 164; classification of Indians by, 167; opinion of the poisoned arrows of Sonora, 168; classification by, of the Sumas, 172 f.; description by, of Casas Grandes, 174 f.

Bañuelos, Baltasar Temiño de, agreement to exploit mines of Zacatecas, 42; claim as discoverer of Zacatecas, 45; petition for assistance, later years, 48; property holder in Zacatecas, 53.

Barrios, Juan de, appointed bishop of Nueva Galicia, 36.

Basques, characteristics of, 3; nobility, 4; soldiers of Ibarra, 113; rebellion of, led by Gamon, 120.

Bazan, Hernando de, lieutenant-governor of Sinaloa, 185; expedition in Sinaloa, 186.

Bernárdez, historian, quoted, 89.

Betanco, Antonio Gotelo de, maestro de campo, 120; in Guatimape, 125; attacks Tôpia, 129; 140; goes to Culiacán, 142; in charge of San Juan de Sinaloa, 143; defence by, of San Juan, 159-160; on the coast of the South Sea, 160; services at San Juan, goes to the Río Mayo, checks revolt, 161; left in charge of San Juan, 163; in Sinaloa, 171; requests Ibarra to return, 180; granted encomienda, 181; letter of, to king, 182.

Beteta, Gregorio de, Dominican friar, 54.

Bolaños, Toribio de, mines of, visited by la Marcha, dispute with Proaño and Martel, 50 f.; mention of, in Ibarra's will, 224.

Boletín de Geografía y Estadística, 76.

Bolsón de Mapimí, 8 f.

Bufa, La Sierra de, in Zacatecas, 41, 45.

Bustamante, Francisco de, Franciscan provincial, 74; comisario general, 79.

Cabeza de Vaca, in Nueva Galicia, 27, 173.

Cabildo, of Guadalajara, 34, 35, 51.

Cacalotlán, *peñol*, 146.

Cacari, Indian pueblo, 231.

Cadena, Diego de la, Franciscan friar, 76, 77; converts the Tepehuanes, 83; founder of San Juan Bautista de Analco, 123.

Cádiz, 239.

Caguacán, native pueblo in Culiacán, 145.

Cahita, native language, 164.

Caja real, royal strong-box, in Zacatecas, 52; ordered transferred from Compostela to